100 YEARS
OF MOTORING

AN RAC SOCIAL HISTORY
OF THE CAR

KAISERLICHES  PATENTAMT

PATENTSCHRIFT
— № 37435 —

KLASSE 46: LUFT- UND GASKRAFTMASCHINEN

AUSGEGEBEN DEN 2. NOVEMBER 1886

BENZ & CO. IN MANNHEIM.

Fahrzeug mit Gasmotorenbetrieb.

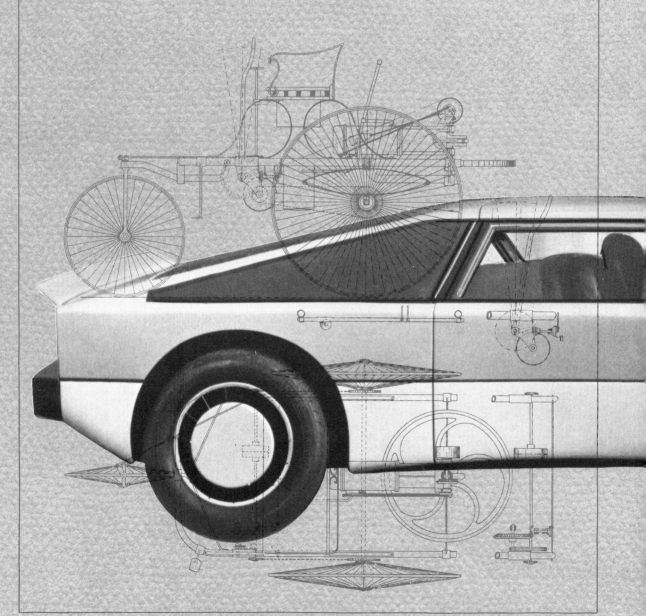

RAYMOND FLOWER
MICHAEL WYNN JONES

Foreword by H.R.H. Prince Michael of Kent
President, The Royal Automobile Club

Preface by Jeffrey D. Rose
Chairman, The Royal Automobile Club

100 YEARS OF MOTORING

AN ♔ **RAC** SOCIAL HISTORY OF THE CAR

Published by THE ROYAL AUTOMOBILE CLUB

in association with McGRAW-HILL BOOK COMPANY

CONTENTS

First published 1981

A McGraw-Hill Co-Publication in association with The Royal Automobile Club

Enquiries should be addressed to
The Publications Manager, Box 92,
RAC House, Lansdowne Road, Croydon,
CR9 6HN

Original Title
One Hundred Years on the Road

RAC ISBN 0−86211−018−1

Art Director: Charles Whitehouse
Editor: David Baker
Managing Editor: Francine Peeters
Designer: Ernst Hodel
Picture Procuration: Ruth Rüedi and the RAC
Production Manager: Franz Gisler
Graphic Artist: Franz Coray

Printed and bound by Mohndruck GmbH,
  Gütersloh, Germany
Composition by: Fotosatz AG, Horw,
  Switzerland
Photolithography by: Actual, Biel,
  Switzerland

Printed in Germany

THE FIRST SPARK

1885–1905

MIDDLE CLASS MOTORING

1914–1935

THE TRIUMPH OF TECHNOLOGY

1945–1960

THE CHALLENGE OF THE CAR

1900–1914

TOWN AND COUNTRYSIDE

1925–1945

COUNTRIES FIT FOR CARS?

1960–1980

No one man 'invented' the motor-car, nor can a single date be given to its birth. But it is true to say that the 1880s saw the crystallisation of ideas, that had been incubating for some time, into a mechanical reality. So in the 1980s we stand at the threshold of our second century of motoring – probably with as little idea of what it will hold as the original pioneers had a hundred years ago. The automobile has, however, affected our everyday lives probably on a broader scale than any other modern invention. Our aim in this book has been to present the development of the car in its social context, avoiding the technical details which have been exhaustively covered by other writers. In that sense it is a book for the 'motorist in the street' rather than for the car fanatic. We would like to express our appreciation of the encouragement and facilities offered by the Royal Automobile Club (whose official views this book does not necessarily express!), and our thanks to Harold Nockolds, to Ronald Barker for his help with the captions, to Lord Montagu for his invaluable comments, to Nigel Cobb, to Harold Catt the Club's librarian, to Elly Beintema for her help with the pictures, and to Paul Frère for contributing some of the car profiles.

RAYMOND FLOWER

MICHAEL WYNN JONES

The joys of motoring 75 years ago: an open road,
but one still better suited to horse-traffic.

Photo: Peter Roberts Collection, London

FOREWORD

by

HIS ROYAL HIGHNESS PRINCE MICHAEL OF KENT

President, The Royal Automobile Club

Very few inventions have affected our everyday lives as profoundly as the motor-car. It is hard to believe that something which we take so much for granted today and which has such an influence on our lives can have been virtually unknown a hundred years ago.

The story of the development of the motor-car since the early days is fascinating and surely of interest even to people whose acquaintance with the car goes perhaps no further than the steering wheel. I warmly welcome this absorbing and comprehensively illustrated social history, and endorse the RAC's encouragement of the project.

Michael

Insignia of The Royal Automobile Club:
(above) for full members of the Club,
and *(below)* for the Associate Section.

PREFACE

by

JEFFREY D. ROSE

Chairman, The Royal Automobile Club

It is appropriate that this social history of the motor-car should be published under the auspices of the RAC, for since its foundation in 1897 the Club has been intimately involved in the social aspects of motoring – both in helping to develop them and in solving some of the inevitable problems that arose. Indeed there is almost no area of motoring over the past eighty-odd years in which the influence of the RAC has not been felt – in the protection of motorists, the development of touring, caravanning and camping, the organisation of motor sports, the encouragement of safety measures and fair legislation, and of course in the whole range of roadside services. The RAC has sometimes initiated important social changes, and always tried to reflect them in its policies. This book is an interesting record of these changes; and it is also, I believe, a significant moment to look back on them – even as we look forward to our second century of motoring.

THE FIRST SPARK

The motor-car arrived in a world that needed it, but was not entirely prepared for it. Over the previous half-century enormous strides had been made in the means of travel: the railroads already spanned continents and the steamship had brought them closer together. Yet local communities remained as isolated as ever. The horse was still the most common form of transport — even the bicycle was regarded with some misgivings. Unlike the railway, the automobile had to impose itself on a road system that was (except in France) inadequate to its needs and which it had to share with the more traditional means of transportation. It also found itself governed by outmoded laws and regulations. Absurd anomalies abounded: an old Prussian law prohibiting 'occupied premises' over a steam boiler was pressed into service to declare steamcars illegal on the grounds that the driver's seat constituted occupied premises! To gain acceptance the motorcar had to prove itself a practical, safe and at least moderately reliable conveyance. The first two decades of its career are the story of the men who demonstrated that it could be.

Infant car: Carl Benz's machines were the first petrol-driven vehicles in the world to go into production. Here is one of the earliest – looking rather like a grown-up version of the elegant pram – an 1891 model Benz, with tiller steering, wooden-spoked wheels, and engine carried under the seat over the rear axle. With the vis-à-vis seating arrangements hardly improving the driver's view ahead, it was probably just as well there were still very few other mechanical vehicles on the road! Within ten years, however, Benz's Mannheim factory alone was producing 600 cars a year.

THE SELF-PROPELLED DREAM

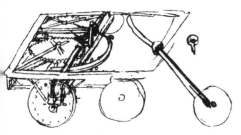

Early inspiration: Leonardo da Vinci's sketch *(above)* for a mechanically self-propelled cart – preserved in the Codex Atlanticus. A dream that got no further than the drawing-board.

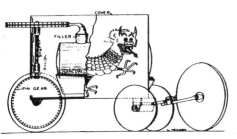

The world's first car? *Above:* A reconstruction of Padre Verbiest's steam waggon of 1672, built for the emperor of China. The original has long since disappeared: only a contemporary account of its apparently successful operation survives.

One summer evening in 1892 Hiram Maxim, the compulsive American inventor, was cycling home to Lynn in Massachusetts. He had been visiting his girl-friend in Salem and was, he guessed, pretty much up in the clouds. He began philosophising on the subject of transportation, and was struck by the idea of what a blessing it would be if his bicycle could propel him rather than the other way round. 'If I could build a little engine and use

its power to do the propelling, and if I could use a regular carriage instead of a bicycle, there would be no limit to where I could go', he wrote, recalling the day forty years làter. 'Towns would become nearer together. More people would intermingle. It would profoundly influence the course of civilization itself....

'I hoped I might be the first to produce an engine-driven road vehicle, which is evidence of how young I was. I was blissfully ignorant that Benz and Daimler in Germany; De Dion, Panhard and a host of others in France; Napier and a few others in England; Duryea Brothers, Haynes, Apperson Brothers, Winton and others in the United States were working with might and main on a gasoline-propelled road vehicle.... As I look back I am amazed that so many of us started so nearly at the same time and without the slightest notion that others were working on the problem. Why did so many different and widely separated persons have the same thoughts at about the same time? In my own case the idea germinated from looking down and contemplating the mechanism of my legs and the bicycle cranks while riding along a lonely road in the middle of the night. I suppose not another one of us pioneers had his original inspiration come to him just as mine came to me. But it has always been my belief that we all began to work on a gasoline-engine-propelled road vehicle at about the same time because it had only just become apparent that civilisation was ready for the mechanical vehicle.'

In an engineering sense he was no doubt correct: almost no great inventions have occurred in a vacuum. Rather they were the result of coalescing existing ideas (often apparently unrelated) when the time was right. But there was, surely, a deeper impetus. The automobile surfaced at the end of the nineteenth century, but the search for it goes back almost as far as recorded history.

Tracing man's preoccupation with this elusive vision you find yourself going back, for instance, to Leonardo da Vinci, whose designs for a self-propelled cart can be found in folio 296 of the Codex Atlanticus. Roger Bacon in the thirteenth century forecast that 'one day we shall endow chariots with incredible speed without the aid of any animal', and for his prescience was imprisoned for being in league with the devil.

Yet for all the Church's scepticism towards technological progress, it was a Jesuit priest at the court of the Chinese emperor in the seventeenth century (whose special passion was mechanical gadgets) who ap-

Far left: The oldest surviving steam carriage, built by Captain Nicolas Cugnot, is preserved in the Conservatoire des Arts et Métiers in Paris (a model of it can also be seen at the RAC Club in London). *Centre:* The first authentic petrol-driven car, demonstrated at the 1873 Vienna Exhi-

parently succeeded in building a steam carriage that *moved.* Padre Verbiest, the Abbé Hué says in *Astronomia Europaea,* 'placed an aelopile upon a car and directed the steam generator within it upon a wheel, on which four wheels were attached. The motion thus produced was communicated by gearing to the wheel of the car. The machine continued to move with great velocity as long as the steam lasted, and by means of a helm could be turned in various directions.' His contrivance, which survived by all accounts in the Winter Palace until quite recent times, has now disappeared. But if one day the dispatches from the Jesuit mission at Peking are exhumed from the Vatican archives, we may find proof that he antedated Cugnot by a full century as the father of the self-propelled vehicle. Captain Nicolas Joseph Cugnot's steam-gun carriage, however, *can* be seen in Paris, at the Conservatoire des Arts et Métiers, a formidable 5 ton tricycle built of wood with a huge kettle-shaped boiler over the driving wheel. Its handling, to put it charitably, was unbalanced: when demonstrated to the Duc de Choiseul in the summer of 1769, it ran proudly under its own steam for twelve minutes at a speed of 6 mph but 'proved so violent and difficult to steer that it knocked down a solid wall'. All the same, in those twelve minutes the history of the car began.

Cugnot was a contemporary of James Watt, and steam was to dominate the

bition by Siegfried Marcus. It is now a museum-piece, unlike the Danish Hammel *(above)* built in 1886 by Hans Johanson, which still bravely takes to the road, and even competed recently in the RAC's annual London-Brighton Run.

9

nineteenth century as a form of propulsion, but all the early attempts to adapt it to the road were doomed to disappointment. A Cornish mining engineer, Richard Trevithick, was the first to make a respectable stab at it: the steam carriage he had put together in a blacksmith's shop at Cambourne successfully climbed Cambourne Beacon on Christmas Eve 1801 with a party of workmen aboard. 'When we see'd that Captain Dick was a 'going to turn on steam, we jumped on as many as could, maybe seven or eight of us', reminisced one of them later. ''Twas a stiffish hill, but she went up like a bird.' Unfortunately the inventor left it overnight in a hotel stable and forgot to extinguish the fire: vehicle and building were burnt to a shell.

Others persisted, like Goldsworthy Gurney, whose New Steam Coach puttered round Regent's Park at a stately 5 mph, belching smoke and smelling like boiled iron, in December 1827. In due course he could be found running a fleet of them on regular services between Gloucester and Cheltenham. In 1834 Walter Hancock had nine such vehicles ferrying passengers between Moorgate and Paddington in London; by 1840 it was possible to travel to Brighton or Hastings and back in a day in Frank Hill's passenger coaches. But as the railways inexorably threw their tentacles throughout the country, these ungainly and uncomfortable steam coaches went out of business – though they left a legacy of mechanical innovations to which the later automobile pioneers were grateful heirs: the change-speed gear (which Trevithick had anticipated though not actually made), centre-point steering, differential gear on the driving axle, driving shafts with universal joints (on James's four-wheel-drive 'tractor' of 1825), and independent suspension on all four wheels (a layout patented in 1832).

Meanwhile another important link in the chain was being forged: the first example of an internal combustion engine was said to have been produced in 1857 at a foundry in Florence. Eugenio Barsanti and Felice Matteuci applied for a patent for 'obtaining motive power by the explosion of gases' through the British consul in Livorno, and exhibited their product at the 1861 National Exhibition in Florence. But their efforts had been pre-empted by Etienne Lenoir, who took out a patent on 24 January 1860 for 'an engine dilated by the combustion of gas', and it is he who has passed into history as the inventor of the first practical gas engine. Lenoir's patent describes a method of vaporising fuel so that the engine could be independent of a fixed gas supply.

To apply this new unit to a road vehicle was a logical step, and in the summer of 1862 he fitted one to a chassis which, he recalls, he often drove from the works through the Bois de Vincennes to his home, 'I took about half an hour to go and about the same time to get back – If we didn't break down. The vehicle was heavy. The motor was 1½ hp turning at about 100 rpm. It was fitted with a large flywheel.' And, he might have added, had a maximum speed of 4 mph. Anyway, by his own admission he soon lost interest in it, and the car itself was destroyed in the Franco-Prussian war.

A year or so later an Austrian, Siegfried Marcus, fitted an engine with an ingenious form of carburettor to a four-wheeled handcart, which ran for a few hundred yards and came to rest in a cemetery. An improved version with wooden frame, four-stroke engine, magneto-electric ignition and belt transmission was shown at the 1873 Vienna Exhibition and in due course became the prized possession of the Austrian Automobile Club, who erected a memorial in Mecklenburg as the birthplace of 'the inventor of the automobile' (without mentioning that Marcus, when he had tested his ma-

Beauty and the beast: Toulouse-Lautrec's 1896 lithograph of his cousin at the controls of his smoke-belching contraption is thought to be the first motoring print. The elegant lady and her dog help to emphasise the gentle parody of the new monsters of the road.

chine on the road, had been warned off by the police as a public nuisance). If the Austrians can claim the earliest existing petrol-engined car, the Danes have the oldest car that still runs, in the shape of a machine that Hans Johansen constructed in a corner of the Hammel works in 1886. With a two-cylinder four-stroke engine, hot-tube ignition and one forward speed, the Hammel did about 6 mph and was driven in the London-Brighton Run in quite recent times.

But none of these early innovators went beyond the experimental stage. A century ago – when our period opens – steam was still regarded as the only practical motive power, and indeed had made some progress. Amédée Bol-

The nineteenth-century heritage. By the turn of the century, although the automobile still had far to go, many of its essential elements were already in place. Indeed, the features illustrated below were in existence long before the first functional motor-car; and they are still to be found as fundamental principles of our current models.

The differential gear train, on the rear axle, allows one wheel to turn faster than the other in rounding corners. This principle – in a much cruder form, of course – was incorporated in Carl Benz's first two-seater tricycle in 1880 and in other early models.

The internal combustion engine, fueled by petrol, became established quite early as the standard source of power for propelling automobiles. Steam and electricity were soon abandoned. The first known petrol engine dates back to the late 1850s, and Marcus, Benz and Daimler helped develop it further.

Universal joints and the propeller shaft, in modern automobiles, convey power from the transmission to turn the rear axle. Many car designers tried other solutions – sprocket and chain (as in the French 1901 Mors shown here), or a belt (the first De Dion) – before settling on the universal joint, which had been proving itself on railway carriages since 1825.

Independent four-wheel suspension. This was another feature which preceded the automobile itself, having been incorporated in railway steam coaches for fifty years before the first real motor-car came along.

Centre point steering. Whereas the horse-drawn carriage had its front wheels locked in parallel, the motor-car required faster turning, with wheels banked at different angles (see the dotted lines). It was the railway train, once again, that provided this fundamental principle of the automobile as we know it.

lée's steam carriage (cheerfully named 'The Obedient' because of its ease of handling) built in his bell foundry in Le Mans in 1873 covered the 230 kilometres to Paris in 18 hours, and astonished the fashionable world as it silently threaded through the traffic on the Champs-Elysées. In the end it was the son of a Mannheim engine-driver who was to provide the first serious challenge to steam. People are only too happy to argue who invented the car. Lenoir, Marcus, Butler all have their supporters, but in truth, of no person can it be said that he alone did it. Yet if the history of the car is taken as having started with the first internal combustion vehicle that was available for sale to the public, then Carl Benz is our man.

BENZ, DAIMLER AND THE PETROL-DRIVEN CAR

The first advertisement for Benz's 1888 two-seater tricycle on sale to the public – just three years after Carl Benz *(below)* had stealthily tested his first model after dark on the streets of Mannheim. 'No danger whatever', the prospectus assures the public.

The son of one the first engine drivers to be killed in a railway accident (this occurred when he was two years old), Carl Benz as a boy was intrigued with clockwork motors. He learned (he later explained) 'to feel the marvellous language that the gear-wheels talk when they mesh with one another', and by the time he was sixteen he had begun to dream about 'a unit that could supplant the steam engine'. After graduating from the local polytechnic, he signed on as a fitter at the Karlsruhe Maschinenbaugesellschaft, a large factory that produced a range of machinery including locomotives and steam engines. In 1872 Benz married, and with the help of his wife's slender capital went into business on his own, opening a small tin-working factory. It was a period of recession in Germany and the firm began to founder, but he continued to develop the stationary engine that he had always had in mind. By New Year's Eve 1880, Carl and Berta Benz were so penniless they could not even afford an evening meal, but the engine on which their hopes were pinned was at last running under its own power.

Convinced that somehow it could propel a vehicle, he spent the next five years resolving some fundamental questions: Should the car have three wheels or four, and be driven by the rear wheels or the front ones? Where should the engine be located, and how should the vehicle be steered? It is worth noting that the earliest vehicle he produced featured several solutions that are still in use. His first two-seater tricycle was certainly a primitive device. But it had a water-cooled, four-stroke gas engine with mechanically operated inlet valves, electric ignition and a differential gear. Most important of all, it performed tolerably well.

By 1885 the car was running and was frequently to be seen chugging round the streets of Mannheim, usually after dark to avoid attracting attention. It frequently broke down and had to be pushed back to the workshop where Berta recharged the accumulator for the ignition by treadling away at her sewing machine stand to which a dynamo had been attached, while her husband made modifications to the design. It was she, in fact, who made the first long journey by car. Stealing out one early morning in 1888 with their two young sons while Carl was still asleep, she drove from Mannheim to her home in Pforzheim. They had to push the car up most of the hills and deal with various mishaps: Berta cleared a fuel line with a hair-pin and used her garters as insulating tape to cure an electrical short. A blacksmith took up the slack on the chains, and a cobbler relined the crude brakes with leather. But at least they completed the 62 mile trip.

Not long after this, the car was demonstrated at the Munich exhibition and attracted enthusiastic comments from the press. However, no flurry of orders ensued, and a leading scientific journal expressed the generally accepted belief that 'the internal combustion engine has as little future as steam for motivating road vehicles'. However, when Benz exhibited the car at the 1889 World Fair in Paris, Emile Roger, a French cycle manufacturer, placed a trial order and began selling the Mannheim-built vehicles under the name of Roger-Benz. But the financial world remained sceptical and the partners in Benz & Cie, fearing that the time and money spent on the development of cars would ruin their stationary-engine business, refused to sanction any further funds for this purpose. After a boardroom battle they both withdrew, and Benz would once more have been left high and dry had two other far-sighted men not come forward with financial sup-

port. As it turned out, the new team was a good one. With F. von Fischer in charge of administration, and Julian Ganss looking after sales, by the end of the century the Mannheim factory was producing nearly six hundred vehicles a year.

One of the minor ironies of history was that, at the very same factory in Karslruhe where young Benz had signed on as a fitter, an engineer by name of Gottlieb Daimler was soon afterwards appointed technical director. By then Benz had moved on and the two men never met, though their respective dreams were to come to fruition at the same moment (and forty years later their two great companies were to merge).

The second son of a well-to-do baker, Gottlieb Daimler was born in Schorndorf on 17 March 1834, and in the spring of 1848 was apprenticed to a gunsmith, where he showed his mettle by producing single-handedly a superb pair of double-barrelled pistols with walnut butts and beautifully chased barrels. He earned a scholarship to a large engineering concern in Alsace which built locomotives, but Daimler was unimpressed with the prevailing steam cult. He believed the slow-starting steam engine to be outmoded, that alternative methods should be studied to produce a unit which, in his own words, 'could be ready for operation instantly'. So when Otto,

In this Cannstatt workshop – as it appeared in the early 1880s – Gottlieb Daimler *(bottom)* worked on the development of his horseless carriage;

literally a standard carriage with an engine fitted into the floor-well, it made its debut in 1886.

13

a pioneer of the four-stroke atmospheric engine, started up the Deutz Gas Engine works, Daimler joined him in 1872 as technical director and engaged as draughtsman Wilhelm Maybach, later to become his right-hand man. Daimler worked with Deutz for ten years, but with the persistent conviction that he could improve on Otto's cherished atmospheric engine. When, with the help of Maybach, Daimler did succeed in designing the first practicable form of four-cycle engine, Otto insisted that it should be named after him. Daimler left to set up in business on his own, and took Maybach with him.

Dawn was about to break on the internal combustion era. But before a high-speed version of the four-stroke engine could be produced, the problem of ignition had to be solved. Working night and day in a small workshop at the bottom of his garden in Cannstatt (with such secrecy that the police raided it on the suspicion that coins were being forged), Daimler finally perfected the 'hot tube' system, whereby fuel was squirted into the cylinder and ignited by the heat of a red-hot platinum tube. Three light, fast-turning engines were built, the forerunners of the petrol engine of today. By carrying fuel in a small tank, these units were independent and did not have to be coupled to the gas mains. With the popular market in mind – that is, the man who wanted personal transportation but could not afford a carriage – he fitted a modified half-horsepower engine onto a bicycle. The device he produced, constructed of wood and steel with the engine slung amidships and the rider sitting on a horse-saddle above it, looked like a nursery hobby-horse. But it was the world's first motor-

Star attraction: the Daimler patent rights were acquired in Britain by Frederick Simms in 1893 (several years before it was even legal to drive over 4 mph). This 1898 Cannstatt Daimler, on its way through an English country town, has quickly drawn an admiring audience.

Coachman's despair: a landau towed by a De Dion steam tractor *(left)* with the Count himself riding in the carriage. This hybrid led all the way in the Paris-Rouen Trial of 1894, but was awarded only second prize – for being 'too difficult to handle'. De Dion later turned to production of petrol-engined cars. First prize in the Trial went jointly to Panhard and Peugeot. In 1891 Armand Peugeot became the first man to produce automobiles commercially in France, most of them four-seater phaetons like this example *(above)* waiting its turn to start in the Paris-Rouen event.

cycle, and in November 1885 his son Paul rode it a distance of about four miles.

Unlike Benz who set out to build a motor vehicle from scratch, Daimler thought in terms of fitting his engine into a carriage and dispensing with the horse. In 1886 he bought an ordinary horse-drawn carriage from a firm of coachbuilders in Cannstatt. After modifications to strengthen the frame had been made in his workshop, an engine was fitted in the rear floor-well to drive the back wheels, and a steering gear erected to direct the front ones. Daimler's genuine 'horseless carriage' (now preserved in the Deutsches Museum in Munich) worked quite well in the initial tests, but it also served to show that Benz was right and that the automobile of the future would have to be a vehicle specifically built for the purpose.

In 1889 he and Maybach constructed a four-wheeled, two-seater machine with a tubular steel frame and a V-twin cylinder engine mounted at the rear. Power was transmitted onto the back wheels through an exposed train of gears that could be varied to suit conditions. The engine was cooled by a water jacket around the cylinders, and interestingly enough the water was cooled by circulating through the tubular frame – a method tried out not so long ago on racing cars to save weight. Demonstrated at the Paris World's Fair in 1889, this vehicle proved to be the catalyst that jerked the nascent French automobile industry into life.

In 1886 a Parisian lawyer named Edouard Sarazin became Daimler's representative in France, and since to keep the patents alive it was necessary to go in for local manufacture, he persuaded his friend Emile Levassor (who together with René Panhard owned a factory making powersaws) to build a few Daimler-designed engines under licence. This done he died, leaving his widow to consummate the arrangement – so conclusively indeed that within a year she became Mme Levassor. The firm of Panhard & Levassor thus gained control of the Daimler patents in France, with farreaching results. For while Emile Levassor had the greatest respect for Daimler's engineering skill, he did not think much of his cars, disliking what he called their 'tremendous vibrations'. Nor did the Benz-type of quadricycle appeal to his engineer's mind. And so he came to the conclusion that he should build a vehicle specifically designed to take a motor, and propelled by proper systems of transmission. Finally, after eighteen months of frustrating but inspired tinkering, he had evolved a machine that was the prototype of the car as we know it. It was crude, certainly, and the transmission was driven by sprocket and chain. But the basic layout of components – radiator, engine, friction-clutch, gearbox and final drive to the rear wheels – which is known as the *système Panhard,* was substantially the same as is still used today in front-engine rear-drive cars. (See profile of 1891 model, pp. 32–33.)

Meanwhile his friend Armand Peugeot had also entered the ranks of constructors. The Peugeot family had been in the hardware business since the French revolution, making everything from farm implements to corsets and coffee-grinders. In 1885 Les Fils de Peugeot Frères opened a works near Valentigney to build cycles, and quickly became one of the largest bicycle

Pioneering motors. Daimler's V-twin cylinder engine *(above left),* unveiled at the Paris World Fair in 1889, helped make the automobile a reality for France and a wide international public. Beside it is shown the 4 hp two-cylinder Panhard-Levassòr motor, which was first developed in Paris in 1891.

Above right:

No room for passengers, however attractive, in Camille Jenatzy's electrically-propelled, bullet-like car. Nicknamed 'La Jamais Contente', it was the fastest car on earth in 1899, having raised the speed record to over 105 kph (65 mph). But the electric car was severely restricted by the range of its batteries, and failed to get into large-scale production except as a briefly fashionable runabout for town use.

manufacturers in France (their cycles were irreverently known as the moulins-à-café Peugeot). Before long they too began to think of motorising them, making an arrangement with Léon Serpollet to fit a 2 hp steam engine into a three-wheeler that was a cross between a tricycle and a carriage. Shown on Serpollet's stand at the 1889 Paris Exhibition, this device gained Armand Peugeot the Légion d'Honneur but was otherwise a dud; the generator gave endless trouble. He was therefore inclined to listen when Levassor suggested that they would do better to use the Daimler engine instead. The engine chosen was a 2 hp V-shaped two-cylinder, which was mounted horizontally at the rear of a four-wheel two-seater. An experimental car followed the Paris-Brest cycle race, successfully covering some 2,500 kilometres at an average speed of 15 kph; and in the next three years, between 1891 and 1894, Peugeot built sixty-eight more cars to the same design (mostly four-seaters) and thus became the first to manufacture petrol-engined cars commercially in France. But while Panhard and Peugeot were establishing the credentials of the Daimler engine – and arguing interminably whether it should go in the front or the back – another apostle was taking up the cause. He was a young man of fashion in the heyday of *la Belle Epoque,* a noted fencer and a sportsman who won or lost thousands at the tables. But above all, Count Albert de Dion, whose ancestor had taken part in the fifth Crusade, was mad about machinery and to indulge his whim to own a steam-carriage, he bestowed his patronage on a small Parisian firm of precision engineers, Bouton & Trépardoux.

His first steam quadricycle was belt driven and the rear wheels steered.

Next, his team fitted a small boiler to a Rudge tandem tricycle. When De Dion's friends saw him driving along a road near the Porte Maillot amid sparks and black smoke, they nicknamed him 'le comte mécanicien'. But when he decided to launch into commercial production, his father, the marquis, thought the joke had gone too far. He obtained a court order to restrain his own son.

In spite of such parental opposition, the partners were to make developments of fundamental importance to the new industry. Their experience in miniature precision work enabled them to produce a light and fast steam tricycle with a rapid steaming boiler. But the turning point came when De Dion began to see the advantages of the petrol engine and – despite the objections of Trépardoux, who quit the firm – developed a small single-cylinder air-cooled four-stroke unit which weighed only 40 pounds and gave ½ hp at 1,500 rpm. Much of the weight saving came through the use of an aluminium-alloy crankcase; moreover the old type of hot-tube ignition was replaced by a coil, battery and contact-maker system, and the mixture was supplied by a surface vaporiser. Ranging up from the tiny ½ hp unit of 1895 to an 8 hp version in 1902, this highly practical engine was fitted to a tricycle (much favoured by ladies of fashion and *demi-mondaines,* who rode them in the Bois de Boulogne), and from 1899 onwards a water-cooled version was used in a small car which soon became the 'mini' of its age. The 3½ hp engine was manufactured under licence in England, Germany, Belgium and America, and gave the impetus for a number of fledgling manufacturers to get into production.

A focus to these disparate activities was provided in 1894 by the Paris-Rouen Trial. Under the terms of this contest, sponsored by a newspaper called *Le Petit Journal,* any type of vehicle could take part provided that it could navigate under its own power; the winner would be the machine which in the jury's opinion was 'without danger, easily handled, and had low running costs'. That this allowed a good deal of latitude became clear from the published list of entrants, which included some unlikely contraptions powered, it was claimed, by means of compressed air, by electro-pneumatics (whatever that might mean), by a system of pendulums and

Well protected from the elements but cruelly exposed to public ridicule, this is how motorists at the turn of the century were seen on the front cover of the French satirical magazine *Le Rire* in November 1900.

The pioneering days of motoring were marked by hair-raising races between Paris and other European capitals. They offered rigourous tests of endurance – and valuable publicity for machines and manufacturers – but as casualties to drivers and spectators grew, so did demands for greater safety measures. Here a Panhard checks in at the Belfort control during the 1902 Paris-Vienna race.

even by 'gravity'. But as it happened, of the 102 hopefuls, only 21 vehicles actually showed up on the starting line at Porte Maillot on Sunday, 22 July. First away was the ponderous two-ton De Dion steam tractor, drawing a two-wheeled landau with four persons sitting vis-à-vis aboard and chauffeured by the huge bowler-hatted count himself. It was followed at thirty-second intervals by thirteen petrol vehicles and seven others driven by steam.

After a luncheon stop at Mantes (where the competitors could scarcely push through the crowds of spectators) De Dion steamed into Rouen having led the whole way. He had, in fact, completed the trip in 6 hours

Naturally enough many early car manufacturers like Peugeot, Darracq and Diort *(left)* graduated from cycle production. The firm of René Panhard and Emile Levassor *(right),* however, began by making power-saws, and were the first to design the basic layout of components which came to be known as the *système Panhard,* still used to some extent in many cars today. Levassor's triumph in the great Paris-Bordeaux-Paris race of 1895 *(far right)* established the company's early reputation.

and 48 minutes, an average speed of 11.6 mph. Yet because the judges considered his machine to be difficult and expensive to handle, the firm of De Dion-Bouton was awarded second prize rather than first, which went jointly to the Panhard and Peugeot companies – 'both employing petrol motors invented by Herr Daimler of Württemberg'. If nothing else, the Rouen Trial made it clear that cars could safely run non-stop over a considerable distance, for with the exception of four steamers that fell by the wayside (one with a burst boiler) the starters all reached Rouen in good order. But what is more important, it sparked the desire to pit the cars against each other in a race good and proper.

A natural course was the long poplar-bordered *route nationale* between Paris and Bordeaux and, hardly had the dust settled on the Rouen Trial, than a group of enthusiasts headed by De Dion, Baron Zuylen de Nyevelt and the Chevalier René de Knyff began organising a race to Bordeaux and back, a distance of 732 miles. Run in perfect weather, the Paris-Bordeaux-Paris was not only the first real race, but one of the longest events in early racing history. Competitors had to check in at various controls along the route, and once the race had started it went on until they got back to Paris. Of the forty-six entries, twenty-three machines were powered by internal combustion engines, thirteen by steam, two by electricity, and there were eight motorised tricycles and bicycles.

From the start at Versailles just after midday on 11 June 1895, Emile Levassor led the pack in a new improved two-cylinder Panhard and was far out in front all the way. When he reached Ruffec well ahead of schedule at three-thirty a.m. he found his relief driver still asleep and simply pressed on. At ten-thirty he checked into Bordeaux, drank a glass of champagne at the wheel and headed back for Paris, once again spurning the relief driver's

services. Alone and begrimed, he reached the Porte Maillot two days and forty-eight minutes after starting, and celebrated his epic run with a bowl of broth and a couple of poached eggs.

Levassor's splendid feat aroused public enthusiasm almost as much as the Dreyfus case that summer, and put the Lumière brothers, who were demonstrating the first *cinématographe*, in the basement of a café on the Boulevard des Capucines, completely in the shade. It established beyond doubt the reliability of the horseless carriage, and in particular the superiority of petrol engines over steam, since eight of the finishers had petrol-driven cars, against a single steamer. At a banquet celebrating the end of the race, a speaker predicted that within a few years the horse would be a rarity; just a luxury or an article of food. More to the point, the little group who had met at the Comte de Dion's house got together and on 5 November 1895 formed the Automobile Club de France, which organised thirty-four city-to-city races over the next eight years – the famous 'dust and glory' classics that created the traditions that were to govern motor sport for at least half a century.

RETURN TO THE ROAD

Sunday promenade in Richmond, 1901, when just the sight of a motor-car parked by the roadside was an excuse to stop, peer, prod or just pronounce on the new phenomenon. It was not long before the car itself became an integral part of the social scene, being used for tea-processions, gymkhanas and automobile promenades in the more fashionable circles.

The Road, for the British at any rate, has always occupied a special place. It was by statute 'The King's Highway', to which no man could be denied access. The gentlemen of the road, villains though they were, were accorded more glory than mere murderers or sheep-stealers (and at crossroads, very appropriately, they were hanged for their pains). In the seventeenth and eighteenth centuries the Road seemed to symbolise a form of romantic liberation. 'My lines and life are free', wrote George Herbert, 'as free as the Road'. It was an idea that the cycling manifestoes in the 1880s also proclaimed to the world, and one that the early motorists endorsed with enthusiasm. But to the average red-blooded Victorian it was not the road that offered such promise of freedom, but the railway. In the first quarter of the last century the main roads of Britain, cherished by engineers like Telford and Macadam, had been worthy of the name, offering fast and regular mail services between the major cities. The journey from Exeter to London, for instance, could be covered in eighteen hours with halts of pit-stop efficiency, during which teams of horses were changed in under a minute. But such expertise dwindled into futility when matched with the convenience of the all-devouring engine. By mid-century scarcely a corner of Britain had not been touched with the iron finger. On one single day at the height of the railway expansion no fewer than three hundred plans for new railway lines were deposited at Whitehall.

Inevitably the great coaching inns, in which Mr. Pickwick and his fellow travellers had gloried, fell into disuse, and the turnpike tolls, which had to pay for the upkeep of the roads, dwindled to nothing. Between 1840 and 1890 the highways fell into a shameful state of neglect, and in the later years the new traffic that did appear – traction engines and cycling clubs – simply made them worse. The official response, however, was not to legislate to improve the quality of the roads, but to pass restrictive laws designed to discourage people from using the road. The most notorious was the 'Red Flag' act of 1865, which obliged any machine-powered vehicle to have a minimum of three drivers and restricted it to a maximum speed of four miles an hour; to add insult to injury it had to be preceded by a footman holding a red flag. After a while the red flag was dropped, but the speed limit and the footman remained, and it was this Act which the early pioneers of motoring in Britain found themselves regulated by (with policemen in plenty to enforce it).

So while exciting developments were taking place in France, the English were still firmly saddled with the horse. British engineers, crippled by the Red Flag act and lacking any stimulus to develop motive power, had concentrated instead on the cycle – to such good effect that Coventry controlled the world's trade in bicycles and tricycles. In fact it was on British tricycles that the continental innovators adapted their early motors. What cars there were in the country in the early 1890s were all imported. H. Hewetson shipped the first car into Britain – a Benz – and was followed by others like Sir David Salomons and the Hon. Evelyn Ellis, who brought cars over from France and put them through their paces in private grounds. Frederick Simms, whose family had an old established business in Hamburg, struck up a friendship with Gottlieb Daimler and

By 1900 the automobile had made enough of an impact for advertisers to adopt it as a symbol of power and prestige. Or did the makers of Lux soap powder believe that mud-coated and begrimed motorists needed the services of their product more than other sections of the community?

Back-seat driver: curious seating arrangements in this Pennington machine of 1896 probably ensured its brief commercial career. The lady in front would have been especially vulnerable – if not to the risks of a head-on collision, then from her close proximity to the petrol-tank!

became a director of the Cannstatt firm, as a result of which he secured the patent rights for the British Empire, and taking the bull by the horns, formed the Daimler Motor Syndicate in 1893. And in November 1895, a full year before it was legal to drive cars at more than walking pace in England, Henry Sturmey, the editor of *The Cyclist*, started a weekly motoring magazine which he called *The Autocar* – his choice of a generic name to replace 'horseless carriage'. As an ex-schoolmaster, he objected to the mixed use of Greek and Latin roots in 'automobile', a term quickly adopted in America and approved by the Académie Française.

The alliance between aristocratic enthusiasts and the cycle trade was elo-

The Hon. C.S. Rolls in 1896, in his first car, a 3¾ hp Peugeot. Clearly this is a set-up photograph: before the repeal of the 'Red Flag' act that year, cars certainly had to be preceded by a man on foot, but for many years he had no longer been required to carry a red flag.

Emancipation *(right):* to celebrate the passing of the new Locomotives Act in 1896 (which among other things raised the speed limit in Britain from 4 to 12 mph) a London-Brighton Run was organised – which for the past 50 years has been continued under the auspices of the RAC. Here the participants drive through enthusiastic crowds at Reigate.

quent enough. But additional muscle was unexpectedly provided by a flamboyant entrepreneur named Harry Lawson, who, having made a fortune floating cycle and tyre concerns, conceived the grandiose idea of cornering the whole of the country's yet unborn motor industry. By buying up all existing and future patents, Harry Lawson launched the British Motor Syndicate in 1895, and in a sense, created an industry from scratch. But it was only in November 1896, that a bill to amend the antiquated Locomotives Act became law and fixed the speed limit at 14 mph (though permitting the Local Government Board to reduce it if necessary, which it promptly did – to 12 mph). Meanwhile the motorists themselves went on the offensive. Sir David Salomons called a public meeting at the Cannon Street Hotel to create the Self-Propelled Traffic Association. Lawson went one better; with the help of Frederick Simms he formed the Motor Car Club, with himself as chairman and his cronies as members.

November 14th, the day that cars could run freely for the first time on the roads of Britain (at up to 12 mph), was celebrated by the famous London-to-Brighton Run that is still going strong today. At the wheel of the Panhard in which Levassor had won the Paris-Bordeaux race, Harry Lawson led off a procession of some thirty solid-tyred, tiller-steered machines through the drizzle. The affair was so disorganised that no two reports agreed on the exact number that took part, nor how many reached Brighton, where a banner flapping in the gale at Preston Park

Above: Gordon Crosby's drawing for the *Autocar* of the RAC's magnificent new Pall Mall clubhouse on completion in 1911. Inspired by Gabriel's Hôtel de Crillon (then the home of the Automobile Club de France), and redolent inside of an eighteenth century French chateau, it stood as a grand monument to the growing stature and importance of the automobile in a spacious era.

assured them that 'centuries will look upon this, your immortal ride'. But the fact was that the motor club had become a vehicle for company promoting. Having bought the rights for numerous products (including those of Daimler from Simms), Lawson was taking advantage of the motor movement to place tempting prospectuses before the public, with the result that several million pounds were invested, only to be quickly lost. When, shortly after the Brighton run, it began to look as though investors might be on the receiving end of a sting, both Frederick Simms, the vice-president, and Harrington Moore, the secretary, felt it was time to resign

Fatal excursion: in July 1899 Edwin Sewell and Major Richie were killed when the rear wheel of their Coventry Daimler collapsed and they were thrown from the car on Grove Hill, Harrow. The motor-car had claimed the first of its many thousands of victims in Britain, and prompted many people to share Queen Victoria's view of it as 'a very shaky and disagreeable conveyance altogether'.

from the Club. They both saw the need for a genuine body to protect, encourage and develop motoring in England. Simms convened a meeting of motorists at a suite of rooms in Whitehall Court on 10 August 1897. The thirty people who attended this inaugural gathering duly approved the proposed rules and appointed a committee. On 8 December 1897 an inaugural luncheon, followed by a display of cars with trial runs, marked the official foundation of the Automobile Club of Great Britain. In the early days 'house dinners', followed by discussions on technical topics, were an effective means of arousing interest in cars. The secretary, Claude Johnson (later to become the driving force in Rolls-Royce Ltd), provided lists of places where petrol could be bought and batteries charged. He also arranged tours and exhibitions. But when in June 1899 the club held Britain's first major Motor Show – a week-long extravaganza in the Old Deer Park at Windsor – the well-advertised race between a horse and a motorcycle backfired as much as the machine; the horse won by a full half-lap. Even S.F. Edge, who sought to retrieve the situation with his De Dion-Bouton over a mile course, only managed a neck-to-neck finish with a trotter pulling a racing sulky, which hardly improved the image of the car any more than the show did for the club's finances. But the club continued to run motoring events. In 1900, at Alfred Harmsworth's suggestion, Claude Johnson staged a Thousand-Mile Trial from London to Scotland and back. It was meticulously organised, and of the sixty-five starters no fewer than twenty-three finished the course. By giving many people up and down the country their first sight of an automobile, this ambitious event turned out to be the catalyst that put motoring on the map in England.

Above: The first motor exhibition at the Royal Agricultural Hall, London, in 1898. It was run as a rival to the National Show at the Crystal Palace, and was continued independently (though under the patronage of the RAC) until the Society of Motor Manufacturers and Traders was formed and organised its own exhibition in 1903 – from which the present International Motor Show is a direct descendant.

THE HORSELESS BUGGY

Light, simple and sturdy, Ransom Olds' automobiles were the first in America to reach a popular market – and cope with the bone-rattling roads. His early runabouts *(below)* gave way in 1901 to the famous Curved Dash Oldsmobiles *(top)* after the disastrous Detroit fire.

Inventors in America, too, had been tinkering with horseless buggies for much of the century, but it was not until 1893 that Charles and Frank Duryea appeared on the streets of Springfield, Massachusetts, with a machine that they could boast 'actually operated under its own propulsion'. Two years later, their second prototype, propelled by a single-cylinder four-stroke engine, won the first American race, which took place in a blizzard, from Chicago to Evanston and back. (The only other competitor was a Benz, whose driver got frostbite and gave up.) But, spurred by this success, they built a further thirteen cars, one of which was exported to Henry Sturmey in England. The brothers then quarrelled, and their business was wound up. Indeed, as late as 1896 cars were still so rare in the United States that the Barnum and Bailey circus displayed a Duryea as its main attraction with top billing over the giant, the fat lady and the elephant.

All the same, the Paris-Rouen run had sparked such interest that hundreds of young engineers were getting busy in their backyards. Hiram Maxim was one of them, expending so much gasoline unsuccessfully cranking his new engine that the proprietor of the local paintshop (which supplied the gas) got very suspicious. 'Let me tell you something you prob'ly don't know, young fellow. Everyone who has ever experimented with gasoline got killed doing it. Not one of them alive today. I'm just warning of yer – that's all.' Nevertheless, by the end of the century there were forty-five registered automobile manufacturers in the States.

Some of them, like Pennington, whose three-wheeled motorcycle was promoted in England by Lawson, were a nine-day wonder. Others, like Ransom E. Olds, Henry Ford and David Buick, laid the foundations of the huge industry that perpetuated their names. They soon found that someone calling himself 'the inventor of the automobile' was putting the bite on them. Back in 1876 George B. Selden, a patent lawyer from Rochester, had seen the Brayton two-stroke engine exhibited at the Centennial Exhibition in Philadelphia and realised that it could be used to power a horseless carriage. Thus inspired, he had drawn up the plans for a vehicle fitted with a modified version of this engine and had applied for a patent, the wording of which covered the use of explosion engine, clutch, transmission and just about everything that made up a car. In 1879, when he filed his application, no one was particularly impressed. Selden was shrewd enough to keep his patents pending until interest in automobiles had quickened, and then assign them to a combine that already held the majority of bicycle patents, which proceeded to exact royalties from every manufacturer building cars. It was not until 1910 that the Supreme Court finally ruled that Selden's patents were 'valid but

THE BARNUM & BAILEY GREATEST SHOW on EARTH

1896

THE FAMOUS DURYEA MOTOR WAGON, OR MOTORCYCLE,
THE IDENTICAL HORSELESS CARRIAGE
THAT WON THE GREAT RACE IN CHICAGO LAST NOVEMBER
TO BE SEEN EVERY DAY IN THE NEW STREET PARADE

not violated'. By that time most of the proceeds had vanished into the lawyers' pockets anyway.

When they finally appeared, most of the early American cars were spindly, spidery affairs with carriage wheels and cart springs, for high wheels were necessary to negotiate the rutted country roads and many of the builders were wagon manufacturers, who found it difficult to separate the idea of the horseless carriage from the horse and carriage. They weren't the only ones. One early motorist arriving at a ferry with a 6 hp machine presented a real dilemma for the ferryman, whose tariff did not provide for any such cargo. After considerable thought he resolved the problem by making out a ticket for 'one go-cart drawn by hand'. Likewise a toll-keeper, confronted by his first horseless buggy, charged the regular fee for two bicycles!

In all the vast countryside of America there were, at that time, only about 150 miles of properly surfaced roads, and these mostly around the cities; for smart town use, light bike-wheeled machines were made, with the engine hidden beneath at the rear to preserve the buggy image. Initially, too, electric cars were popular, being slow and easy (no cranking!) though only suitable for a turn in the park, while steam cars were considered smoother and more practical than the internal combustion engine, despite the time it took to heat up and the tendency for the boiler to explode. It was just as well, perhaps, that New York, which as late as 1901 had its own 'red flag' ordinance prescribing that a 'mature male' walk one-eighth of a mile ahead of a steam carriage, discreetly overlooked that old ruling. Other legislators, though, were more apprehensive and dreamed up the weirdest regulations to keep the new monsters at bay. One New York alderman introduced (unsuccessfully) a measure to ban the presence of

Top of the bill: the Duryea brothers' pioneering automobile found itself exhibited, like a freak, by Barnum and Bailey after it had won the famous Chicago-Evanston race in 1895. Others *(below)* thought the horseless buggy a joke, and submitted designs to reinstate at least part of the faithful horse!

all gasoline within the city limits, while in Chicago it was decreed that persons wearing eyeglasses should not be permitted to drive automobiles lest they should fall off.

Not surprisingly, Ransom Eli Olds experimented with steam and electric engines before he made his famous Curved Dash runabout and proved that the petrol-engined car could be sold in the thousands. Various prototypes were made, including a mini-runabout of extreme simplicity and lightness that could be turned out at a cost of only about $300. To Olds' partners it hardly seemed a real car at all, and they opted to launch a much heavier model at $1,250 on an already price-conscious market.

Marketing the American automobile. From the very first years of the century, the car was part of the American scene, with its own prominent place in advertising. Both the automotive and the advertising industries seem to have come of age together – and to have developed a mutual dependency that continues today. Adverts helped associate the car with a wide range of social functions. Here we see the automobile linked to business (the Federal), to cross-country touring (1904 Franklin) and to women drivers (1901 Toledo).

However, on 9 March 1901 (a date never to be forgotten in Detroit), the entire plant and its contents were destroyed by fire, except for the experimental runabout that a young tester managed to push out of the burning building. No alternative being available, the little single-cylinder two seater – know as the Curved Dash on account of its elegant, scroll-shaped dash – was put into production and became an instant commercial success. It was the success of Ransom Olds' little car that anchored the centre of the automobile industry in Detroit, until then a virtually unknown town a few miles from the Canadian border. With the factory destroyed, it became necessary to contract out for parts, and local businessmen became involved. The operation of assembling parts led to the first instance of mass-production within the industry, which was introduced by Olds (and copied by Thomas B. Jeffery with the Rambler) long before Henry Ford developed it into a fine art.

Henry Ford also started with steam, bolting an engine to the bottom of an ordinary horse buggy. But doubts about the safety of the boiler led him to give up the attempt. 'To be seated on a high-pressure engine which might explode is not a pleasant thought', he observed sagely and took a job with the Detroit Edison Company. Yet the itch remained, and he spent his nights developing his first petrol-engined machine, a water-cooled twin with belt drive. Early one fine morning Henry took it out on test, only to discover that he had forgotten to fit a reverse gear and could not

28

SCRIBNER'S for MARCH

NOW READY · PRICE 25 CENTS

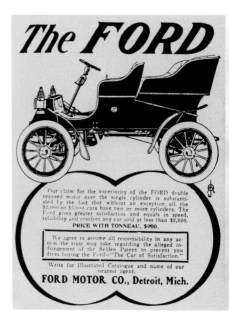

The FORD

Our claim for the superiority of the FORD double opposed motor over the single cylinder is substantiated by the fact that without an exception all the $2,000 to $5,000 cars have two or more cylinders. The Ford gives greater satisfaction and equals in speed, reliability and comfort any car sold at less than $2,000.
PRICE WITH TONNEAU, $900.

We agree to assume all responsibility in any action the trust may take regarding the alleged infringement of the Selden Patent to prevent you from buying the Ford—"The Car of Satisfaction."

Write for Illustrated Catalogue and name of our nearest agent.
FORD MOTOR CO., Detroit, Mich.

Ford, founded in 1903, seemed to be avoiding type-casting or specific 'images' in this 1904 ad – no ladies or businessmen (as on opposite page) impinge on the classic profile of the automobile in its purity. Shades of the no-nonsense Model T of later years. Meanwhile, *Scribner's*, a fashionable magazine, demonstrated in this poster ad from 1907 that the car was already enjoying a chic status in the States and that the machine could be compatible with glamour and even a touch of gallantry.

turn without pushing it in the direction he wanted to run. Not for another three years was his next car completed, a comparatively low-built job with wire wheels and solid tyres (and this time with reverse). Disregarding his father's advice to 'stick to his $350-a-month job rather than tinker with automobiles', Ford scraped together all the money he had, and with the help of a few friends formed the Detroit Automobile Company. A wearing period of development followed; the small capital of $5,000 soon vanished in experimental work, and the firm had to be reorganised as the Henry Ford Motor Company. With the co-operation of Tom Cooper, an ex-racing cyclist, some racing cars were built. The first of these scored an unexpected victory over Alexander Winton's heavyweight at Grosse Pointe, and later 'Barney' Oldfield hit the headlines with the famous 999. All the same, Ford had to sell out in 1900 to Henry Leland, who renamed the ailing firm Cadillac (after Antoine de la Mothe Cadillac, the founder of Detroit) and began making high-quality 6½ hp vehicles.

But the wave of popularity generated by his racing cars enabled Ford to found his third concern, the Ford Motor Company, in 1903, with $28,000 put up by a dozen venturesome but fortunate subscribers, who subsequently saw their investment increase into millions. The first model A had a Ford-designed two-cylinder engine which cranked at the side, two forward speeds, plush leather seats and gleaming brass headlights. It was known as the Fordmobile, and 1,700 were sold at $850, or 100 dollars more than

Testing the first Curved Dash Oldsmobiles outside Detroit in 1901. The strange equipment – called a teetertotter – was designed to examine the car's control and stability by manoeuvring the central vehicle so as to create equilibrium.

the Cadillac. Ford's first four-cylinder, the Model B, had the engine in the front, planetary two-speed transmission, and cost $2,000. It was followed by the six-cylinder K at $2,500. But the limited success of these expensive cars convinced Ford that the secret was not high price but high volume. In 1906 he undercut Oldsmobile with a four-cylinder model N runabout; by selling 8,432 of them at $550 the Ford Motor Company made a million dollars, and became the world's largest manufacturer even before the immortal Model T was announced in 1907.

At Grosse Pointe Club, where motoring lore abounds, they will tell you that while Henry Ford was still experimenting with his first early cars the patriarchal figure of Henry B. Joy appeared in the humble premises of the Detroit Automobile Company and offered to buy one. Ford demurred, saying that first he must iron out the bugs, and since the New York and Ohio Company, under the presidency of Colonel James Packard, had just brought out their first 12 hp Packard, Joy bought one of these instead. Although following the traditional buggy styling, the Packard had an unusual gearbox, giving three speeds forward and two in reverse, as well as an automatic spark advance and 4-inch pneumatic tyres. Joy was so pleased with his car that he promptly bought a controlling interest in the concern and transferred the plant from Warren, Ohio, to Detroit. With the wealth and social weight of his old established family behind it, Packards moved into the top end of the market. In 1903 a 12 litre model designed on European lines sold for a hefty $7,500 and led to the Model L, the first car to bear the classic Packard radiator. The famous 30, which really established Packard's reputation as a quality car, appeared just as Henry Ford was launching his 'Lizzie'. Half a century later, in 1954, Packard was to link up with Studebaker, who traced their origins back to 1854 when the brothers Henry and Clem Studebaker started a wagon building business in South Bend. The first Studebakers were electrics, and the model C petrol-engined car appeared in 1904. Sadly, these two great marques discontinued production in the megabuck atmosphere of the sixties, just as Winton did in 1925. And yet, when Alexander Winton switched from bicycles to automobiles, his cars quickly became the yardstick by which the others were judged. His first effort was massive and looked like a tub, but even in 1896 it had a self-starter. His second set a record by covering a mile in 1 minute, 48 seconds. With his third, Winton drove from Cleveland to New York, a distance of over 700 miles. In 1898 he turned out a lightweight model. Twenty-one were sold, which put him at the top of the production league.

By the turn of the century it was patent that, whatever you may have thought of automobiles in America, they could not simply be ignored. You might, perhaps, like the editor of the *Louisville Courier-Journal* in 1900, look forward to the quick return of the horse and buggy: 'The present fad in locomotion is the automobile. It is a swell thing, and the swell people must have one. But if it should displace the horse it will only be for a time. The bicycle threatened the thoroughbreds, but where are the bicycles?' Alternatively you could, like the editor of *Horseless Age*, look forward to a golden era ushered in by the motor-car: 'In our motor world the noise and clatter of the streets will be reduced, a priceless boon to the tired nerves of this over-wrought generation.... Streets will be cleaner, jams and blockades less likely to occur, and accidents less frequent.'

Frontiers of touring: few American motorists were tempted far beyond the town limits in the early days of motoring. Road often just ran out and direction signs were a luxury. These tourists in Ohio in their 1905 Rambler were fortunate to have come across even this primitive effort. The absence of signs, one motoring journal complained, made it 'easier to find one's way into a town than through it or out of it'.

PANHARD-LEVASSOR
1891

Lounging in one of GM's ornate 'personal luxury' Oldsmobile V8's it is hard to believe that 80 years ago Ransom E. Olds got Detroit going with a single-cylinder runabout. In fact, his factory might have been at Newark, across the river from New York, had he not met a copper-miner named Smith on the platform of Detroit station who offered to finance him if he stayed right there. Olds' factory – the first plant designed specifically for car manu-facture – was erected near the Belle Isle Bridge on East Jefferson Avenue. During the autumn of 1900, when sales of the few large cars he made were falling off, Olds built a small prototype vehicle with a curved buggy-style dashboard. His idea was that a little runabout that cost about $300 to manufacture and retailed for $650

would appeal to city residents for local trips. But his backers disagreed, until on 9 March 1901 – a date that has tremendous significance for Detroit – the works were destroyed by fire. The only car saved was this experimental Curved Dash machine, which was pushed out of the burning building by a time-keeper called James Brady (who later became mayor of Detroit). And so suddenly this lightweight vehicle, with its single-cylinder water-cooled engine mounted at the front and operating through an epicyclic gear-change and chain drive, was all that was left for the firm to produce. With the factory gone, moreover, subcontracting of parts became an urgent necessity. So local contractors were called in. Leland & Faulks made the engine, John and Horace Dodge built the

transmissions in their machine shop, Benjamin and Frank Briscoe supplied the radiators, and Barney Everitt the bodies. The little Olds was an immediate success: by driving one from Detroit across Canada to New York in seven and a half days, Roy Chaplin (a tester who later became U.S. Secretary of Commerce) secured orders for 1,000 cars. In 1901, 425 Oldsmobiles were made; by 1906 produc-tion was running at the rate of 6,500 a year. Result: America had its first volume-produced car, the suppliers flourished, and (with the help of Henry Ford and a few others) the small city of Detroit became the motor centre of the USA.

MERCEDES 'SIXTY'
1903

'C'est brutal, mais ça marche' ('A rough ride, but it moves'): the words were spoken with a smile by Emile Levassor one day in 1890 after his prototype Panhard-Levassor finally spluttered into action – and into automotive history. Not that this was the first automobile, by any means – Cugnot, in Lorraine, claimed that honour more than a century earlier. Levassor's wasn't even the first gasoline powered internal combustion motor-car – a milestone achieved in 1864 by Siegried Marcus and followed up by Benz and Daimler. Levassor is remembered in the history of the automobile because he turned the Daimler model into something quite different, which has remained the basic concept of the automobile. Daimler's car had one fundamental flaw: it was in fact a

horsedrawn carriage, minus the horse, with a motor rudely superimposed upon it. Levassor saw that, while it might be easy to fit an engine into a rowing boat and convert it into a motor launch, you could not do the same with a carriage – which was far too flimsy to support the weight and propulsive movement of a petrol engine. What was needed, he decided, was a vehicle designed from the outset with the motor in mind, and having the appropriate transmission system.
His answer: a front-mounted engine, a foot operated friction clutch, sliding-pinion gear-change (this was the 'brutal' bit), a differential and chain drive to a live axle. The chassis was of wood.
The first outings in the car were disastrous, and Levassor had to be pushed back to

the works again and again. But by 1894 the P-L was making the Paris-Rouen Trial, and in 1895 Levassor drove one of his own cars singlehanded from Paris to Bordeaux and back, at an average speed of 11 mph, to win the world's first real motor race.
The basic layout of components established by Levassor in 1891 laid the ground rules for automobile architecture that were followed, and progressively refined, by other manufacturers until Porsche defied the convention with his rear-engine Volkswagen. But in front-engine rear-drive cars the *système Panhard* – radiator, engine, clutch, gearbox, transmission and rear axle, in that order – prevails to this day.

OLDSMOBILE CURVED DASH
1901

It was, in a sense, the outcome of a happy conspiracy between customer and constructor. Emile Jellinek, a rich Austrian with a passion for cars, visited Daimler's Cannstatt works in the hope of persuading the factory to build a lighter, more powerful model than his Phoenix-engined Daimler. He found Maybach with a car full of new ideas on the drawing-board, and agreed to place an order for no less than three dozen – on the understanding that the new car would be named after his daughter, Mercedes.
Unveiled at Nice Week in 1901, the Mercedes 35 introduced the world to pressed steel chassis, honeycomb radiator, mechanically-operated inlet valves and gate-change gearbox. It set new standards of refinement and performance which

eclipsed any opposition, and even at a price of over $2,000 the rich of the Riviera rushed to buy. By 1903 Mercedes had developed an even more powerful version in the form of a touring model 'Sixty' with elegant 'Roi des Belges' bodywork, curvaceous and copiously buttoned.
The Sixty had a 9,236 cc engine with cylinders cast in pairs; the drive went through a scroll clutch, and the four-speed gate gearbox was combined with the differential, final drive being by side chains. The result was incredible. 'When the throttle is opening', wrote one admirer, 'a series of giant impulses, smoothly delivered but each individually appreciable, give an impression of irresistible power and communicate an intoxicating sense of omnipotence to the driver. Now one can

understand why the Sixty although good drivers declared it to be the safest car that at that date had been built, was the death of so many less experienced owners.'
Even to-day to drive in a Mercedes 60 is unforgettable. Climbing into the driving seat, you sit looking down at a wide and shapely bonnet, without a suspicion of windscreen. In front of you are eleven drip feeds on the dash, four foot pedals, outside gear and brake levers, a bulb horn and side lamps. You can almost count the engine revolutions – twenty-two, twenty-two, twenty-two – and though the steering is brutal, the gear-change is finger-light, and the old monster accelerated in top up a hill on the outskirts of Bath leaving modern traffic behind as if tied to a post.

THE CHALLENGE OF THE CAR

By the turn of the century the automobile was beginning to assume its own identity rather than masquerade as a motorised version of the horse carriage, and the petrol engine was emerging as the most practical form of propulsion. It could be a brute to start sometimes, and to keep going, even to stop. But it worked, and there were already the foundations of a flourishing motor industry. The next battles were to be fought on the road, against prejudice and fear and class hostility – for the motorists were still a clearly defined group, upper-class, rich and dedicated enthusiasts. They formed themselves into clubs of impeccable pedigree – the Royal Automobile Club's new premises in Pall Mall, London, were hailed on completion as 'the finest gentlemen's club in Europe'. But at the same time the RAC (like its counterparts in other countries) acted as a springboard for many of the significant developments in motoring – campaigning against repressive legislation, advising the government on the scale of car taxes, providing driving tuition, sponsoring experiments in road improvement, setting up a framework for motor sports. By the outbreak of war, the motor-car had made its challenge and it looked as if nothing was going to withstand it.

Make way for the new: an old-fashioned hansom-cab with flagging horse is overtaken by a new motor-taxi in London in 1907. The first one had appeared on the streets of the city three years earlier. They now numbered over 700 and many of the horse-cab drivers had applied for the necessary month's training. In 1906 taximeters came into use on the motor-cabs, thus dispensing with the hallowed tradition of haggling over fares – though some passengers complained that less scrupulous taxi-drivers omitted to put non-skid bands on the wheel attached to the meter, so that in wet weather the taximeter registered up to an excess of 50 percent.

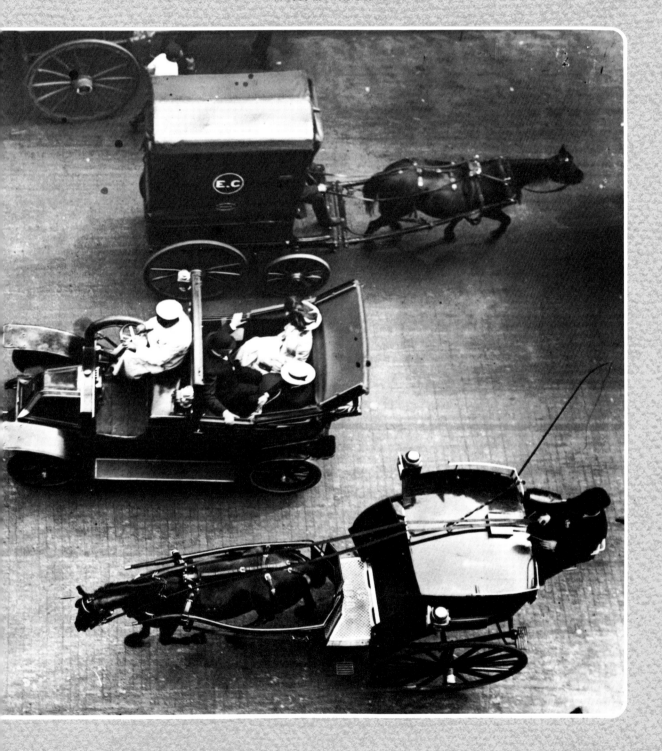

MOTORPHOBIA

THE CAMPAIGN AGAINST THE MOTOR-CAR

The dream of motoring: a family picnic in the Ardennes in 1903. Early motoring writers were constantly extolling the 'liberating' virtues of the motor-car... 'the milestones, the hedgerows and wild flowers to smell' (wrote one). 'The hidden beauties suddenly revealed by the curving road, the stop for lunch, the arbitrary stoppage to enjoy the silence and the peace: For this French family the idyll was not cheap – their car, a De Dietrich with custom-built coachwork, was one of the most expensive on the market. That same year Charles Jarrott drove a 24 hp De Dietrich in the-ill-fated Paris-Madrid race, covering the 343 miles to Bordeaux in 361 minutes.

'What will become of coach-makers and harness-makers, coach-masters and coachmen, inn-keepers, horse-breeders and horsedealers? Is the House aware of the smoke and noise, the hiss and whirl which engines passing at the rate of ten or twelve miles an hour will occasion? Neither the cattle ploughing in the field or grazing in the meadows can behold them without dismay. It will be the greatest nuisance, the most complete disturbance of quiet and comfort in all parts of the kingdom that the ingenuity of man can invent.'

This philippic was delivered (by one Sir Isaac Coffin) in the House of Commons, not in 1896 when Parliament was deliberating on the regulation of motor-cars, but in 1826. The monster that was going to throw honest men out of work and stampede the cattle was not the motor-car, but the railway engine. None of Sir Isaac's prophecies were fulfilled, yet each one of his arguments and many more besides were arrayed once more against the motor-car seventy years later (not least by the very gentlemen who had made their fortunes in railway shares).

Many far-reaching inventions have been greeted initially with suspicion, apprehension or abuse. But the depth of hostility aroused by the early automobiles was remarkable in itself. The pioneer drivers came to expect it,

The nightmare of motoring: curiously this almost surrealist vision of 1899 was dreamed up in order to sell De Dion cars. The advertisement seems to contain virtually every indictment made against the automobile by motorphobes: reckless driving (as one can well understand when your passenger chooses the open road to breast-feed the baby), the frightening of horses, near-massacres of animals and complete disregard for other road-users. The underlying theme however – the arrogant domination of the highway by car-drivers – must have appealed to the French sense of humour, since it recurs constantly in advertisements at the turn of the century.

and classified each outburst as another manifestation of the malaise they called 'motorphobia'. It was, as they came to realise in time, a complex reaction arising from a variety of causes: fear or ignorance, justifiable indignation, vested interest, class conflict. Under its impact motorists began to feel they were a persecuted minority, misunderstood and deprived of rights. In retaliation, the motor-owners formed themselves into associations, clubs and pressure-groups to protect themselves and further the cause, and until the outbreak of the First World War the two entrenched factions confronted each other, in the press, in the courts, in Parliament and state legislatures, and most frequently on the open road.

The car first became identified as a social 'problem' in France in the mid-1890s. By 1897 there were already several thousand motorised vehicles on the streets of Paris, and the Bois de Boulogne could be particularly hazardous at certain times of the day. After one incident there, Monsieur Hugues le Roux claimed to have been knocked down by a motorist 'going at the speed of an express-train' and penned an angry letter to the Prefect of Police, denouncing motorists as 'mad dogs' and warning that in future he intended to carry a revolver in his pocket and shoot anyone driving a car. The letter found its way into several Paris papers, and evoked some apoplectic responses. The motoring magazine *La Locomotion Automobile* (the first of its kind in the world) retorted that if pedestrians were going to carry revolvers in the streets, then motorists would arm themselves with machine-guns.

Undoubtedly speed, and the absence of effective regulations, were the main causes of public hostility in France. There was *(La Locomotion Automobile* disarmingly admitted) an obsession with speed and performance, which was encouraged by the great Napoleonic legacy of *routes nationales*, and which was only tempered by the tragic series of accidents in the 1903 Paris-Madrid road race. Meanwhile in rural areas summary retribution was meted out to errant motorists by local inhabitants according to their of-

The uninvited guest: an illustration from *Le Petit Journal* depicting a contretemps in Boulogne in 1903, when an errant motorist 'provoked a riot' by running into a wedding procession. The magazine had continued to take a rather morbid interest in motoring affairs ever since a letter had appeared in its columns in 1893, suggesting a competition for the new horseless carriages. The letter was in fact the work of the paper's editor, but it bore fruit the following year when the first-ever car rally, from Paris to Rouen, was held.

fence: the driver in Boulogne who interrupted a wedding procession was mobbed by the guests; the automobilist who ran down a pedestrian at Fontainebleau watched his car being burnt to a cinder.

Elsewhere antediluvian regulations were themselves the cause of friction. In Switzerland, where a four-mile-an-hour limit in towns survived well into the twentieth century, hundreds of motorists were punitively fined for an offence they could scarcely help committing. The cumulative effect was to brand *all* motorists as law-breakers, and many inoffensive drivers found their cars being stoned or themselves lashed with whips. Switzerland may have been an extreme example of reaction, but no country really came to grips with the problems of legislation, if only because events were overtaken by the meteoric development of the car between 1895 and 1905. By the time the speed-limit had been raised in many countries to around 20 miles an hour (15 in some states of America) in 1903, the mighty 60 hp Mercedes – capable of speeds up to 80 miles an hour – was already appearing on the roads.

Bitterly though some motorists objected to the existence of any kind of speed-limit, what undoubtedly united them all was the ways in which the limit was imposed. It was, they complained, nearly always arbitrary and quite unscientific. In France they experimented with a system of 'instantaneous photography', which involved two exposures of a moving object within a given time: it worked well enough on carriages proceeding at a sedate pace, but was hopelessly inefficient for the scorchers it was aimed to trap. The Germans likewise hit on the bright idea of fixing a visual speed indicator on the *outside* of every car, until tests proved that the faster a car was going, the less readable the indicator was. In the end no substitute

was found for the traditional method of a measured distance, two policemen and a stopwatch.

The 'police trap' became the focus of all the motorists' frustrations. Conviction naturally depended on the word of local police officers, and their zealousness was evidently a reflection of the anti-motorist feelings of local authorities. Unfortunately in Britain it rapidly became clear, after the Light Locomotives Act of 1896, that certain magistrates' benches were prejudiced beyond reason, especially in the counties of Surrey, Sussex, Kent and Middlesex. It was, perhaps, no accident that these counties all embraced major roads leading out of London, and were therefore reluctant hosts to the increasing exodus of joyriders from the capital. Motorphobia, in its early years, was partly a crystallisation of an age-old rural-urban conflict, of the town 'invading' the country.

Rural magistrates – not unreasonably – objected to their threadbare roads (which had to be maintained by local rates) being turned into quagmires by strangers, who contributed nothing, and consequently felt quite justified in

The dust fiend: a typical propaganda production from the antimotoring press in Britain in 1902. That year saw intense lobbying from car-drivers to have the 12 mph speed limit abolished, but their opponents succeeded in keeping it down to 20 mph in the Motor Car Bill introduced into Parliament the next year. As *The Times* commented: 'the number of drivers of motor-cars who are not gentlemen would seem to be unduly large. There is no turning a cad into a gentleman, but there is such a thing as making even cads fear the law.'

levying the heftiest fines on motorists who came before them. Village communities also objected to the car for its dust, its noise and for its dimly-perceived threat to an established way of life. In some notorious districts motorists literally ran the gauntlet. S.F. Edge, the famous racing-driver, recalls driving past Crawley in the winter of 1900 and being hit on the head by a rock. Spotting the 'yokel' in the light of his acetylene headlamps, Edge stopped the car and gave chase through the snow. Two fields later he caught up with the culprit and relieved him of all his clothes, except pants and shoes, which he deposited at the next village. It was, he added with satisfaction, one of the coldest nights of the year.

The terrible motor-collision at Pompignac – another front page from *Le Petit Journal,* which even in 1907 continued to regale its readers with its version of spectacular accidents from all over France.

American motorists had their local Dogberries as well. Their special wrath was reserved for Magistrate Kellogg of Yonkers, whose flying squad of bicycling speed-cops provoked *Automobile Topics* to frenzy in 1902. 'Encouraged by his petty despotism [wrote the editor] every village constable in the northern suburb now seems to regard himself as a heaven-sent lawmaker, confident that whatever legal freaks his brain may engender, a ready sponsor will be found on the local bench.' Equally feared was Mayor Dennis of Glencoe, Illinois, whose speciality (until he was sued) was ordering steel cables to be strung across the main road to stop all automobiles entering his jurisdiction. Deprived of his cables, he then contracted for the road to be dug up into artificial bumps – fiercer ancestors, no doubt, of modern rumble strips.

But motorists themselves were far from being blameless before the law. There was a tendency for speeding drivers not to stop when accosted by an officer: on Chicago's North Shore Drive policemen began to open fire on scorchers who ignored their speed-traps – prompting *Motor Age* to comment grimly that 'war' had been declared. In New York, Vanderbilt, flamboyant in his huge red tourer, made a sport of out-running the police around the streets of Manhattan – until one day he came to an ignominious halt in a swamp in Harlem. A cause célèbre of 1905 was the hit-and-run on Park Row, which was eventually tracked down to Pierpont Morgan's coupe: the victim was reported to have withdrawn her complaint when she learnt that the multi-millionaire was a passenger! The motor-car was still the plaything of the rich man, and the problem was that toys plainly carried no social responsibilities. As Woodrow Wilson, later to be president of the United States, summed it up: 'Nothing has spread socialistic feeling in this country more than the use of the automobile. To the countryman they are a picture of arrogance of wealth, with all its independence and carelessness.'

These were sentiments echoed in England, by the president of the Local Government Board (whose function was the imposing of local speed-limits), who wrote: 'There is an embittered feeling in the general public against all persons who use motor-cars which, as a dangerous class feeling, is, perhaps, without parallel in modern times.' The motoring lobby laboured hard to demonstrate that car-users were not a privileged minority, but it made little impression on the general public. And its case was in no way improved when, on one notable morning, four titled gentlemen (including a Lord and a Member of Parliament) were arraigned before the Bench at Odiham for speeding.

The fact was there was a gulf of misconceptions separating the motorists

German version of the speed-trap. A parody (from the journal *Lustigen Blatten)* on the official zeal in pursuing the motorist. 'Of all the countries in Europe' (commented a touring manual in 1907) 'Germany is the most difficult for the motorist.... What you have to do when touring in Germany nowadays is to keep out of the country. If you venture it, prepare for quick payments and small returns.'

Pedestrian power: *Punch's* answer in 1910 to the London roadhog – a potent counterploy against the new pneumatic tyres, with which most cars had begun to be fitted.

41

Priority to the sheep: a hazard of the High Street in Lewes (England) in 1908. Even in large cities animals being herded through the streets were a common sight – motorists were required by law to stop their cars, switch off the engine and wait till the animals had passed before they proceeded on their way.

Above right: De rigueur – a motoring coat for the upper classes from a French motorist's catalogue. But note that the gentleman still holds on to his riding crop: not to beat his horse-less carriage into submission, but because whips were considered a normal fashion accessory in those transitional days and some models of car had brackets fitted to hold driving whips!

and the administrators: the courts talked of public amenity, the car-users of fair play. It was not very sporting of the police, the motorists submitted, to hide in ditches and pig-sties or to set their traps on long, isolated downhill stretches of road: such tactics smacked of persecution rather than serving the needs of public safety. In turn the motorists set out to nullify the effects of the speed-trap – car magazines published maps of how to avoid the most notorious ones, the RAC campaigned vigorously for the abolition of all speed-limits, the Automobile Association was formed expressly to organise platoons of bicycle scouts, who would stop motorists and warn them of imminent police-traps. The activities of the AA scouts aroused the implacable anger of chief constables and came perilously close to constituting an obstruction of justice. Prudently, in 1909 the Association revised its advice to members: 'When a patrol does *not salute,* stop and ask him the reason'. (The reason being patently obvious, most drivers didn't bother to ask, but simply slowed down.)

But when the anti-motorists referred to the 'car nuisance' it wasn't merely the dangers of reckless driving they had in mind. One of their principal complaints was pollution, the saharas of dust trailed by cars in the countryside which made life in roadside cottages extremely unpleasant. Even town roads – except those constructed as in France with teeth-rattling *pavés* – could give off a veneer that made suburbs look like limestone quarries. To this charge the motorists had no defence, except that it was the fault not of their cars but of the roads, which had been badly neglected during the heroic era of the railways. Self-evidently the answer was better roads, but of what kind and at whose expense? How these questions were resolved we shall see in due course, but first car-owners were preoccupied with a struggle to establish their right to use the public highway on equal terms with other road-users. It was a right that was far from being taken for granted by pioneer motorists.

It might seem curious to find a judge in America – in the twentieth century – having to remind a jury that automobiles had a *right* to be on the roads

Meet my motor-car. The recommended way to accustom a horse to the car, according to a contemporary writer, was 'to stand the vehicle round it in gradually decreasing circles. The driver should talk soothingly to the horse....The horse will follow with his eyes the movements of the car, and in a little while will allow it to be driven close by without any further signs of fear!'

at all. Summing up in a case where a local doctor and his wife had been injured when their horse had been panicked by a passing car, Judge Russell said in 1901:

'The day is past in the history of New York State when we are obliged to give up the use of the highways entirely to the use of carriages propelled by horses or oxen. Whatever we may think about the value of steam carriages or carriages propelled by electricity or any other motive power aside from animal power, the time has come when those carriages have a right to go on the public highways for reasons perhaps of utility as well as pleasure....'

Perhaps the judge's reminder was necessary, because the jury came to the conclusion that the car should have stopped to allow the doctor's carriage to pass by. It was an opinion that became enshrined over the next few years in many state laws, which ordained that should a person riding a horse on the public highway raise his arm 'the operator of a motor vehicle must stop, silence the motor and, if necessary, assist the person riding the horse to pass'. This put the onus squarely onto the motorist, who took the view that, while there were undoubtedly 'motor-cads' who exercised little common sense in the vicinity of horses, there were infinitely more incompetent horse-riders who were unable to control their horses. It meant, in short, that in any incident involving horses it was the car-driver who was at fault if his vehicle was moving (and sometimes even if it wasn't).

An early (1904) anti-pollution cartoon, from the Austrian magazine *Schnarferl*. Motorists were very aware of the suffocating dust-storms raised by cars, but argued that the answer was to improve roads rather than penalise motorists.

In this respect the motorists were fighting the same battle with the horse lobby as the cyclists had in the 1870s, when they had been obliged to dismount on encountering a horse-carriage. In France the courts ruled that it was the horse-owners' responsibility to accustom their animals to the car before they put them on the road. But in Britain the friends of the horse were well organised and vocal: in the shires the fox-hunting gentry stood firm and in London a Highways Protection League was formed in 1903 (whose platform included a mandatory prison sentence for speeding and a reduction of the speed limit). Gamely the RAC ran courses to show how easily a horse could be trained to the car (apparently by driving the ma-

The advent of the motor-bus – by democratising this new form of travel – helped to break down the prejudices against the car. For several years a war raged between petrol, steam and electric buses in Britain: the 'Vanguard' service with its Daimler engine proved the most economical, durable and (in spite of this accident at Hand Cross Hill in 1910) reliable.

chine in ever-decreasing circles round the animal), but was sadly disappointed with the response. So the motoring interest launched a counter-offensive to prove that, even in the hands of an experienced coachman, horse traffic was more dangerous than the car.

Up and down the country a series of 'stopping trials' were organised, matching horse against motor. Predictably perhaps the results were unanimous and comprehensive: cars could stop in half, sometimes a quarter, of the distance required by a horse vehicle to come to a standstill. In a test held at the Crystal Palace a butcher's cart travelling at 12 mph took 50 feet to pull up; a 15 hp De Dion at the same speed stopped in less than 10. At 20 mph a 90 hp Napier required 26 feet; a trotting sulky, 43. At another demonstration, in Hertford in 1903, it was reported that the coachman at the reins of a four-wheel dog-cart was so humiliated by a Lanchester that he broke down and wept.

But in general the carters in their juddering juggernauts which could thwart all attempts at overtaking, and the sharp-tongued horse-cabbies were thicker skinned. Even in France, as the motoring writer Baudry de Saunier explained, wagon drivers paid no attention at all to car-horns (he suggested carrying a loud-hailer). Whether or not their truculence betrayed fears for the future of their time-honoured form of transport, the harsh reality was that by the coming of the war, horse-carriers were rarely to be seen on the streets of major cities, and hansoms and horse-buses were extinct. And as *Crown* magazine pointed out: 'To the man in the street the motor-car must have remained a pernicious and unwholesome thing for ever, had it not been for the happy advent of the motor-omnibus. You cannot go on very well hating motors when you are constantly taking penny rides in them.' The irony was that as the motor-car became too commonplace to denounce and the motorphobes' prophecies of doom died down, the real inconveniences and dangers of the car became apparent. As we shall see.

The ending of an era: this poster for the Detroit auto week in 1910 has little sympathy for the decrepit-looking horse which has the misfortune to find itself in the centre of America's automobile industry. Even if a little premature in its assumption that a new car-generation had been born, the advertisement clearly reflects the industry's confident vision of the car's future.

AUTO
WEEK
JAN. 24-29
1-9-1-0

"LOOK MAMMA, THERE'S A HORSE!"

THE BEAST IN THE STABLE

THE PROBLEMS OF BEING A CAR-OWNER

Trained mechanics, like this gentleman presiding over a 1903 24/30 hp De Dietrich engine, were thin on the ground in those early days. In the event of a breakdown at home, carowners had to resort to tinkering as best they could and getting spare parts worked by the blacksmith. For major repairs, however, manufacturers had to send out their own mechanics to the furthest parts of the country, and despatch components after them by train.

By the turn of the century the motor-car was smoothly shedding its horseless carriage image, even though the influence of the coachmakers lingered on for some years in the shape of phaetons, landaulettes and hansoms for the town-carriage set. (Indeed, in our motoring vocabulary we still carry the legacy of coaching in the 'dashboard' for instance, and the 'boot'.) But, for car-owners brought up in the horse tradition, the transition could be less than comfortable. Many still thought of their machines as a replacement for the horse, and continued to talk of hind wheels and motor-stables. But the relationship turned out to be very different: horses served, the new beasts (as people very soon discovered) dominated.

If you were fortunate, your brand-new automobile was delivered in working order by a trained mechanic from the manufacturers or their agents, who could initiate you into its mysteries. If you were less fortunate, like the Irish customer whose De Dion was shipped over by ferry, you had to rely on local know-how. In his case a mechanical genius duly arrived (presumably from the hunting-field), sat the owner upon his mount and ordered him to 'give a twist to the wheel, two blasts from the horn, and away she'd go!' Even the makers' handbooks – for all their comforting assurances – acknowledged it was harder than that. By 1902 many features were beginning to be universally adopted: the steering wheel, electrical ignition, acetylene headlamps, and pneumatic tyres, at least on the front wheels. Equally, over a whole range of basic components the customer was confronted with a bewildering array of claims and innovations. The gearing arrangements alone (a strange enough concept anyway to one brought up to change speeds with a whip) could range from a reasonably simple system of floor pedals working a planetary transmission in the Oldsmobile to the refinements of Daimler's gate-change gear-lever. Some models might have a quite separate lever for engaging reverse; others, like the Lanchester, came with two sliding gear-levers *and* a gear-trigger – with the intriguing and ever-present possibility of engaging two gears simultaneously!

However, as all the driving manuals cheerfully pointed out, the owner's first hurdle was to get his car started. Having digested the ominous warnings of dislocated thumbs from an incorrect grip on the starting-handle, of broken wrists from inducing a backfire and of hernias from standing in the wrong position, the novice could then address himself to the task in hand. Provided, that was, that he had previously jacked the car off the ground if it was his first outing (as one popular textbook recommended). The routine might then be summarised as follows: check petrol and water tanks, turn on tap to the carburettor, switch on accumulator, engage brake, disengage clutch, place speed-change lever in neutral, open throttle, retard ignition,

BOSCH
Zündung

ROBERT BOSCH - STUTTGART

Devilishly clever: this advertisement for an early Bosch magneto with its rather demonic motorist was characteristic of the period, when manufacturers liked to stress the 'magical' aspect of their products by filling their adverts with assorted warlocks, gremlins and demons. In this case Bosch have also emphasised their international success, by introducing racing cars from all the major European nations that competed on the racing circuit at the time. The advertisement dates from about 1912.

tickle carburettor float, insert crank and pull up against compression. Having cranked for some time in vain, the owner might return to his instructor and (if it was Mr Filson Young) read the comforting words:
'It may be, however, that the handle will be turned for a considerable time and yet the engine will not start. In this case it is no use to go on working oneself into a heat at the handle, and it is better to look round and see whether something has not been overlooked.' It might be, of course, that he has overlooked the fact that his model was fitted with a sparking-lever, or with a starting control lever which reduced compression by opening the valves slightly, or with a removable connecting plug which was a primitive form of anti-theft device.
Assuming, as we must, that the driver is at last on his way, he must prepare himself mentally for anything to happen. Before he started he should – if

he had listened to the experts – have equipped himself with an awesome list of spares:

'Not less than two new outer tyre covers should be carried as well as, say, half a dozen inner tubes.... Bolts and nuts of every size and shape: two spare inlet and two exhaust valves; sparking plugs (six) if the ignition is high-tension, and a complete magneto, if by magneto; a spare battery fully charged, for high-tension ignition; plenty of insulated wire, copper wire, rubber tubing of the same gauge as the copper piping of the water system; a spare water-pump; belting for the fan (if belt-driven).'

And that, by contemporary standards, was an extremely modest catalogue.

One American correspondent, writing in 1905, was highly dubious that any significant journey ought to be undertaken with less than seventy separate items of repair! In the case of tyres the advice was well heeded, since it was an absolute certainty that the motor-owner's largest item of expenditure during the year would be on tyres, and his hours of patching and pumping by the roadside prodigious.

Solid tyres, which could transmit every shock of the road with spine-jarring precision, were by now confined to heavy commercial vehicles. But the price the motorist paid for his relatively smooth ride on pneumatics was expensive on the nervous system. The familiar names of Michelin, Dunlop and Firestone were considered reliable – within the narrow limits dictated by appalling roads bristling with nails (shed by generations of horses' hooves) – but until the advent of detachable rims or wheels in 1906 and the low-pressure balloon tyre after the War, changing a tyre could be a nightmare. A puncture on your journey (and two or three could be commonplace) would set you back half an hour, because the cover had to be forced off the rim with tyre-levers on the spot, the inner tube mended, then the beaded edge of the cover fitted back into the matching groove on the wheel, fastened with safety bolts and finally pumped to a pressure at least double that used on modern cars (since it was the air-pressure for the most part that kept the tyre in place).

Manufacturers soon realised that the smooth, round tread of their early tyres was almost inciting punctures – not to mention that dreaded affliction, the side-slip. On the best of surfaces cars with a high centre of gravity and embryonic brakes were hard enough to control: on granite-paved streets, where a light rain had softened up the layers of horse manure, they could be virtually impossible. Tram-lines and wood pav-

Outside the larger cities the first local garages were grafted onto existing blacksmith's shops or cycle engineers, like Victor Ashby's ivy-clad premises *(far left)* at Towcester in the early 1900s. The high class of his clientele – they include two Daimlers and a Mercedes – obviously allowed him to specialise in automobiles early on. By 1910, however, enough car mechanics had been trained (either by the manufacturers themselves or by bodies like the RAC) for metropolitan garages, such as this one in London *(left)*, to cope with most aspects of repair and maintenance.

ings in town, and unexpected stretches of chalk road in the country, could also cause embarrassing pirouettes. How to avoid the side-slip became a preoccupation of the motoring world: tests and side-slip trials, involving every conceivable combination of studded belts, chains and moulded tyres, were held in many countries, while the tyre companies themselves would invent all kinds of tread-patterns for the motorist to try. In the same spirit of improvisation the 'Stepney wheel' was invented by Dunlop as a makeshift device to get a punctured motorist home. It was indeed a spare wheel, but one that was clamped onto the offending wheel to save roadside repairs. When the idea of simply substituting wheels gained currency, the Stepney went into permanent retirement.

That manufacturers themselves were painfully aware of the motor-car's vulnerability may be inferred from the eulogies they bestowed on their own product. 'As perfect a piece of machinery as can be built', said the makers of the Santos-Dumont unblinkingly. 'The acme of automobile perfection' turned out to be the soon-to-be-forgotten Starin. The public knew different, of course, and celebrated the automobile's frailty in a succession of

popular songs that harped embarrassingly on one theme: 'Get a Horse' was one of the hits of 1905, while that love's lament 'He'd Have to Get Under, Get Out and Get Under' is still remembered today. (Almost in self-defence the car-makers took to commissioning their own songs, some of which lurched rapidly into obscurity like 'The Studebaker Grand March', though 'In My Merry Oldsmobile' was revived several times, and made the manufacturers very happy indeed.) The problem – as the car-makers saw it – lay in the drivers themselves. In competent hands their cars were capable of anything, as their advertisements repeatedly reminded the world. They could be driven up the steps of the Capitol, like the 1904 Cadillac, or pitted in strength against a team of horses, like the 1905 Autocar. They could jump chasms or negotiate aqueducts. Provided of course you knew what you were doing.

Only on the open road did a car's caprices and limitations eventually reveal themselves. It was an endearing habit of pioneering motorists to keep a log-book, or motor-diary, of the triumphs and catastrophes that befell them at the wheel: they make salutary reading for the modern motorist.

What civilised motorist would have been without his patent cigar-shield *(above)*, designed to protect his smoke while belting along at 20 mph? Other examples of car artistry were more decorative: a serpentine bulb horn, a travelling flower-vase. All the same, methods of refuelling one's motor-car remained primitive – petrol was sold by the kerbside in cans and poured into the tank with the aid of a funnel. *Above right:* The scene in a busy Paris suburb in 1904.

For two years after he acquired his first motor-car in 1901, a De Dion voiturette, Kenneth Murchison diligently kept a motor-diary. When things went wrong for him, they really went wrong, as his account of a trip in North Wales in 1903 shows:

'Left Menai 9 a.m. Called at Bangor for a new tyre, could not get one: ran over a sheep: at Bethesda changed gears so rapidly that I broke the connecting rod of the steering gear: being at the top of a long hill there was nothing for it but to go down the hill backwards in the hope of getting to the bottom alive, and finding a blacksmith: this was done: slate quarry workers on strike and much interested in car: after wait of 2½ hours blacksmith finished his job, but the product of his labour was 1/16th of an inch too small: waited another 2½ hours: this time successful result. Going round a sharp corner nearly ran into a big lake....'

Less stoical, but just as resilient was another of his contemporaries who also kept a log-book, Dr H.E. Tracey of Willand, Devon. His 10 hp Peugeot arrived in September 1907, and his entries for October speak for themselves:

'*October 8.* Ran over and damaged S.H. Thomas' dog. Its own fault entirely owing to almost complete deafness.

'*October 10.* Near hind tyre went down. Valve was torn off by riding on the rim.

'*October 12.* Rotten French tyre burst through puncture in Cullompton. Stuck on two awful hills. Got her up empty.

'*October 17.* A broken bottle cut a tremendous gash in our Dunlop cover right through. Put a rotten French tyre in its place. This promptly punctured again in Toverton and had to be mended at a garage there. Farmer Frost's horse reared at the sight of motor at Brick Houses, and fell, breaking a shaft. No-one hurt.

'*October 25.* Met a herd of cows 3 miles the other side of Totnes. Bent axle, steering rod, lamp brackets. Damaged lamps, much of this by striking hedge after striking 2 or 3 cows. Rubbed the Dunlop tyre a lot, crippling into Totnes where we had the steering rod and wheels straightened. It was pitch dark.'

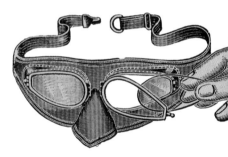

Amateur inventor's paradise: car accessories soon became an industry in their own right, pampering the motorist with weird and wonderful gadgets – a mechanical hand *(above)* which lit up as a direction indicator, transparent ear-protectors, combined goggles (with interchangeable lenses) and nose-guard! Nor was the car itself forgotten. One company *(left)* offered for a sale a mobile garage, which presumably had to be towed behind the car wherever it went. Did the driver have to climb out of one of the windows?

Dr Tracey's brakes obviously left a lot to be desired, but to be fair, nearly every motorist did his best to avoid using his brakes. In most cases they were hand-operated, contracting band brakes (which got over-heated if used for long), often fitted only to the back wheels (which could, if you weren't careful, put you into an alarming spin) and only really effective in a forward direction. Above all, this made grinding to a halt on a hill something of a gamble, for the chances were you might find yourself and your machine inexorably sliding backwards and gathering momentum.

The answer to this recurring problem was an impromptu device called a 'sprag', which was simply an iron spike that hung below the chassis and could be let down – with luck, to dig itself into the road – by unhooking a chain on the steering column. To operate it successfully called for great presence of mind by the driver, for should he let down the sprag after the car had started to roll back, the whole machine might leapfrog over the bar and do dreadful damage to the frame. Rather than attempt this manoeuvre, some motorists preferred to disgorge their passengers at the bottom of a hill and arm them with bricks to stick behind the wheels; others went to great pains to avoid the steeper hills altogether.

Woman's work: to the lady driver on her own who suffered a puncture, Dorothy Levitt's advice was 'drive very slowly on the rim to the nearest repair-shop', but the invention of the Stepney spare wheel and then detachable wheels *(below)* made it less impracticable for ladies to carry out their own roadside repairs – in spite

of the petticoats and flowing dress! Engine failure, though, was another matter: these ladies *(right)* whose 1903 Fiat has broken down were quite content to amuse themselves with the fashionable game of Diabolo, and let the man sort the mechanical intricacies.

But however prudent a motorist you might be, sooner or later you would break down and would have to work out your own salvation. Outside the large towns there were no commercial garages, and the best you could hope for in smaller communities was an enlightened blacksmith or a progressive cycle engineer. Hotels might offer to sell you petrol or the use of an inspection pit for your own repairs – equally well, they might refuse to take in both you and your car: 'No Automobiles' was a not uncommon sign in the early years of the century. The ultimate solution, as enthusiastically recommended by the motoring press, was a fully-equipped motor-house of your own, which could easily end up costing more than the car itself. 'Any damp or dirty shed will not do for the purpose', fulminated one publication. It had to be dry, well ventilated and well lit; it should be equipped with sloping floor, inspection pit, workbench, electricity, fire-buckets and water-supply. Petrol cans, which were the only means of purchasing fuel, were to be stored in a separate building some distance away (in practice many owners merely dug a hole in the garden and buried their supply of petrol

cans). The advertisements and department-store catalogues of the day offered a huge range of gadgets for the home mechanic – vulcanisers and valve-grinders, patent lubricators and accumulator-chargers. And from there it was but a short step to tempting them to more sophisticated accessories – klaxon-horns of truly symphonic complexity, motor-stethoscopes ('for locating knocks') or electrically-heated steering wheels!

By the end of the first decade it seemed that a huge peripheral industry had been built up on the shortcomings and discomforts of the motor-car. But these were growing pains, for which new cures were being found every year, and which the motorist bore with a certain philosophical pride – perfectly epitomised by that ardent pioneer, Rudyard Kipling:

'I like motoring because I have suffered for its sake. My agonies, shames, delays, rages, chills, parboilings, road-walkings, water-drawings, burns and starvations at which you laughed.... all went to make your car today safe and comfortable. Any fool can invent anything, as any fool can wait to buy the invention when it is thoroughly perfected; but the men to reverence, to admire, to write odes and erect statues to, are those Prometheuses and Ixions (maniacs, you used to call us) who chase the inchoate idea to fixity up and down the King's Highway with their red right shoulders to the wheel. Yes, I love because I have suffered. Suffered, as I now see, in the cause of Humanity.'

Even Regals got stuck in the mud sometimes. Nor was this untypical of American country roads in winter ca. 1908. One character in Faulkner's *The Reivers* even kept his stretch of road well-watered in the dry season, so that he could hire out his mules to extricate motorists from the mud.

Blow-out: back in the days of non-detachable wheels there was no alternative to jacking up the car, prising off the tyre and mending it on the spot. But at least the driver of this Peugeot *(below)* had the foresight to bring a bottle of compressed air with him, to make pumping up to the required very high pressure a bit easier.

THE ROOTS
OF MASS PRODUCTION

The first drive-in snackbar? This Coca-Cola advertisement, which appears to date from before 1910, shows the motor-car already enshrined in the American consciousness – and ripe for commercial exploitation – as a status symbol. The car and its association with 'gracious living' were obviously intended to help make the drink acceptable and desirable.

At the turn of the century France was not only the centre of motoring, but also the biggest producer of cars – turning out in 1903 almost half the world's total production of 62,000 vehicles. By then the great names were showing regularly at the Paris Salon de l'Automobile. There was a waiting list of two months for a Darracq, six for a Delahaye or a Peugeot, eight for a Mors and a year and a half for a Panhard. By this time the classic pattern of the car had emerged, and although there were still flirtations with steam and electricity, the petrol engine had virtually taken over.

A number of manufacturers had graduated from the cycle business. Alexandre Darracq built Gladiator bicycles before founding the company at Suresnes that was rapidly to achieve prominence and be one of the first to turn out cheap cars in fairly large quantities – in 1901 some 1,200 of Darracq's 6.5 hp models were produced. Adolphe Clément likewise started as a riding instructor, selling his bicycles to each pupil. He began making cars himself in 1901, was later joined in a British venture by the Earl of Shrewsbury (whose family name was Talbot), and the fruit of this liaison was the Clément-Talbot.

In contrast, the great Renault empire owes its origin to a young man's hobby. André Maurois thought he 'had the face of a poet', but Louis Renault had other ideas in mind. Instead of writing verses he fitted up a well-equipped home workshop, in which he turned a De Dion tricycle into a Renault quadricycle. Having then come to the conclusion this wasn't the right answer, he made a scaled-down version of a large chassis in tubular steel, and fitted an engine in the front. Better still, he conveyed transmission from the three-speed gearbox by a universal jointed shaft to a differential on the back axle. The car had been built for fun, but it appealed to his friends. The family lawyer, who was given a ride to the Place du Tertre in Montmartre, is said to have taken forty gold coins out of his pocket, placed them on the table of a café and become Louis Renault's first customer.

Thus encouraged, Louis and his elder brother Marcel started Renault Frères with a capital of 60,000 francs on the family property at Billancourt, and built about 25 units of this first model, using the ¾ hp De Dion engine. Believing that the reliability of a vehicle depends on the strength of its weakest part, they put the same engineering skill into their light cars as the older firms did into their big machines, and proved the point by a series of racing successes. By the end of the first year the works were employing 100 men; a new model was introduced using a stronger frame and the new 3½ hp water-cooled De Dion engine, with vertical radiators each side of the bonnet. With this they went on to win the Paris-Toulouse-Paris, and gave such an impetus to the light car vogue that 350 units were built and sold in 1900.

ROLLS-ROYCE 40/50 SILVER GHOST

1906

When at the age of forty Henry Royce acquired his first car – a second-hand Decauville – he was so disgruntled by its crudity that he set about fashioning a similar machine in a way that satisfied his own high engineering standards. Royce's car appealed immediately to the Honorable C.S. Rolls, and the first result of their partnership was a rakish 20 hp four-cylinder two-seater with which Rolls won the Tourist Trophy in 1906. But his preference was for larger, more luxurious cars, and it was the 40/50 which appeared later the same year that established the reputation of Rolls-Royce. About the design of the Silver Ghost there was nothing very innovative. But the immense flexibility of the understressed six-cylinder engine gave it an uncanny feeling of silence and superiority. The Silver Ghost whispered along, and indeed on one celebrated occasion was driven from London to Edinburgh in top gear. The same regard

for quality regardless of cost was reflected in every component of the chassis. Each non-machined part was polished all over and examined through a magnifying glass to detect any possible flaw.

Although Hives drove a lightly-bodied chassis round Brooklands at over 100 mph, and James Radley finished the 1914 Alpine Rally in a Ghost without loss of marks, it was not a tearing performer. From a capacity of 7.4 litres it gave the modest output of 48 bhp at 1200 rpm, with a maximum crank-shaft speed of 1500 revs. The secret lay elsewhere. Royce was not seeking new or unconventional solutions, or dramatic performance. He was applying existing knowl-

edge to best advantage, to combine, as Pomeroy says, '*ordre, luxe, calme, volupté* and *beauté* in a degree not rivalled by any other make or model'. And so the Silver Ghost won its reputation of being the best car in the world, though in fact Rolls-Royce did not build complete cars, but only chassis, until after World War II. When you consider that Royce only began to think about the problems of automobilism in 1903, that 24 months after building his first unassuming model he had designed and developed a car that was to maintain its supremacy for twenty years and become a world-wide symbol of quality, you are bound to agree that it was a most extraordinary achievement.

FORD MODEL T

1908

To designate his cars, Henry Ford used letters of the alphabet, starting with the A in 1903 and the B in 1904. Both of these were conventional machines, and it was only with the N model, introduced in 1906, that he set out to win the mass market. This four-cylinder had features which were later to gain the T its sobriquet of 'spider' – notably large wide-tracked wheels with a small body mounted high above the ground. And indeed when the legendary T Model was launched on 1 October 1908, most Americans were struck by its apparent fragility. But here the

eye deceived, for the car was built largely of vanadium steel, the lightness of which enabled the chassis to be reduced to proportions that could withstand the buffeting a cross-country vehicle is expected to cope with today. The 'Lizzie' could bounce over every sort of terrain – and 15 million of them produced during the next twenty years did just that – putting America and much of the rest of the world on wheels in the process. It was powered by a 2898 cc four-cylinder, water-cooled engine that produced 20 bhp at 1600 rpm and a top speed of

40 mph. Ignition was by flywheel magneto running in an oil bath, and transmission consisted of an epicyclic gearbox with only two speeds engaged by stamping on a pedal. While other motorists controlled their machines much as we do now, the driver of a Lizzie went through a series of unusual procedures that often provoked some curious kangaroo leaps. The T Model, incidentally, was the first Ford with left-hand drive. More important, it was the first car to be made on a moving assembly line, which Ford installed in his factory at Highland Park in 1913, along with power-driven conveyers for sub-assemblies. Initially, the body was made of wood and the T came in red as a tourer or grey as a roadster, costing $850 to $875. In 1908, the year the Lizzie was born, there were 200,000 cars in the United States. Five years later there were that many T's. By then the body was made of sheet steel, and Ford was experimenting with a moving assembly line – inspired, it was said, by the overhead trolley systems that the beef-packers used. You could have any-color-so-long-as-it's-black, and the price was $600. By 1915 this had gone down to $440, and Ford had made his millionth auto-mobile. Later, the Lizzie retailed for under $300. These constant reductions in price were perhaps its most revolutionary feature.

In other countries too there were brothers tinkering away to good effect. In Britain the Lanchesters, Frank and George, produced the country's first full-scale practical car in 1897, a saucy-looking machine with one or two novel features like epicyclic change-speed gears, tubular frame and wire wheels attached to axles supported on cantilever springs, which won them a gold medal at the 1899 Richmond Trials. In Germany the sons of Adam Opel of sewing-machine fame presented the first model off their drawing-board (a 10/12 hp) at the Hamburg Show in 1902: on it Fritz and Carl Opel won at least 100 sporting victories to become two of the leading drivers of the day.

But some of the most fruitful of those pioneering partnerships were between men who had little in common except their passion for machinery, such as that between Napier and Edge. D. Napier & Son had made printing machinery in Soho since the days of George III, though it was little more than a shell when Montague Napier purchased the plant from his father's executors in 1895 and teamed up with an Australian, Selwyn Francis Edge, to build motor-cars. Napier's first petrol engine was fitted into the famous 'Old No. 8' Panhard, and from this neat piece of grafting, with a few modifications to the coachwork, the 9 hp Napier was born which Edge drove (still unpainted) in the 1,000 Mile Trial to win a bronze medal.

An even more significant fusion of talent and enthusiasm was to take place a few years later at an historic meeting in a Manchester hotel. An electrical engineer of outstanding skill who started his career as a telegraph messenger and newspaper boy, Henry Royce pooled his resources with another young man, called Claremont, and with £75 capital set up a factory in Cook Street, Manchester, to make electrical appliances. From switches and

Henry Ford built his first asembly-line plant at Highland Park, Detroit, in 1911 and within two years had installed the first complete moving assembly-line, with the result that in five years the price of a Model T almost halved to $440 and his workers' wages were doubled. *Below:* Bodies being fitted to the chassis at Highland Park.

fuses they graduated to electric cranes and dynamos; then in 1903 Royce bought a second-hand two-cylinder Decauville. He liked it well enough, but to his fastidious mind it was noisy and spoilt by poor workmanship. Reckoning that he could do better, he began designing a car along similar lines, but with new criteria of silence, lightness and durability. On 1 April 1904 the first Royce emerged from Cook Street and did not stop running until its creator reached his home at Knutsford, 15 miles away. On a rather different social level, the Hon. Charles Stewart Rolls, third son of Lord Llangattock, began motoring in earnest while still up at Cambridge. He competed in both the Paris-Berlin and the Paris-Vienna on a Mors (ending

up against a tree in the latter), and having collected a special gold medal in the 1,000 Mile Trial, began to combine pleasure with business in the form of a small, private company called Rolls and Co. dealing in imported cars, notably Panhard and Mors.

The meeting took place during the first week of May 1904, when the little experimental Royce made an immediate impression on Rolls. An agreement was reached that C.S. Rolls & Co. would take all the cars made by F.H. Royce & Co. and market them under the name of Rolls-Royce. At first a variety of models was produced. Rolls disliked small cars, and the original 10 hp twin was soon joined by a 15 hp three-cylinder, a 20 hp four-cylinder and a 30 hp six-cylinder. In 1905 Rolls entered one of the 20 hp cars in the Tourist Trophy on the Isle of Man, where he achieved the dubious honour of being the first driver (and surely the last) to strip the gearbox of a Rolls-Royce. In 1906 Rolls-Royce was registered at Somerset House to take over the business and assets of C.S. Rolls and Co. and the motor side of F.H. Royce Ltd. An advertisement by the new firm, appearing on 12 May, stated its intention of building 'not one of the best: the Best in the World', an ambition which the *Motor Trader* greeted as 'an estimate of future prosperity about as tangible as the Aurora Borealis'! It is true that had the local bank manager not arranged a £20,000 overdraft the firm might never have got going. But previous models were abandoned in favour of the 40/50 Silver Ghost, which arrived for the Olympia Show in November 1906, when it was immediately hailed, not as a dramatic performer, but as the pinnacle of engineering precision.

At the 1906 Olympia Show there was a bewildering choice of 434 different

From 1909 Model T's were assembled in Britain *(abo·e left:* engines and chassis being tested), and in 1911 the first foreign Ford assembly plant was built at Trafford Park, Manchester, giving Britain its very first glimpse of volume production.
But even in Detroit the horse was not immediately made redundant: delivery of bodies *(above)* continued to be made on these enormous horsecarts in the early days.

models at prices ranging from £150 to £2,500. Filson Young was quick to warn that 'many of the English cars that look so attractive in their advertisements are constructed largely from the old discarded stock of some foreign makers, and are by no means built up of newly designed parts'. Which unhappily was true. Since components were readily available, many small firms were tempted to take the plunge and assemble cars with more wishful thinking than knowledge, with the result that back axles broke and some models were fundamentally unsteerable. This artisan approach (which also produced some memorable cars) was to linger on well into the twenties. Even as late as 1913, some 65 constructors contributed to the total British

New clients for the Railway Inn: these well-laden Lanchesters appear to be taking this ferocious hill in their stride. Pioneer motorists had made a point of avoiding steep hills, or at least shedding all passengers before attempting them. By 1907, however, even the services of the sprag had largely been dispensed with.

output of just over 26,000 vehicles a year, an average of about 400 from each works.

It was a long way yet from the point where the customer simply chose his car and drove it off. At a time when motoring had come to be regarded as the natural pastime of a gentleman it was normal to have one's car made to measure, like one's shirts and one's shoes. Many manufacturers supplied the bare chassis as a matter of course, and recommended a coachbuilder who would make the bodywork to the owner's specification. This meant that he chose every detail of the body, from the shape and design to the materials that would be used – the upholstery, the fittings, the lamps, even the dials on the dashboard. And of course, the colour scheme, often intricately devised. Timber, which played an important part in the interior of the car, would be selected with much care, and seasoned. After a long period with expert joiners, the body passed to skilled metal workers who carefully built the panelling. External rivets and bolts were plated or polished; the fittings were mounted by hand. Finally 16 to 20 coats of paint were lovingly applied. Nothing was hurried, and craftsmanship was all important.

And of course a coachbuilder was precisely what the name implied, using the time-honoured methods and techniques of the carriage trade, for whom comfort meant strength, and strength meant weight – a recipe that placed intolerable strains on practically every component of the chassis and engine. Supercars clothed in limousine bodies suffered most. Their whippy frames twisted, cracking the coachwork, while their lofty rooflines, designed to accommodate top hats and female finery, caused them to roll excessively and swerve sideways at a sudden puff of wind. So for practical reasons people preferred an open touring car. Filson Young recommended 'a roomy side-entrance body of the type known as the Roi des Belges, with high upholstered backs, and a light Cape-cart hood on the back to keep the dust out and set up in case of heavy rain; this, with a proper provision of waterproof clothing, is all the protection that the ordinary traveller need want.'

By 1909 the general trend towards a modern open car was already apparent. There was a windscreen, front and back seats were at the same level, and the bonnet was about a third of the vehicle's length. All the same, the high bodywork, with low doors to the rear seat and none in the front, not to mention the steeply sloped scuttle, still kept an aroma of antiquity. This was quickly shed, if not overnight, at least during the following season, as body sides and bonnet were brought into parallel line, front doors were fitted, and a hood and sidescreens provided weather protection. 'By 1910', says Kent Karslake, 'the debt to the past had been paid, and the horseless carriage had been replaced by the true motor car.' And not just in appearance. The year 1910 was a critical, even epochal point in automobile development, because the cars built immediately after this had more in common with those of twenty or even thirty years later than with their immediate ancestors of five years before. The faster cars of 1911 had a performance comparable to that of a 1931 model, or indeed of a normal production car built immediately after World War II. They certainly showed an enormous advance on anything available ten years earlier.

In 1911 more than 170,000 spectators crowded in to see the exhibits at the Paris Salon de l'Automobile held in the Grand Palais. They admired the stately Delaunay-Bellevilles, the superb Rolls-Royce Silver Ghost Tourer,

The first Mercedes. The young lady whose name is perpetuated by the most enduring of the Daimler range: Miss Mercedes Jellinek.

The imperial Mercedes. King Edward VII on an official visit to Germany rides with Kaiser Wilhelm in his Mercedes. King Edward, a keen motorist like the Kaiser, became Patron of the Automobile Club of Great Britain and Ireland in 1903 – which in due course came to be the Royal Automobile Club.

the aristocratic Napiers, and the Panhard 'Skiff' designed by Labourdette for Rene de Knyff, with its long smooth bonnet flowing into a low inclined windscreen, sparkling wire wheels, and canoe-shaped bodywork made of light three-ply wood sheathing. But few of them could afford to buy, or indeed to run, such ornate and expensive machines, for which the tyres alone would cost £500 a year. So the sporting young enthusiast would have been more likely to covet an Hispano-Suiza or an Isotta Fraschini, both of which had made their mark in voiturette racing.

Léon Bollée first coined the term 'voiturette' for his three-wheelers in 1895, but it soon came to mean any small car. From 1906 onwards voitur-

The fruits of mass production: rural America took to the car very early. This is main street, Henderson, Texas, where virtually every car in sight is a Model T Ford. By 1920 there were some nine million cars on American roads and every second car coming off the production lines was a tin Lizzie.

ette racing really grew in popularity when events like the Coupe de l'Auto, the Sicilian Cup and the Catalan Cup attracted wide entry lists, and saw the first successes of such famous marques as Delage, Hispano-Suiza and Sizaire-Naudin. True, the *Autocar* thought in 1908 that 'the long line of square-ended voiturettes resembled so many blunt-nosed beetles in a high state of detonating agitation', but the high performance and reliability of the early voiturette engines was not to be denied, and there is no doubt that the real development of the light car engine can be dated from these small formula races. The light car itself began to appear around 1910 in the shape of such successful models as the Darracq, Renault, Grégoire, Mors, Phoenix, Peugeot, NSU and Riley, that were relatively inexpensive to purchase and run, and attracted increasing numbers of middle income buyers. Indeed, by 1910 the *Autocar* had done a complete volte-face and was remarking that 'there is no longer the same demand for powerful, costly touring cars, and these have given way to the lighter class of vehicle, which fully satisfies the requirements in speed and comfort and is, besides, much more economical'.

By 1910 the basic design of the light car had been established, and would continue to be followed for many years to come. Though chain drive still survived fitfully, it had for the most part been replaced by the universally jointed cardan shaft and differential rear axle. The old epicyclic change speed gear had been superseded by the sliding spur-type of gearbox. Front-wheel brakes began to appear from 1910 onwards, but most models were

still content with a pedal-controlled brake on the transmission shaft, and hand-lever controlled bandbrakes on the rear wheels.

High tension magnetos had replaced the old coil and battery ignition, but illumination was still largely by oil or acetylene lamps, which required a ceremony with carbide and water at lighting-up time. And to advertise one's presence it was still *de rigueur* to squeeze a large rubber bulb, though the raucous tones of metal scraping against metal from an electric klaxon were beginning to be heard. Herbert Austin, who started his own factory in 1908, announced a 10 hp four-cylinder model in 1911, and the first Morris Oxford appeared late in 1912 to compete with other British light cars. France produced the De Dion-Bouton, Peugeot, Renault, Clément et Charron, Mathis, and the Corre 'La-Licorne', while in Germany the choice lay between the 1163 cc NSU and the 1140 cc Wanderer.

Early warning of traffic congestion to come: a New York street in 1911 – not a horse-drawn vehicle in sight and with motor-taxis, automobiles and buses already at a standstill. Note that left-hand steering was not yet uniform; indeed it only started to become popular after 1908.

How did they perform? Motoring papers in England did not yet conduct road tests (perhaps because of the 20 mph speed limit?), but Anthony Gibb recalls the 1913 9½ hp Standard two-seater he owned as an undergraduate. 'It had the old, very vertical Standard radiator done in brass with a very large Union Jack', he says. 'I had to crank it, of course, and I have no idea at what speed it went because it didn't have a speedometer; the gear-change was, naturally, in a gate on the right, and the clutch was so heavy that if you wanted to go, say, from third into top, you had to count ten before you could think of putting it in. One other thing it did have was an extra air valve worked by a knurled knob on the steering wheel. This set up a tremendous hissing which made passers-by turn their heads.'

In the United States, Sears Roebuck & Company tried to tap the mass market with their Sears Motor Buggy, which was sold between 1909 and 1912 at $395. This was an interesting little machine with a horizontally opposed twin not dissimilar to the VW power plant. But it was doomed from the start. With its tiller steering, high wheels and solid tyres, it was as archaic as the Curved Dash Oldsmobile or the Orient Buckboard. By now buyers were looking for faster, heavier, more comfortable transport, and Henry Ford (who had made a few false starts himself) provided the answer with his Model T. The design was one of revolutionary simplicity. Transverse semi-eliptic leaf springs attached to the chassis located the front and rear axles and served for suspension. Engine, transmission and universal joint were all enclosed in one solid casing, and the epicyclic gearbox had three pedals sticking out of it. These pedals became famous. When the left one was held halfway with the handbrake on, the car was in neutral; if stamped on, in low; if released, in high. By holding it gently in mid-position and depressing the second pedal, one could make the car go backwards, or slow it down. The right-hand pedal was a transmission brake. Under the steering wheel was the hand throttle. Pull it down, give a kick with the left foot, and the car would lunge forward. Release the pedal, and it would

Feminine attraction: these early examples of advertising art seem to be soliciting the ladies' approval rather than their participation, by appealing socially to the American grande-dame *(above)* and aesthetically to the German art nouveau lady.

catapult directly into top gear. In theory it was as easy as automatic drive – but some Bronco Bill bounds would ensue if one didn't look out.

There were three ways of stopping. One could depress the brake pedal and pull the handbrake which also disengaged the clutch. Or one could kick on both the brake pedal and the gearchange pedal, thus engaging low gear to help slow the car down. Or, more drastically, one could brake and engage reverse simultaneously – a manoeuvre that would cause a normal gearbox to disintegrate. (See the Model T profile, p. 55.)

Thanks to Ford's efforts, the United States had cars before she had roads. More than 15 million Model T's were made, and the Tin Lizzie became part of the national folklore. She might shimmy and rattle and wheeze, but she was all things to all men. 'Someone should write an erudite essay on the moral, physical and aesthetic effect of the Model T Ford on the American nation', declared John Steinbeck in *Cannery Row*. 'Two generations of Americans knew more about the Ford coil than the clitoris, about the planetary system of gears than the solar system of stars. With the Model T, part of the concept of private property disappeared. Pliers ceased to be privately owned, and a tyre pump belonged to the last man who had picked it up. Most of the babies of the period were conceived in Model T Fords, and not a few were born in them. The theory of the Anglo-Saxon home became so warped that it never quite recovered.'

The Michelin brothers were pioneers of the pneumatic tyre – and patrons of art. Their new London headquarters *(above)*, opened in 1910, was built in the classic art nouveau style and decorated with illustrated tiles. The Michelin Man ('Bibendum') soon became – and remains – their famous trademark, here mounted with his friends on a car to advertise the company's new building, all of them looking suitably inebriated.

DUST
AND EXOTIC
FASHION

A priority for all passengers, women and children, was to dress to keep out the dust and the cold. For the really dedicated motoriste in 1903 *(above right)* there could be no compromise with fashion, and for the rally-driver *(below)* protective wear could match the wildest fantasies of science-fiction.

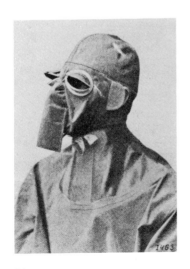

The biggest single nuisance of the new horseless era was dust: the squalls of dust from the roadway that dogged every passing vehicle, that enveloped passers-by and settled like a grey shroud on houses and gardens. Two generations or so have now lived with dust-free roads, and in retrospect the outcry against the dust menace seems slightly unreal. Nevertheless, when a Royal Commission on motoring was held in Britain in 1905 a seemingly endless procession of complainants came forward: farmers reporting that their crops had been ruined, doctors asserting that throat and eye infections had increased, a housewife who dared not hang her washing out any more, even a lady novelist whose typewriter had broken down by being clogged up with dust!

At first it was thought that the design of the car was at fault – and in some early trials cars were penalised for the amount of dust they raised. All manner of palliatives were devised and attached to vehicles: one optimistic inventor even devised a suction-chamber between the rear wheels to devour the offending dust! But gradually common sense prevailed, as it was recognised that the only permanent answer lay in better road surfaces. It was not that the art of roadmaking was utterly derelict – in many towns there were adequate surfaces of cobble or granite setts, even of hardwood blocks. And in the last quarter of the nineteenth century, compressed asphalt had been widely experimented with. But beyond the town limits (with the honourable exception of France which, even before the automobile's arrival, boasted over 40,000 miles of reasonable highway) all sophistication vanished. In Britain most roads were of compacted stone or gravel, neglected for decades and worked loose by horses' hooves; in America even these were a luxury, most routes being merely dirt tracks imprinted by the usage of time and transformed into quagmires by the slightest rainfall. The time-honoured method of 'laying the dust' was by sprinkling the road with water, and on some major mail routes pumps had been set up at intervals of a mile for just that purpose. But as the mail-coaches disappeared, so did the organization for tending the roads. It had anyway been a futile exercise, because what surfaces needed was not more water but water-proofing. A visitor to California in 1902 reported on the success of a new method being tried out on the west coast, oiling the roads:

'The effect of oil sprinkling is to make water run off quickly and it is a most effectual preventative of dust. I rode for the greater part of a day over roads in the neighbourhood of San Francisco which had been oiled two months before, and they were entirely free from dust although a brisk breeze was blowing.'

For several years after that, much money and ingenuity was expended in discovering the magic formula and a number of patent road-sprays came onto the market – which only served to demonstrate that what might work in the balmy climate of California was not necessarily suitable in the changeable seasons of western Europe. The obvious answer was some form of surfacing that would seal the road completely. This already existed and had done so since the mid-nineteenth century in the form of tar-spreading, but with the puny horse-drawn tar-spreaders then in use, it would have taken an eternity to surface every important road. By 1907, however, when the RAC held its celebrated Tar Trials, tarring on a large scale had become a practical proposition and by 1910 had become the approved method of treating all principal roads. And as the dust settled, so did the protests against the car.

No-one was more relieved than the motorists themselves, who were constantly exposed to the dust thrown up by their own machines or any other driving up to half a mile ahead. There was something of a dilemma here: they could have protected themselves, like the well-to-do, by enclosing the car, but the motoring authority Filson Young advised 'do not have a covered-in body because this adds greatly to the weight and raises a shocking

A Sunday outing in Paris, 1909 – a view on the Pont de Suresnes by Sabattier, with the prevailing fashion among ladies for 'bee-keeper' bonnets much in evidence. *Below:* Another monster from motoring's chamber of horrors ca. 1904.

The "Non-Concussion"

Right: What the well-dressed motorist was wearing. Rainproof overjacket with over-leggings to match — though it is not entirely clear how they stayed up! A distant relation of the jodhpurs.

The "Twinpeak."

The "Motogog"

Above: Latest styles in motoring caps from Gamages catalogue, ranging from prototype crash helmet to floppy hat with built-in goggles (that could be tucked under when not required).

Driving gloves complete with storm cuffs — a very practical accessory for the gentleman who didn't have to mend the punctures.

Gent's Fine Grain
Tan and Black Cape Leather
Gauntlet Gloves.

Chamois Leather
Undertaking

Far left: Driving underpants — not one part of the anatomy was left unprotected (either from cold or from the profusion of projecting levers). Also seen here are chauffeurs' leggings in real pigskin.

The "A.W.G." Motor
Spring Legging.

The "Marlborough."

The "Contessa"

Left: The conflict between the dictates of fashion and the bulk of clothing needed for protection from the elements exercised the ingenuity of fashion writers, whose columns appeared in all the motoring magazines.

Motoring bonnets were a particular problem – they had to stay on in the wind, keep out the dust *and* look pretty.

Latest Pattern Foot Muff.

Above: Foot muffs were particularly welcome when the wind whistled up through the floorboards. Other models could be filled with hot water before a journey.

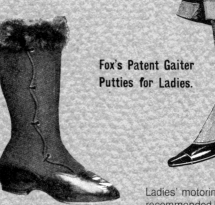

Fox's Patent Gaiter Putties for Ladies.

The "Invicta" Overboot.

Ladies' motoring putties – also recommended by the manufacturer for mountaineering and shooting wear!

The correct car for the correct occasion. In 1909 Rolls-Royce commissioned from Charles Sykes these paintings to illustrate their range of bodywork, which emerged as cameos of Society before the First War. Customers were recommended to use the open tourer to go shooting in the coverts *(top)*, the landaulet with folding hood for a good view of the hunt *(above)*, the limousine for turning up at the golf club in style *(right)*.

amount of dust'. Besides, he added for the benefit of any milksop who might still be tempted, 'one surely loses one of the great pleasures of motoring if one is not in the open air.'

Minimal protection could be available from a folding canvas hood if the car was stationary, and windscreens were provided from about 1909. Even then it was difficult to drive in rain without a mechanical wiper and that did not appear till after the war. (Meanwhile chauffeurs depended on rubbing the screen with a raw potato or apple!) The only real protection from dust or rain and, above all, the cold lay in one's motoring wardrobe. The earliest garments were 'borrowed' from another outdoor sport, yachting: peaked caps, double-breasted greatcoats, waterproof leggings. But the needs of automobilists clearly went beyond this, and very soon a vast peripheral industry had been spawned. Huge toe-length fur coats with voluminous collars appeared in the catalogues, for which hordes of raccoons, wombats and otters had allegedly been slain.

Leather and rubber also had their supporters. Gamages of London offered a comprehensive range of aprons – the Sack Apron (or 'motor envelope') into which one literally climbed, the Passenger Apron into which one was laced, indeed even an Overall Apron which stretched out over an entire car and allowed up to six passengers to stick their heads through holes. Peaked caps gave way to helmets of every hue, with built-in visors, goggles, earmuffs and sometimes 'anti-collision protectors'. Gauntlets, gaiters and foot-muffs were doubtless optional extras, but what self-respecting driver would not have felt naked without his chest and lung protector ('natural-colour best pine felt') underneath it all, or his motorist's under-pants ('from selected chamois skins')?

For ladies, whose fate was mostly to attend as passengers, the problem was to reconcile the inevitable frumpishness of motoring clothes with the dictates of fashion. You could of course, make no compromise and travel incognito by donning one of many veiled confections on the market, which left the wearer looking like an itinerant bee-keeper. But that rather spoiled the joy of motoring, which was to be seen in a car. Weekly in society papers and the motoring press, fashion columnists, with *noms-de-plume* like Madame Le Pip-Pip and Boadicea, grappled with the delicate questions of what to wear *en auto*. Their advice rarely coincided, which was hardly surprising since as one fashion writer put it bluntly: 'The fact that women

Further episodes in the life of a pre-war Rolls-Royce owner. For a day's salmon-fishing *(above left)* he would no doubt require the elegant Roi des Belges coachwork with its buttoned upholstery. For an evening at the opera *(left)* the enclosed limousine wouldn't crease the evening dresses, while the rear-extension laundaulet, complete with luggage rack, was most suitable for travelling to a country-house weekend *(above)*.

motor and care for it as much as they do is a great tribute to their lack of personal vanity, for try as hard as they can it is almost impossible to make the dress they have to wear a becoming one.' Even more ominous perhaps were the cautionary words of Lady Jeune in her *Dress for Motoring:*

'If women are going to motor seriously, they must relinquish the hope of keeping their soft peach-like bloom. The best remedy is cold water and a rough towel, and that not used sparingly, in the morning before they start.... Appearance must be sacrificed if motor-driving is to be thoroughly enjoyed. Those who fear any detriment to their good looks had best content themselves with a quiet drive in the Park.'

HIRED ASSASSINS

THE CHAUFFEUR QUESTION

Like his predecessor the coachman, a chauffeur's livery had to be distinctive lest he be mistaken for anything but a servant! Peaked cap and button-down jacket were standard. Boots and breeches too were normal, though some chauffeurs were permitted shoes like those worn by this one *(abo 'e right),* posing with his master at the wheel of a Delaunay-Belleville in London, 1910.

'Les Chauffeurs', so the French newspaper *Le Figaro* maintained, were originally eighteenth-century terrorists who specialised in arson and disguised their faces with soot. Hardly less lethal – the writer went on – were the scorching chauffeurs of the early twentieth century, who burned up roads rather than houses and whose favoured cosmetic was oil rather than soot. In fairness, the newspaper was not in fact impugning motor-servants in particular, for 'chauffeur' at that time, and for some years to come, embraced the whole of the motoring classes, owner and employee. Just as the car laboured under a variety of descriptions in its pioneer days, so did the men who drove it: automobilists they were to some; to others, voiturists, autocarmen, locomobilists, motorists or chauffeurs.

This last title was the most curious of all the attempts to coin a word, since a chauffeur was strictly a fireman, whose function was to stoke the boiler of a locomotive. Nonetheless, many a duke or baron proudly accepted the

title of chauffeur, who would no more have dreamed of pricking out the burners of his steam-car than he would of lighting his own drawing-room fire. A paid chauffeur was more properly known as a mechanician or motor-man, which perhaps gave a clearer indication of his status – though in practice the chauffeur (as he will be known from now on) was a vexing anomaly within the rigid domestic structure of nineteenth-century households. The hierarchy below stairs, which had been established for at least a century, had no place for such an intruder. If he were formerly the coachman, trained and translated into a car-driver he was already the highest paid of the liveried servants, with a measure of independence.

Some authorities insisted that coachmen made the best chauffeurs, since they were already skilled at maintaining coachwork and had a well-devel-

The chauffeur as star: cars rapidly became the central feature of many popular romantic novels, melodramas and revues (like this one at the Metropol theatre, Munich, in 1898). Inevitably the chauffeur acquired some of the reflected glamour – even if the 'chauffeur' with whom the heroine fell in love was usually a millionaire incognito!

This is your passenger speaking. Davenport's patent communicator dispensed with the tedious task of having to give verbal directions from the back of the car to the chauffeur. Like a captain on the bridge of a ship, the owner instructed the driver, with a flick of the lever, to 'stop' or 'return home'.

oped 'road-sense'; others found that the mechanical expertise required called for a different breed of man altogether, one who was not trained for the social niceties of domestic service.

Here lay the root of the 'chauffeur problem', which reasserted itself continually in the correspondence columns of the motoring press before the First World War – at least in Europe. In America where the motor-car very quickly became a democratic machine, chauffeurs were rather more respected and by 1902, in some states, had formed their own union, which was commendably active in defending its members' rights in the courts. In the Old World the problem really boiled down to one of over-familiarity: at least in the old four-in-hands the coachman was conspicuously segregated from his passengers. In the infant years of the automobile, it was very often the master who drove and the chauffeur who was driven, his presence required only for the menial duties of cranking, changing tyres and crawling under the car. Lest there be the faintest possibility of anyone mistaking the chauffeur for anything but a chauffeur, in the more rarefied echelons of society it was not unknown for the poor fellow to have to sit on the floor.

The real value of a chauffeur was in ferrying the mistress of the house about her business. There were, even in the earliest days, hardy automobilistes like Alice Roosevelt, who was often to be seen spinning along the streets of Washington, but in general the mechanical complexities and the effort of cranking discouraged most women from taking a car out on their own. In vain did the redoubtable Dorothy Levitt try to rally her sex: 'There may be pleasure in being whirled around the country in a car driven by your chauffeur; but the real, the intense pleasure comes only when you drive your own car', she wrote in a book that sought to explain the mysteries of the carburettor and the glove-compartment to society ladies. But too many feared the fate of Mrs Hamilton Fish who, on taking her new Runabout out for the first time on the streets of New York, felled a pedestrian and contrived to run over him twice more before bringing the car to a stop. On her return home she ordered that the infernal machine be banished forever from her sight.

The idea of motoring as a masculine pursuit persisted up to, and well into, the war. The feminine approach was summed up in an advert for the Chal-

Image and reality: this 1908 satire on the 'off-duty chauffeur' *(right)* characterised popular sentiment that many chauffeurs spent their leisure taking parlour-maids for a spin, scorching along in their employer's car. The chauffeur in fact was a useful scapegoat on whom other motorists could blame the excesses complained of by the motorphobes. The reality of a chauffeur's life was rather more mundane – less time was spent on the road than engaged in routine chores, as in the case of this chauffeur *(abo e)* maintaining a 1903 De Dietrich.

mers Motor Company, written and signed by Lady Duff Gordon, who had been engaged to design the furnishings and fabrics for the new model.

'I am not interested in the exterior of this Chalmers town-car... neither am I concerned in the least with the motor. I know not and care not whether it be what mechanical men call a six, a 22 or a 3400. *Les détails m'ennuient.* I leave those to Monsieur Chauffeur. My only interest is in the vitally important thing – the interior. More important because that is where I have to sit. It is my sun-parlour on wheels, and if colours clash or upholstery fabric grates on my nerves, how am I to love the car? Nothing can recompense for poor taste.'

So while Madame critically appraised the decor of her wheeled sun-parlour, it was the chauffeur who crawled underneath. It was a relationship that, for a time, intrigued playwrights and romantic novelists who worked some updated permutations on the theme of Kingsley's *Ravenshoe* – the high-born heir seeking anonymity as footman, or rather now as a chauffeur. Even advertisers capitalized on the social nuances. 'Charles the Chauffeur' one popular advert was entitled, which then broke into verse (which could in fact be sung to the tune of 'D'ye ken John Peel?'):

Charles the Chauffeur and Milady, Juliet,
The dashingest pair of the autoist set,
All primed for adventure, are out for a spiel,
On this fine country road, in their automobile.

Romeo – sorry, Charles, then brings the car to a halt at the top of a grassy slope. What is going on? Well actually Milady has a fly in her eye, and has requested Charles to hand over Murine ('a tonic for Auto Eye'). Vision restored, they continue on their innocent pleasures. Such copy may have boosted chauffeurs' status with parlour maids, but they still had to perch on the dickey-seat when the master was driving.

Nevertheless, a chauffeur *was* a skilled man and by the turn of the century – when car-ownership was no longer confined to the mechanical enthusiast – his salary was at least double, even treble, an average industrial wage. For that he would have to be an efficient driver and engineer, attend to the minutiae of several cars and probably act as gentleman's gentleman in the hours he had left. But the situation began to change very rapidly as more manufacturers joined the market and more shop-floor workers became acquainted with the inside of the car. The trickle of men from the factories and workshops became a steady stream of applicants for the coveted post of chauffeur: inevitably, as the market increased, wages dropped and so did the calibre of the aspiring chauffeurs. The affluent owners, who could not tell a cylinder from a crankshaft, increasingly found themselves under the tyranny of their chauffeur's incompetence. 'Much of the horror of motoring is centred in the chauffeur', moaned a correspondent in 1906.

'It is his convenience that must be consulted, it is he who gives the word to stop and to go on, he who decides that you must sleep at Coventry when you had intended to go on to Shrewsbury. You may not make plans without consulting him; he is ruthless in his discouragements; he spends your money with a fine liberality, and you learn to dread his statement of accounts, presented on the oily page of a notebook. He smokes the

Getting the push: a few helping hands get this car *(abo_e)* on the move in Sutton Place, New York, in 1905, but the services of a Swansea tramcar were less welcome in 1910 *(left)*. The siting of tramways in British towns was a constant source of complaint by motorists – like this indignant chauffeur – for many years.

73

vilest known cigarettes – there seems to be a brand especially blended for chauffeurs: he eats and drinks expensively, and at the wayside inns where you put up he monopolises the service.'

The litany of complaints runs through the journals of the day with constantly recurring themes: 'May I protest through your columns', wrote one incensed employer to *The Car*, 'against the growing habit of motor-men smoking while in charge of their masters' car?' He had apparently witnessed three cases that day in Piccadilly, one of them puffing away at an old clay pipe. Nothing was worse for the image of automobilism, he submitted, than 'to see an untidy, dirty-faced mechanic smoking a cigarette mere-

The back seat of a 1913 Delahaye with the hood down is perhaps not the most private place for Madam to adjust her stocking, but at least James is being a paragon of discretion (which is more than can be said for the photographer).

ly for the purpose of swagger'. Another indignant owner wanted the Automobile Club to 'suppress the tendency of chauffeurs to take out their masters' cars without permission, and running riot in every direction'. Yet another was shocked to find chauffeurs taking their fellow-servants out round the neighbourhood on joy-rides.

In an age when the motorist himself was besieged by prejudice and persecution, it was perhaps a small comfort to be able to deflect some of the abuse onto a ready scapegoat. Wrote a justice of the peace in 1905: 'I am open to take a short shade of odds, and I say that 75 percent of accidents, inconsiderate driving, and offence to others are the acts of the 'paid drivers' who, in my opinion, have...most objectionable natures.'

He would have got no odds at all from the editor of *Automobile Topics* in America, whose calculations came out even higher. He proclaimed: 'Ninety percent of the obloquy attaching to the sport today is undoubtedly owing to the chauffeurs who are hired to run private cars. Not one in a thousand owners cares to risk either his life or his property by indulging in scorching, while on the other hand it would seem to be the ambition of every second chauffeur to get a reputation for dare devilry.'

There is no objective evidence to suggest that these gentlemen were doing anything but exaggerating. Unlike the owner-drivers, chauffeurs normally had to produce certificates of their competence to drive, either from manufacturers who ran training courses, or from a motoring organisation (like the RAC, which opened a chauffeurs' school in 1904) or from one of the 'driving academies' which were springing up with varying degrees of qualifications. The system didn't always work, of course. In the first years of the century it was very fashionable to hire French chauffeurs in America – until a widespread racket in forged certificates was uncovered.

The chauffeurs had few opportunities to plead their own case publicly, but when they did they made some very telling points. In 1910, during yet another round of chauffeur-bashing in the English press, a number of them spoke out roundly (an indication, surely, of the growing egalitarian mood of the times). 'Chauffeurs are treated more like slaves on the whole', commented one who would only commit his initials to the letter. 'My idea is that a chauffeur who has sole charge of and drives a valuable car is entitled to ask and get the same respect and esteem as the skipper of a gentleman's yacht.' In *The Motor* another down-trodden motor-man echoed these sentiments:

'Though when driving and for his general conduct the chauffeur is principally subject to the wishes and whims of his employer, he is still largely differentiated from the domestic class.... Reputable repair garages and manufacturers are always able to supply men well fitted for the post. But these men must not be expected to exchange regular and congenial hours of employment for erratic hours of labour and to be subjected needlessly to the whims of an unreasonable car-owner, for the wages of a coachman. Chauffers, like their employers, need at times a place in the sun.'

The early stirrings of emancipation – if not exactly a portent of liberation (between the wars a chauffeurs' strike actually precipitated the revolution which brought Somoza to power in Nicaragua), but a long way from the dictum as articulated by *Motoring Illustrated* in 1903: 'The fact that a man drives a car for its owner rather than a pair of horses does not level class distinctions.'

'My sun-parlour on wheels': thus did one lady of fashion describe her car in the days of the First War. The cushioned interior of this 1908–1912 Lanchester could be better compared to a drawing-room. The exterior – not to mention the mechanical aspects of her car – mattered far less to Madam than her own comfort, and she would not have dreamt of driving the thing herself.

THE HEROIC AGE
OF MOTOR RACING

New York society arriving in their autos for the 1905 Vanderbilt Cup race. Crowd control – not to mention carriage control – proved so difficult that Vanderbilt eventually constructed a private Parkway on Long Island on which to continue the event.

In the Paris-Rouen Trial, it had been creditable just to finish the course, and even in the early races that followed, speed was less of a criterion than reliability. Levassor won the Paris-Bordeaux-Paris at an average speed of 15 mph; De Dion took first place in the Paris-Dieppe at 24.6 mph. You could argue that the comparatively low performance of the cars contributed to their reliability, and that in effect all petrol engines of the period ran at one speed (with a bit of variation by manipulating the air and ignition controls). But this could not last. A few days before Christmas 1898 a *concours de vitesse* was held in Achères Park, just north of Paris. Various

Heroes or hell-raisers? Two contemporary views on motor racing. *Far left: The Car Illustrated* celebrated the 1904 Gordon Bennett Cup race (held in Ireland) with truly Olympian fervour. *Punch (left)* took a more jaundiced view of the tragic Paris-Madrid race in 1903 – in which five drivers and some spectators were killed – with this bitter satire.

cars were put through their paces, but Count Chasseloup-Laubat's electric-powered Jeantaud easily beat its petrol rivals, covering the flying kilometre in 57 seconds. This was slightly slower than the existing bicycle record.

The peak of the electric car's achievement came when Camille Jenatzy finally turned up with a cigar-shaped creation made of aluminium alloy and powered by two big electric motors driving directly to the wheels. 'La Jamais Contente', as the car was called, brought the time for the flying kilometre down from 38.8 to 34 seconds, which broke the 100 kph barrier. And there, at 105.88 kph (65.79 mph), the matter rested, for although electric machines packed a lot of punch, their range was limited. Even so, it was three years before petrol caught up with these speeds. To make their petrol cars go faster, designers had resorted to sheer brute

Although a Stanley steam car held the land speed record in 1906, the steamers soon disappeared from the racing scene. This 1907 White Sprint car at Fort George was one of the last of the breed.

One of the first and most enduring of the European motor races was the Targa Florio, a nerve-chilling circuit of Sicily's mountain roads, instituted by Count Florio. This was the scene at the 1908 event, with crowds flocking round Tamagni at the starting line.

Agony and ecstasy: reaching Bordeaux in the fatal Paris-Madrid race of 1904, Louis Renault learns of his brother Marcel's death. *Bottom left:* Pit stop 1910-style in the Vanderbilt Cup race. *Bottom centre and right:* Death Curve on the Santa Monica track in 1914 taking its toll, with a

Sunbeam overturning and a Mercer losing its front wheel. *Opposite:* Like impatient dragons, cars line up for the start of a race at the first (1909) meeting at the Indianapolis Speedway. After three days' racing the dangerous dirt track began to break up and had to be replaced with 3 million bricks.

power. A fearsome 13.72 litre Panhard appeared in 1902, and Mors, a great name in the early days, was fielding a 10.1 litre monster in 1901. (It was in a 60 hp Mors that William Vanderbilt finally won the land speed record with a petrol-driven car.) This hairy machine was built for the town-to-town marathons which turned motor racing into a national French sport. Clearly the race was now to the swiftest, and to those who could persuade manufacturers to build ever larger and faster models. 'Commercialism, the curse of the 20th century, is the ruin of the sport', wrote Charles Jarrott almost before the century had started.

He may have been right. Perched precariously somewhere above the rear axle and the thrashing chains, behind a roaring, unsilenced engine and without wind-shields, mudguards or protection of any kind above ankle level, drivers had to wrestle to keep control of their monsters down unsurfaced roads and through clouds of dust or blinding rain. They had to contend with mechanical breakdowns, incessant blowouts and a hundred hazards on the way. When a weight limit of 1000 kg was imposed in 1902, on the theory that if cars were lighter they would be easier to handle, and with the result that already flimsy frames were pared down still further just as larger engines were put in them, the result was lethal.

Over 100,000 spectators crowded into Versailles to see 179 cars start on the ill-fated Paris-Madrid race in 1903, and something like 3 million people turned up to watch along the roadside. The uncontrolled crowds certainly contributed to the accidents that followed, but the uncontrollable cars were the cause. Blinded by dust and with practically no means of stopping anyway, drivers were involved in collisions with dogs and livestock and other competitors. At least ten people were killed – including Marcel Renault and Lorraine Barrow, a popular British sportsman – and by the time the authorities stopped the race at Bordeaux a trail of broken vehicles was littering the route.

The immediate effect of the tragedy was to spell the end of these city-to-city blinds, and to open an era of closed circuit races. These continued to be on open roads, but closed to other traffic and preferably with a modicum of crowd control – a pious hope more energetically expressed than

acted upon. The Vanderbilt Cup Race, launched by the millionaire in 1904 and run through the hamlets of Long Island, attracted the flower of New York society in such numbers that supervision proved impossible. Dressed (commented one observer) either for a hunt or a Roman chariot race, they munched their sandwiches as the mighty monsters roared through the villages.

On the continent the sport blossomed. The Circuit des Ardennes had been held successfully in Belgium since 1902. In 1905 Count Florio inaugurated his Targa around a mountainous course in Sicily, and the following year the Automobile Club de France organised the first Grand Prix at Le Mans. It

Speed was not the only criterion: the early years of our century also witnessed a whole series of long-distance endurance records – from San Francisco to New York (1903), from Paris to Constantinople (1905), and the most famous of all: the Peking-Paris race sponsored by a French newspaper (postcard, *above right*) in 1907. *Above:* Prince Borghese in his 35/45 hp Itala during the Peking-Paris event, which he completed in sixty days.

Opposite: Driving was often out of the question in rallies such as the Peking-Paris event which traversed all but impassable terrain. These automobiles on their way from China to Paris required a good bit of towing – and at times had even to be carried. Total distance was some 10,000 miles (14,000 km). Prince Borghese estimated that, of the first 150 miles he covered, he was able to drive no more than about 50. Nevertheless these exploits contributed greatly to the mystique of the automobile, and to public interest in motoring.

comprised six laps of an immense 64 mile circuit on two successive days, and by tacit agreement the following year's event at Dieppe was discreetly pruned. Even in Britain, where the government refused to close the public highway for the benefit of racing cars, a circuit was found in the Isle of Man (which was autonomous in such matters), and the first RAC Tourist Trophy was held in 1905.

It can be argued, of course, that normal development would have established the principles of automobile design without all these junketings, but there is no doubt that racing accelerated the process. When Hugh Locke-King opened a 2½-mile speed bowl on his estate at Brooklands in 1907, with scientifically angled curves that allowed a car to tear around them without deflection of the steering, a valuable amount of experience was gained from the strain that all-out running imposed on engines, cooling systems and tyres. And the extremely bumpy surface at Brooklands placed a premium on rugged contruction, the benefits of which quickly percolated through into normal road cars. It was the road surface that almost killed off another purpose-built speedway, the Indianapolis Bowl, opened by a group of local businessmen in 1909. After the first races the gravel track began to disintegrate, accidents multiplied and there was talk of giving up racing there. But with the vision that characterised so many of the early enthusiasts, the promoters decided to invest in some 3.2 million paving bricks to surface the entire course. Today Indianapolis remains not just a national institution, but the oldest racecourse in the world to have operated without a break.

TOURING AND OTHER GAMES

The mecca for motoring pilgrims: en route to France in 1910 *(below),* where motoring was unrestricted and the roads the best in the world. Passengers crossing the Channel relax on deck alongside their Vinot et Deguingand while the chauffeurs swap experiences of foreign travel, no doubt.

'The fact that motor-car driving exerts an extremely beneficial influence on the health of those engaged in it is one that is obvious to all who have any experience of the matter,' wrote Dr F.W. Hutchinson in 1902. He recommended 'driving at speed' to all those suffering from phthisis, sleeplessness, liverishness, bad digestion, asthma and cold in the head. 'A tonic once experienced, never forgotten.' His enthusiasm may be forgiven, since a vocal body of anti-motoring opinion insisted that driving was positively dangerous to the health. There were even those who claimed – in spite of all the evidence to the contrary – that human beings could not breathe at speeds in excess of twenty miles an hour!

Many other motorists – albeit fur-wrapped and begoggled – would have endorsed the doctor's theories. Perhaps the most celebrated of these was

In the earliest days of touring the cross-Channel ferries – like the *S.S. Queen* on the Folkstone-Boulogne run in 1909 shown here – carried cars as deck cargo and unceremoniously hoisted the precious machines (in this case a 1908 Mercedes) aboard by crane.

By 1904 motoring tourists were numerous enough for the railway companies to offer special continental services. The customs were not always quite so obliging.

Charles Glidden of Boston, whose self-confessed motive for a whole series of marathon international car tours was to lose weight. Between 1901 and 1908, accompanied by his stoic wife, he drove over 46,000 miles in no less than thirty-nine countries. Their various Napiers conveyed them beyond the Arctic Circle, through the jungles of Java, the deserts of North Africa and across the continent of America: when the roads ran out, they simply fitted flanged wheels onto the car and bowled along the railroads (occasionally being shunted into a siding to allow an express through). Always immaculately dressed, Mr Glidden was daunted by no obstacle, whether geographical or bureaucratic. His Napier, he claimed, could go anywhere, and motoring journals were inundated with testimonials – written on postcards from the most outlandish places – to prove that it did. In 1908 he ceased his globetrotting, just marginally short of the fifty thousand miles he had promised himself and, sad to say, not an ounce lighter.

The extent of the Gliddens' achievements in trailblazing across the world may be measured by the experiences of other contemporary 'tourists', whose ambitions outstripped their performance. In 1902 Dr E.C. Lehwess – one of the founder members of the RAC – set off from Hyde Park Corner in a very curious Panhard pantechnicon to tour the entire world. Experts studying his itinerary pronounced emphatically that he would get no further than a few miles beyond Nizhni-Novgorod in Russia. And sure enough, at the very point where roads and civilisation ran out the Panhard's cylinder blocks cracked in the sub-zero cold. Dr Lehwess had already taken nine months to get that far.

Stranded in a foreign country: this party of British tourists find their 24 hp Fiat in a spot of trouble somewhere in France in 1904. If they were members of the RAC they could, even then, have had recourse to the Club's French motoring dictionary! But it was not until the following year that an office was opened in Paris.

Above right: The proud owners of this 1905–1906 Singer pose for the obligatory photo. Such pictures were constantly being taken at the time – usually to demonstrate ownership and the ability to drive, but sometimes as proof that car and driver had indeed made it to an exotic locale 20 or perhaps 200 miles from home.

However, for these pioneer tourists time could scarcely be a consideration when even a minor breakdown could entail cabling the manufacturers for a spare part, then sitting down to wait in the back of beyond until their 'man' arrived with it in person. One particularly reckless German, Paul Graetz, set off in August 1907 to cross Africa from Dar-es-Salaam to Swakopmund in German South-West Africa in a 40 hp Gaggenau, and reached his destination twenty-one months later – which included three months' enforced camping in the veldt while a new axle and cylinder block were shipped from Germany and transported by native bearers. When, in 1905, Robert Jefferson – already a veteran explorer by bicycle – determined to drive from Paris to Constantinople, even he could not have dreamed of the procrastinations of the Balkan frontier officials. To enter Serbia with a car, he discovered, he was required to submit a sample of his petrol to the government laboratories for analysis. How long would that take, he enquired. Shrug. Ten days, perhaps. Little wonder that at the next frontier, the Bulgarian, he decided to drive straight past the guards, saluting smartly as he did so.

Inexorably the automobile challenged, and overcame, fresh tracts of the earth's surface. In 1903 Nelson Jackson drove a Winton from San Francisco to New York in two months, for a fifty-dollar bet. In 1907 Harry Dutton belaboured his Talbot across Australia from Adelaide to Darwin in fifty-one days. The next year Shackleton shipped an Arrol-Johnston fitted with skis to Antarctica, where with moderate success it ferried men and supplies through the pack ice. Of all the endurance tests the car was submitted to in these years, the one that caught the public imagination – because it included an element of international competition – was the Peking-Paris 'race' in 1907.

It was not strictly a race, since the entrants (three French cars, one Dutch and an Italian) prudently made a pact to stay close to each other in case of emergency. Earlier in the year the Paris paper *Le Matin* had issued a challenge to any motorist who could drive the 10,000 miles from Peking to Paris and had received an entry from, among others, the flamboyant Prince Scipione Borghese. It was largely through his determination and diplomatic muscle that the contest got started at all, for the Chinese had their own atavistic notions of world geography, could see no intrinsic merit in exploring China in an automobile and therefore assumed that these foreigners who had arrived in their midst with their diabolical machines must be spies. After protracted protest and negotiation the Chinese government concluded that perhaps, after all, the quickest way to get rid of these 'spies' was to let them drive off, and so they did, straight into some of the most daunting terrain in the world. Prince Borghese later estimated that of the first 150 miles, his vehicle (the Itala) drove only about 50; the rest of the way it was towed or carried by coolies.

Such proved to be the pattern for the long journey through Mongolia, Siberia and Russia. Even in that god-forsaken wilderness someone always turned up to extricate the cars from disaster – a troop of Mongolian horsemen to save the Itala from being devoured by a swamp, a gang of Russian railway workers to manhandle it out of a gorge when a wooden bridge collapsed. Borghese arrived in Paris sixty days after leaving Peking, and three and a half weeks before the other cars. A magnificent achievement, but what had it proved? Only, said some of the cynics, that you *couldn't* drive from Peking to Paris yet. Nevertheless *Le Matin* felt sufficiently encouraged by the adventure to co-sponsor, with *The New York Times,* an even more hare-brained scheme: a round-the-world race from New York to Paris.

In a sense, it had to be done sooner or later. But at least the improvident organisation of the event ensured that it would not be attempted again for many years. The chosen route was speculative beyond the dreams of metaphysics: among other things the contestants were going to have to drive

It's the man with the car that gets the girl. A German postcard series, published in 1906, exploring the amatory advantages of owning an automobile – in this instance a Piccolo voiturette.

Last resort for the skier – propping his skis on the running board of a 1908 Piccard-Pictet (a Swiss model known as a Pic-Pic for short). Nevertheless they made it up the mountain.

through Alaska and then over the iced-up Bering Strait to Russia! The mayor of New York forgot to turn up to send the six official entrants on their way on 12 February 1908; two of the cars retired barely beyond the state border and three weeks of battling through snowdrifts later the rest of them had only reached Chicago. First to San Francisco was the American entrant, the Thomas Flyer, whose crew then set sail for Alaska to discover for themselves what everybody else already knew – that Alaska was impenetrable and there was no way across the Bering Strait. The organisers hurriedly revised the rules to permit the teams to sail direct to Japan (to the dismay of the Americans who were still on their way back to San Francis-

Rallying point: a lady passenger in a 3.6 litre Peugeot deposits her token at a check-in point during a 1905 Belgian rally. A more strenuous form of exercise was the car gymkhana (centre) – here being held in Bombay in 1904. The ladies' passenger race involved plucking the lady out of her seat, completing an obstacle course and returning her 'home' safe and sound.

co). At Vladivostok the 'race' was called off, though prizes were still offered to the first three cars to get to Paris – an academic point, as it turned out, since the French team had by then sold their De Dion to a Peking merchant and resolved to go home by boat!

The Thomas Flyer broke its gear box as it juddered along the sleepers of the Trans-Siberian railway. The Italians in a Zust were thrown into prison for spying in Omsk, where they had tried to send a telegram in Italian. The German team in a Protos was the first – after 170 days – to reach Paris to a deafening silence: the committee was horrified at the German success and contrived not to award the first prize to them, on the grounds that they had not crossed Japan. By that time, anyway, everyone had publicly disqualified everyone else.

For the vast majority of motorists these herculean feats were just part of the mythology of motoring; there was adventure enough in achieving a modest hundred miles a day along real roads, with the prospect of a clean hotel at the end of it. Signposts, for a start, were a luxury. L.C. Boardman, vice-president of the New York Road Association, driving from New York to Chicago in the autumn of 1901, pronounced himself 'aggravated' by the entire absence of directions and the fact that 'but two people in the entire 1,086 miles between New York and Chicago could give them any informa-

Demonstration: an automobilist showing his paces by climbing the Odessa steps in 1905 – only a few months before a far more lethal demonstration took place in this very spot: the Potemkin massacre.

A little out of line: a competitor taking part in a car carnival at Ostend in 1908 fails to keep the front wheels of his Porthos on the painted lines. The fronds and flowers adorning the vehicle were typical of such events at the time.

Sensation of the season: Miss Mia Alix looping the loop in her car on rails at the London Hippodrome in 1903. Such feats of daring were highly popular, and the following year an even more intrepid artiste 'jumped the chasm' as well, in a Paris music-hall.

Early motorists left no stone unturned *(above)*. These gentlemen, attempting to take a car up Ben Nevis for the first time in 1911, appear to be proceeding in reverse.

Each new conquest called for a photograph – like the Cadillac seen here reaching the top of the Pordoi Pass in Italy, 7,340 feet up. A comfortable journey nowadays but in those days (1914) it was truly an achievement.

tion regarding roads in either direction'. Every township in the state, he proposed, should erect guideposts when requested to do so by six or more citizens. But inevitably in the end it was the motoring organisations which took up the challenge. André Michelin's great *Guide* first appeared in 1900, the RAC's Touring Department opened its doors in 1903 and in America the *Automobile Bluebooks* became the bible of those prepared to brave what roads there were. Among the less orthodox methods of navigation was the short-lived Chadwick Automatic Road Guide, an ingenious arrangement of perforated discs and cables which rang a bell when the motorist was approaching a road junction.

By 1904 touring had become a highly fashionable pastime, its popularity among the rich reflected by a sudden upsurge in touring handbooks. The Argyll Motor Company, in a shrewd piece of propaganda, sent a representative off on a ten-day tour of Britain by car: in that time he covered 1,353 miles which, as diligent analysis of Bradshaw's timetables proved, would have taken him three weeks by train. Motoring writers concentrated less on the convenience of the car than on the lyrical pleasures of the open road: 'I am at no man's beck and call – the car will annihilate distance for me: north or south, east or west, it shall carry me tonight to some sure haven such as this, where young men and maidens will laugh through the twilight, where the streets will be narrow and steep, the church a shrine of glorious antiquity. And this liberty is my holiday – these hours the roses which my car shall gather', wrote Max Pemberton in 1905, in what surely must be the archetype of modern travel-brochure prose.

The mecca for all tourists abroad was France ('where the very children babble of mechanical mysteries') and in particular the Riviera, where even then the famous Lower Corniche was under construction – though that redoubtable *motoriste* Baroness von Laurentz did remark that it was really 'no place for motoring, being quite spoilt by tramlines and overcrowded with motor-cars'.

The Riviera remained Lionel Rothschild's favourite destination in his Mercedes 60, so his chauffeur remembered years later, though he could scarcely have seen much of the countryside between the Elysée Palace Hôtel in Paris and the Hôtel de Paris in Nice, since the entire journey took him only eighteen hours. Mr Rothschild's idea of a jolly good tour was often to beat someone else to their destination: in 1905 he took on the Engadine Express in a race to St. Moritz, fell asleep at the wheel near Belfort and finished upside down in a ditch.

It must be said that the hazards of continental touring were normally less fraught with danger than frustrating. One of the most frequent mishaps was to find your petrol tank filled with lamp oil, or worse. Then there were the apparently arbitrary regulations which dictated on which side of the road you were required to drive – not only could these vary from country to country, but from region to region (as in Austria) or even city to city (in Italy). And one matter on which all the guide-books were unanimous was the need for patience and tact with customs officials, and indeed to negotiate the maze of regulations called for quite a bit of skill. Mechanical examinations of the car were required, tests of competence to drive, licences to 'circulate' and duty payable at frontiers against the car being sold abroad. Only after the International Association of Automobile Clubs got under way in 1904 and adopted the all-purpose triptich (invented by the Swiss A.C.) as the motorist's passport did things get easier.

Touring in one's own country was less formidable, but still required some detailed planning. 'Two ladies' (who strangely wished to remain anonymous) described their car tour of the West Country in *Car Illustrated* in 1902: the over-riding problem, they discovered, was that their vehicle could not accommodate all their hat-boxes *and* the chauffeur. They solved the dilemma admirably by dispatching hats to various post offices along their route and returning the used headwear via the royal mail! Baroness von Laurentz – whose more ambitious tours included trips round the Alps and the Pyrenees – tackled the luggage problem in a more professional way. She personally designed trunks that could be strapped to the back of

her car, anticipating the day when the rear end of the automobile would blossom into a built-in 'trunk'. And Dorothy Levitt, whose practical little book *The Woman and the Car* published in 1909 rather oddly offers no advice on luggage at all, had one firm recommendation to all lady motorists. That was to carry a small revolver.

Touring was, as one motoring apologist put it, 'a recreation which no horse-rider – except he have the constitution of a Cobbet – would have seriously contemplated'. Nevertheless, a great many upper-class pastimes were still centred on the horse: hunting and polo and show jumping were obviously safe from the encroachment of the automobile. However, the new car-owners were quite prepared to adapt social conventions to suit their expensive machines. In Paris the time-honoured *promenade* of car-

Touring in America before the First War could be a hazardous adventure, with roads un-made and gas supplies few and far between. At least this 1908–1909 Packard driving through the Rockies has found a tolerable track.

riages in the Bois de Boulogne had long been infiltrated – and taken over – by self-propelled vehicles, and the society papers were taking to reporting on the fashionable five o'clock 'tea processions' of motors at Versailles and Chantilly. Even in Atlantic City, reported *Automobile Topics* in 1901, 'the automobile parade on the Pacific Avenue driveway is becoming a daily feature of society. Prince Yee of Korea is usually seen in the daily parade, accompanied by a party of friends.' But it was Washington that boasted the most exotic parade of all. The magazine went on: 'The Celestial Minister, Mr Wu, is thoroughly imbued with the automobile fad. In his flowing garments and picturesque head-dress he cuts quite a striking

As early as 1906, the Scottish Trials evoked strong participation. This competitive touring event put the many eager motorists and their motor-cars through a range of difficult paces, including hillclimbs through the Scottish terrain. The race was to the quick – but just plain endurance was often enough for victory, under these circumstances.

figure as he flits by on his "no-pushy, no pully" contrivance, which he manoeuvres with a fantastic grace.'

In many European resorts the 'motor carnival' soon became established as a popular event, in which motor-owners paraded their vehicles, lavishly gilded with flowers and translated into exotic fantasies, and which would end in anarchic battles of flowers with drivers and spectators alike tearing the extravagant creations to shreds, and pelting one another with the blooms. Even so, there were limits beyond which gentlemen should not go – as *The Car* reported after the 1905 Worthing motor carnival:

'The most elaborately decorated vehicle was undoubtedly Mr John Parker's Daimler, surmounted with a figure of Cupid, and adorned with roses and white lilies. It was universally regarded by the spectators as an easy winner, and surprise amounting to mystification was created when the judges – Earl Russell and Sir James Duke – suffered it to pass with scarcely a glance in its direction. The explanation lay in the fact that the flowers with which it was adorned were...artificial!'

Even more popular in Britain and the colonies was the motor gymkhana, where – short of jumping over fences – motorists put their mounts through all the disciplines of the show ring. Events included 'Cleaving the Turk's Head', a motorised version, presumably, of the light cavalry; 'Gretna Green Stakes', in which dashing automobilists eloped with as many young ladies as time permitted; 'Antivibration Races', which were run off with glasses of water attached to the bonnets of the cars and 'The See-saw', a

test of balance and manoeuvrability comparable in its way to *dressage*. While the gentry were playing musical chairs and obstacle races with their motor-cars, ordinary folk too were getting their amusement – if only vicariously – from the novelty of the machines. Romantic novelists took the automobile to their hearts, making it the 'hero' of untold acres of pulp fiction. Well, the real hero of course was a millionaire or lord (often disguised as a chauffeur) who pursued the girl of his dreams in a handsome tourer through the playgrounds of Europe or America, or at the very least an Honourable who through sheer horsepower tracked down and cornered the masked maniac with his futuristic self-propelled monster. The more stylish of the genre, like the Williamsons' *The Lightning Conductor* of 1902, became international best-sellers. Theatre managers, too, quickly discovered that to put an automobile on stage was a predictable crowd-puller – at one stage there were no fewer than twenty-nine plays running in New York in which a car appeared or was the central theme – and variety theatres vied with each other to present more and more spectacular car 'acts'. At the London Hippodrome in 1903 a gigantic apparatus was erected on which an intrepid young lady nightly looped the loop in her machine. In the lesser music-halls, where the audience were inclined to a more jaundiced view of the rich man's plaything, the 'collapsing car' was a long-standing favourite and the discomfiture of its occupants was a guaranteed belly laugh. Curiously, it is one of the dramatic manifestations of the car which has survived, in the circus, to the present day.

MIDDLE CLASS MOTORING

The First World War had an anomalous effect on the development of the automobile. In Europe it brought many thousands of men (and women) into contact for the first time with the combustion engine; but it also re-awakened some of the ghosts of 'motorphobia' that many thought had been put to rest. In America – almost untouched by the war until 1917 – the full impact of the new mass production techniques began to be felt, and it was not long before the whole nation aspired to be on wheels. Car-ownership began to be a symbol of the American way of life, and throughout the twenties the automobile fostered a social revolution which affected tourism, rural life, courtship, crime, industry, advertising and many other areas of life. By now the machine itself was more reliable, offered protection from the elements, and (with the advent of the self-starter) could be comfortably driven by women. Nevertheless it still provided that 'sensation' of motoring which old hands look back on with such nostalgia, of being in contact with one's surroundings, of motoring for motoring's sake rather than just to get somewhere else.

UNPATRIOTIC PLEASURES

THE CAR AT THE FRONT AND AT HOME

Lull before the storm: idyllic afternoon in the country for an officer and friends in their 2-cylinder GWK sports car, during the summer of 1914. With the coming of war and petrol shortages, pleasure motoring came to be considered unpatriotic and, in the absence of proper government controls, the familiar spectre of motorphobia was to rear its head again.

The war in Europe was barely a month old when the German army under von Kluck was poised at Meaux for the final advance on Paris: only a swift counter-attack could hope to save the French capital from falling. With the boldness of desperation the military governor, General Gallieni, gave the order for all the taxis in Paris to be requisitioned, and six hundred Renault cabs rushed five battalions of infantry from Les Invalides to the Front. All night they shuttled back and forth ferrying the troops, and the French attack from Nanteuil at dawn took the Germans completely by surprise, throwing them back the same day. The gallant little two-cylinder 8 hp Renaults were known thereafter as 'the taxis of the Marne'.

But as a practical demonstration of mechanised mobility so early in the war, it was wasted. For the next two years military transport figured almost not at all in the strategy of either side. By the end of 1914 the opposing armies had already got bogged down in the mud of Flanders and the trenches stretched clear from the coast to the Swiss border. To the generals on both sides the only answer to this impasse seemed to lie in attrition, in massed manpower and heavier artillery – their vision of the military potential of the armed and armoured car was strictly limited. The Germans, to be sure, had used cars for communication duties since the turn of the century and Kaiser Wilhelm's Mercedes was a frequent spectator at army manoeuvres. And if the French propaganda is to be believed, one whole department of

94

the German civil service had spent the weeks preceding the invasion diligently copying out Michelin maps of northern France!

Intermittent attempts to turn the automobile into an offensive weapon had taken place in the years before the war, but nearly all had foundered on technical problems or official apathy. As early as 1901 the indefatigable E.J. Pennington had invented a tub-shaped 'fighting autocar' with armour-plating and mounted machine-guns, which was said to have made its debut rumbling up Broadway in the early hours of the morning before being imported and studiedly neglected by Britain's War Office. And in 1906 the Austrians unveiled a surprisingly modern-looking armoured car topped with a domed revolving gun-turret, which must have looked like something from outer space to the hidebound Imperial army. It got no further than the prototype: the sheer weight of the armour made such vehicles at that time suicidally ponderous and vulnerable – a point well taken by the French General Staff who, while not actively discouraging the Charron armoured car, concentrated their efforts on equipping Peugeots and Panhards with machine-guns. At worst, they offered a faster moving target.

In fact the Charron, first developed in 1902, was the first armoured car to go into action: one of two ordered by the Russian government helped to put down the riots in St Petersburg in January 1905, and its effectiveness, ironically, is said to have inspired the Germans to produce one of their own. The Ehrhardt BAK appeared in 1906 with the rather modest label of 'anti-balloon gun', but with its very limited field of fire the German authorities must have decided the odds were heavily on the side of the balloon, and no more was heard of it (until it re-appeared as the more sophisticated E-V/4 in 1915). The fact was that, even during the war, armoured cars presented a somewhat primitive aspect of rivetted steel plates hung on a conventional chassis, such as the French 60 hp Hotchkiss and the British

Taxis of the Marne: some of the 'gallant little Renaults' that were recruited from the streets of Paris in September 1914, to ferry troops to the Marne to try to halt the German offensive against France.

Archduke Ferdinand *(below)* on his fateful journey through Sarajevo in June 1914. As he drove through the city in his open Graf und Stift, first a bomb was thrown at the car and, when that failed, a student with a revolver stepped forward and shot both the Archduke and his consort.

15 hp Napiers, which distinguished themselves by charging, cavalry-style, against hostile tribesmen in North Africa. The Italians produced Lancia armoured cars (with their gaily painted turrets) from 1915, and the Americans·a Davidson-Cadillac which did sterling work winkling out Mexican guerrillas. Not quite so conventional were the Rolls-Royce six-wheelers (a conversion which the company had reluctantly undertaken for a Welsh eccentric in 1911) and the Russian Austin-Putilov half-track cars, actually based on a design by the Czar's chauffeur! Chasing zeppelins or conveying staff-officers from headquarters, the armoured car could claim to have been a useful accessory to the armies. But on the Western Front, confronted by shell-craters and six-foot dugouts, it was virtually impotent.

Behind the lines, however, there was every conceivable form of transport pressed into service: heavy tractors to tow siege-guns, cyclecars to carry stretchers (a prospect more alarming, surely, to the wounded than going over the top), double-decker buses trundling ever more regiments to their fate, private cars towing field-kitchens or ambulance trailers. By the end of the war a huge reservoir of trained drivers and mechanics had been created on both sides — which in peacetime was to affect significantly the move to cheaper, more democratic cars. But at the outbreak of war the armies had

Standing room on top: in the absence of regular troop carriers, London Buses were enlisted for war service — here carrying soldiers of the Royal Warwickshire regiment to the front during the first battle of Ypres in November 1914. By the end of the war practical armoured cars had been developed — though in the trenchbound years of confrontation they played only a limited role at the front, being used largely

as infantry support vehicles like this French armoured car (centre) at the battle of the Lys in April 1918. The tank did not actually 'win the war' as some persons claimed, but it did have an effective try-out beginning in 1916 and produced some impressive results. Its widespread application — revolutionizing modern warfare — still lay in the future.

found themselves embarrassingly short of motoring men and machines, and not least the British army. In spite of – or more probably because of – the madcap manoeuvres of the semi-official Motor Volunteer Corps (in which Earl Russell was a private and was chauffeured about in a steam-brougham by his own servant), Whitehall's only contingency plan was a subsidy system, whereby a number of car-owners were paid a retainer to hand them over to the Services in time of emergency. However, with characteristic improvisation, the motorists themselves solved the problem: three days after Germany had invaded Luxembourg an appeal appeared in *The Times:* 'The Royal Automobile Club will be glad to receive the names of members and Associates who will offer the services of their cars, or their

services with their cars, either for home or foreign service in case of need. It is requested that the make and horsepower should be stated.'

The response was immediate, and on 24 August 1914 a detachment of owner-drivers with their cars was sent to GHQ in France. In time a register of some 13,000 cars throughout the country was compiled, and an emergency fleet of 300 cars was kept in readiness day and night for special service. Nevertheless, even allowing for all the other private cars that had hastily been painted khaki and dispatched to their doom on the Front, this represented only a fraction of the 140,000 licenced cars in the country. At no

Above left: A convoy of Model-T ambulances destined for France in 1915. From the deserts of Palestine to the mud-locked roads of Flanders the 'flivvers' proved their endurance and versatility throughout the war. Fiat's speciality was in building heavy vehicles, like these huge guntowing tractors *(below)* which came into service in 1915.

time during the war did the government actually place a ban on all non-essential motoring though, had it done so, it would probably have been doing a service to motorists. For as it became clear the war was not going to be won at a stroke, and the ideal of austerity took root at home, the motor-car once again became the symbol of luxury and indulgence. Just when it looked as if the motor-car had been accepted as a legitimate and convenient means of transport, drivers once again found themselves subjected to torrents of abuse from the public and the press. Pleasure motoring took on the status of a national crime, and joy-riders were branded as 'traitors' in outbursts of the same moral indignation that was otherwise reserved for those who had failed to take the king's shilling. Led by *The*

Times and *The Daily Mail*, the national newspapers penned vitriolic editorials against selfish motorists and even argued for the abolition of all non-commercial motoring. Car-owners retorted that their vehicles were essential in keeping the business of the country running (and that petrol licences had been issued by the government on precisely that basis), that the only recreational motoring they were guilty of was taking wounded soldiers out for a spin in the country. The newspapers simply pursed their lips and published photographs of serried ranks of cars in the enclosures of race-meetings (which the government had also omitted to ban). When things got really tough in 1916 – car-taxes were trebled, petrol tax dou-

Angels with oily hands: the drain on manpower from the factories and into the army made it necessary for women to take over what had formerly been exclusively men's jobs. Not only did women work on armament production-lines, they also became mechanics in garages *(right)* and in effect opened up a new market for cars after the end of the war.

bled and fuel eventually rationed – many thousands of motorists laid their cars up for the duration.

There were restrictions in France too, of course. Motorists had to re-apply for a driving licence each month, and should one even inadvertently stray into the war zone he would be summarily put in prison and his car confiscated. But there was no petty persecution and petrol was still relatively cheap – too cheap as events turned out, for by the autumn of 1917 there was not a drop of spirit left in the country for the private motorist, who in many cases was forced to hand his machine over to a dealer with orders to offer it for sale at an exorbitant price, simply to avoid the new and crushing car taxes. In Germany as well the streets were empty of all but official cars (as much for lack of rubber as for fuel), but the surviving British motorists kept themselves on the road by exploiting all manner of petrol substitutes. The most popular was coal-gas, being a home-grown product. For £20 a vehicle could be converted to run on it, and 'gas-depots' were opened in most of the large cities. Very soon cars, vans, even buses were sprouting huge gas-bags like monster mushrooms – on the roof, in the back-seat, or trailed behind on carts. They were unsightly and the very devil to manage in a high wind, but they were moderately efficient and the motoring press even began to talk a little smugly about petrol being 'superseded'. But if the gas-baggers thought that the strange new growths on their cars would allay all doubts about their patriotism, they were soon disappointed: the police made a point of stopping them to check they weren't hiding secret pipes and petrol tanks under all the canvas! And meanwhile at the Front the opposing armies continued to pound each

A new face on the wartime buses in London was the conductorette as here, on the Islington run in 1917. After the war women continued to look for, and find, work on the buses.

other into extinction by sheer weight of munitions – much of which was, ironically, being produced in car factories which had been hastily retooled at the beginning of the war. Throughout Europe indeed the motor-trade had ceased to exist, since even those firms still producing engines or vehicles were doing so exclusively for the Armed Forces (and incidentally employing large numbers of women, whose introduction to mechanics on the factory floor was to open up new markets for manufacturers after the war). The big breakthrough in armoured vehicles came in 1915, when a body mysteriously called the Land Ships Committee was set up to investigate an idea Mr Winston Churchill had been pressing on the government, namely a 'traction engine with feet' which could straddle trenches and, who knows, even break the deadlock in France. The first specimens were hopelessly heavy, but by 1916 a model known as Big Willie was approved and went into production. The project was so secret that the authorities – in a flash of inspiration – decided there should be no secrecy at all. Instead of sentries and barbed-wire compounds, they simply announced that the work at Hatfield was to fulfil an order to the Russian government for a large number of mobile water-tanks – which was how the land-ship colloquially became a 'tank'. The Tank Corps first went into action on 15 September 1916 with exuberant results: the village of Flers was captured without a single casualty. The French Schneider and Renault tanks appeared the following year, and the German response – mostly with captured machines – came too late to affect the final outcome. It might be an exaggeration to claim, as some observers did, that the tank won the war; but it did at

In the face of petrol shortages and strict rationing many drivers converted their machines to run on coalgas, like this French motor in 1918 with its unwieldy gas-bag aloft *(above)*. In Britain the government urged owners not to use cars for inessential journeys. *Below:* The scene near Admiralty Arch in London, 1916.

least ensure that warfare would never again be conducted in a wilderness of trenches stretching across Europe.

* * *

While British and European factories were turned over to armaments, American production of automobiles soared across the Atlantic. In 1915 nearly a million cars and trucks were constructed: Ford himself produced his millionth automobile, and Willys-Overland alone produced 141,000 cars. Cadillac unveiled a V-8 engine and Packard went one better: their fantastic Twin Six was the world's first production 'Twelve', and one of the first to use aluminium pistons. It was so smooth that the car could run in top gear at 3 mph and accelerate from zero to 30 mph in ten seconds. Police had to keep the crowds in line when it was first exhibited, and Enzo Ferrari later reminisced that it left him forever hankering after a twelve-cylinder car.

In a less lofty vein Dodge coined the word 'dependability' (which found its way into the dictionaries) and achieved a major breakthrough by replacing hardwood frames with the first all-steel body. Edward Gowan Budd's concept of a body built from steel pressings was perhaps the most fundamental piece of automotive re-thinking since Benz. Budd realised that pressed steel, if correctly used, could form a lighter and cheaper substitute for traditional coachwork. It is true that some 1,200 small pressings went into an open tourer body, but General Motors, Studebaker and Willys-Overland were also quick to adopt the new method. By 1917 Budd had developed an all-steel saloon body, which Dodge put into production in 1919.

Militarily uninvolved until April 1917, the United States grew into a giant store for the supply of Allied needs and American factories took the lead in both production and design. The staggering quantities of cars produced during the war were achieved by the use of standardised parts, and often the specifications of different makes were surprisingly similar: engines for instance were nearly always side-valve 'fours'. To European eyes the American cars of this period all had the same tinny look. Their radiators were painted and the bodywork sloped upwards so that the gap between the rear wheels and the wing was twice that in front; they had wooden spoked wheels with 'demountable rims' and the spare demountable rim was a recognisable feature of the back. Even the Packard Twin Six was subject-

The buildings may be in ruins, but this German ball-bearing manufacturer *(below)* assured the public that it was keeping the army staff-cars on the road. For the Allied top brass a staff-car meant a Rolls-Royce Silver Ghost: Sir Douglas Haig is seen *(bottom)* arriving in his to review the French infantry.

ed to severe criticism by the *Autocar* which, while enthusiastic about the chassis, wrote that the body was quite unsuited to the English climate and taste. Against this, electric lighting and self-starters using the new Bendix drive off the flywheel were standard equipment on all models, not to mention such refinements as folding or divided windscreens, side windows, dashboards with proper fuel gauges, even ignition locks. These mass-produced Americans might owe more to the press than the loving hand of the panel-beater, but in comfort and convenience they were way. ahead of the stodgy English pre-war models.

American connoisseurs, too, who until now had tended to favour European cars, began to discover the charms of home-bred marques such as Packard, Cadillac, Pierce-Arrow and Locomobile. But the most significant aspect of these war years was the manner in which automobile production became locked into the national economy. In addition to producing cars and trucks the industry built tractors, aircraft engines, submarine chasers and an enormous range of specialised material. Dodge, for example, managed to mass-produce mechanisms for French field guns, Henry and Wilfred Leland developed the Liberty engine, and Ford created a complete ship-building operation from some very dubiously drawn-up blueprints. Meanwhile his 'tin Lizzie' continued to bounce through the mud of Flanders and the sands of Sinai, a testimony to millions of serving men that the car was a workhorse quite as much as a rich man's toy. By the time the war came to an end not only had the car changed, but so had many people's attitudes to it.

A quick getaway: the main square in Antwerp in October 1914. Machines, horses and men prepare to evacuate the city before the arrival of the German army. At the outbreak of hostilities, under the auspices of the RAC many car-owners had volunteered their machines, and their services as army drivers; the first detachment had arrived on the continent at the end of August.

THE AMERICAN GIANTS AND
THE EUROPEAN RESPONSE

Shedding war memories with elegant aplomb, the 1919 Salon de l'Automobile was all luxury and *faste*. Of the handful of superb designs that set the tone, the most outstanding was the new 37.2 hp H6B Hispano-Suiza. 'Open as a yacht, it wore a great shining bonnet, and flying over the crest of this great bonnet, as though in proud flight over the heads of scores of phantom horses, was that stork by which the gentle may be pleased to know that they have escaped death beneath the wheels of a Hispano-Suiza car, as supplied to His Most Catholic Majesty.' So wrote Michael Arlen, for whom the H6B set off a green hat to perfection. Isotta Frachini's straight eight was almost as opulent, with an added touch of massiveness that made it heavy to handle. (In contemporary fiction Isotta tended to get into the hands of the villain, who was chased and overtaken by the hero in his Hispano.)

Then there was Delage's six-cylinder Type CO, designed by Lovera. But perhaps the most novel engine in the Salon was the 6½ litre twelve-cylinder Lancia (with its two banks of cylinders inclined at a 22 degree angle in a single casting). Although it proved uneconomical to manufacture, the monobloc narrow-angle principle was to figure in Vincenzo Lancia's unforgettable Lambda, introduced in 1922 (see profile on page 107). Some of the famous marques had a distinctly déjà-vu air – which was something that could not be said of one popular model bearing the 'chevron' motif.

André Citroën was by no means a newcomer: as chief engineer at Mors he had rallied that firm after a depression in 1908 and boosted production to 2,000 units a year. In 1913 he quit Mors to start his own gear-cutting firm, and during the war had turned out shells in prodigious quantities for the Allied artillery. Even so, when he formed Automobiles Citroën early in 1919, announcing his intention to mass-produce cars at the rate of 100 per day, no-one took the project very seriously. Few in the trade believed he would even get into production, but his critics were proved wrong. Adapting American mass-production methods, Citroën was already turning out 35 cars a day in the old Mors works when the Salon opened in November. His Type A was a 10 hp 1.3 litre tourer, and at 7,950 francs (about £320) it was attractively priced. Though this was later increased to 12,500 francs with full equipment, some 20,000 orders were placed when the car was unveiled. Within a year, using the first fully-fledged assembly-line in Europe, Citroën had built 10,000 units. In 1922 he acquired the old established firm of Clément-Bayard, and introduced the famous Clover-leaf 5cv (a popular three-seater), which was soon coming off the lines at the rate of 250 a day and forcing Renault and Peugeot to pull up their socks.

A month after the Paris Salon it was London's turn. When the war ended there were only 78,000 cars left on the roads of Britain, and a host of new hopefuls joined the established manufacturers to meet the demand from a car-starved public. New makes were as thick as starlings at dusk: 134 British marques and − in spite of the fact that the McKenna duty of 33⅓ percent on imported cars (imposed during the war, ostensibly to preserve shipping space) was still in force − 130 foreigners displayed their offerings at the Olympia Show in November 1919. Among the profusion were a good many warmed-up pre-war models. Among the newcomers were the 1½ litre Aston Martin and T.G. John's 10/30 Alvis, both of them destined for fame in the sporting world. But even their successes were to be eclipsed by the handsome, bulldog-looking tourer with a winged B on its radiator

that heralded in, and exactly spanned, the period we now know as Vintage. Indeed the term 'vintage car' is symbolised by an open green Bentley with outside gear and brake levers, emitting the purposeful burble of four big cylinders. W.O. Bentley set out to build fast, reliable cars for the rich sporting motorist, backing meticulous workmanship with a five years' guarantee: how well he succeeded (though not, alas, financially) was shown by the five victories at Le Mans and countless other competitive awards. The first post-war signs that a vast new market was opening for cheap transport came with the arrival of small, cheap cyclecars that (along with the motorcycle and sidecar combination) became popular in the 1930s with the British working-class. They may have been democratic, but for the

Symbol of the States. *Above:* Ultra-modern gas station in Daytona in 1923, with automatic pumps selling the new 'anti-knock' petrol. A ubiquitous Model T on the right gets its tankful, while an expensive Scripps-Booth tourer waits its turn.

THE PERFECT PRODUCT OF MODERN SCIENCE
MORRIS CARS

ROLLS-ROYCE

AS SILENT AS ITS SHADOW

Just as the old Inn has stood the test of time, so have the Dunlop Tyres that bring you to it. They have both been *built to last*.

Avec une 10 HP CITROËN
Vous pouvez avantageusement habiter à 50 kilomètres de vos affaires

USINES CITROEN 115-143 QUAI DE JAVEL PARIS

Some inter-war images of the automobile *(above),* with Rolls-Royce not deviating from its elegant classicism but Morris opting for a curiously nightmarish vision! Citroën appeals to the new suburbanites of Paris, Dunlop to the fresh-air fun-seekers – but shouldn't the cars be driving on the other side of the road?

most part they were rickety devices combining, as one critic of the day put it, 'the comfort of a cement-mixer, the noise of a pneumatic drill, and the directional stability of a chicken with its head off'. Of course they were built to a price: the natty little Carden sold for only £100 and King Alfonso of Spain bought one at Olympia (to sling as a lifeboat on his Hispano-Suiza, said the wits).

If cyclecars flourished briefly in the early twenties it was because the euphoric hopes of 1919 were dashed by subsequent events. Supply problems and labour unrest meant it was a long time before customers could get their hands on the models they had chosen. (In fact on both sides of the Atlantic a lucrative black market flourished: the simplest trick was to put your own, and other people's, names down on dozens of waiting-lists, take delivery from the official dealers, then sell off round the corner for an extra £500.) The strikes of 1920 caused lengthy delays in the delivery of parts, with the result that prices rose persistently and the value of pre-war used cars, which filled the small-ads of the motoring press, soared. A good eighteen months went by before supply caught up with demand, by which time recession had reduced orders to a trickle and many firms had gone to the wall.

Curiously the 'roaring twenties' opened and closed with a slump. Japan, for instance, experienced a financial panic on 17 April 1920, and in May that year credit tightened throughout the U.S. automotive industry. Ford weathered the storm by slashing the price of the Model T to $395, well

DODGE BROTHERS
TOURING CAR

In city traffic or on the open road, this new touring car impresses you instantly with its exceptional riding comfort.

The seats are deeper and lower. The body has been lengthened to afford more leg-room. Its low-swung design reduces side sway and increases the car's stability at all speeds.

The front springs are wider, and built of more and thinner leaves; the rear springs—now under-slung—have been materially increased in length.

In fact, the comfort of the car is comparable in every way with its good looks and the well known character of its performance.

The price is $880 f. o. b. Detroit

MORRIS
AHEAD AGAIN for 1933

The road ahead: two advertisements showing the evolution of traffic signals over ten years. When Dodge brought out their ad in 1923 manually-operated stop/go beacons were still in use at many city intersections in America (to little effect, apparently). By 1933 automatic traffic lights were revolutionary enough in Britain for Morris to adopt them as their symbol of progress.

below cost. He ended the year on the brink of disaster with a $50 million loss, but by loading his dealers with unsold cars against cash payment he emerged solvent. For the man at the end of the chain it was a ruthless tactic. Some years later a Ford dealer from the Midwest wrote his 'confessions' and recalled the black days of 1920:

'If anyone wants to know what hard times are he ought to try to do business in a Western farming community during a panic....From September to January that year I sold exactly four cars. But the worst was yet to come. All of a sudden came notice that a shipment of fifteen Fords was on its way to me, and that I would be expected to pay for them on arrival. I thought there must be some mistake, and got the branch manager in the city on the long distance. He was a pretty hard-boiled egg named Blassingham. "Those are the orders," he snapped, "and my advice to you is to pay for those cars when they arrive." '

A lot of dealers didn't manage to survive, and even a firm as big as Maxwell went into receivership and was reorganised with Walter P. Chrysler in charge. The Maxwell name remained on its cars for another four years, until the exciting new Light Six Chrysler with a high-compression engine and other innovations was unveiled at the Commodore Hotel in New York in 1924 (see profile on page 111). Thus the Chrysler Corporation was born, and by selling $50 million worth of cars in its first year joined Ford and General Motors as the 'Big Three' of the automobile world.

3 LITRE BENTLEY
1919

When the Hispano-Suiza Company was founded in Barcelona in 1904, partly financed with Swiss capital, it hired a young Swiss engineer named Marc Birkigt who had been working in Spain for a company making electric buses. Hispano-Suiza, which specialised in high class luxury cars, also produced racers which proved successful in the Boulogne event (near Paris).When war broke out in 1914, Birkigt moved to the Paris branch of Hispano-Suiza and began designing V-8 airplane engines that made the competition look prehistoric.

With this experience under his belt, Birkigt proceeded after the war to design a completely new, high class H6B model which virtually shook the world when it was first unveiled in 1919. For one thing, its

100×140 mm six-cylinder engine with full pressure lubrication and a 7-bearing crankshaft exactly reproduced the technique of the famous aero engines. Its chassis, bristling with brilliant innovations, was an architectural masterpiece. Not only did it boast four-wheel brakes (very rare at the time), but its large brake drums were cast iron linered aluminium, operated by a gear-box-driven mechanical servo (later used by Rolls-Royce who acquired the licencing rights and who still use it on their Phantom VI). The use of light alloys and highly tensile steel resulted in an exceptionally lightweight chassis for its size. The 1919 Hispano-Suiza was truly the supreme splendour of the classic age. Though most H6B chassis were fitted with large limousine bodies, a light two-seater was also produced for the sports-minded.

The latter group included a very able gentleman driver named André Dubonnet (still remembered for the apéritif that bears his name), who in 1921 began a run of three straight Hispano victories at the Boulogne meets which by then had become famous. In 1923, the winning car was the new H6C model, which had an engine bored out to give a capacity of 8 litres. The H6C scored a stunning victory, driven by the famous French coachbuilder C.T. Weymann, in a 24 hour challenge race on the Indianapolis track, against an American Stutz, in 1928.

The H6B and H6C were produced almost unaltered well into the thirties and retained Birkigt's original chassis with only minor modifications.

LANCIA LAMBDA
1923

Probably no other automobile company in the world acquired such fame in so short a time as Bentley Motors. In operation for a total of only ten years, Bentley produced just over 3,000 cars, of which nearly half are still running today, cherished by fastidious owners, a half-century after the company's demise.

Having raced motorcycles and cars in a number of British speed events before the First War, Walter Owen Bentley, better known simply as W.O., went to work for Rolls-Royce and Sunbeam, designing and developing the successful Bentley Rotary aero engine, but had already made plans to found his own car manufacturing company and begun some rough designs. These materialised at the end of 1919 in the first experimental 3 litre Bentley, the 'Ex. 1'.

A straightforward but very clean and well-detailed design, the Ex. 1 featured a very long-stroke (149 mm) 3 litre engine of 80 mm bore, with a single overhead camshaft, four valves per cylinder and twin magneto ignition, and a separate, four-speed gearbox. It was to set the pattern for all future models produced by the Bentley Company. These are the cars which prompted Ettore Bugatti's famous comment: 'Mr Bentley is an excellent engineer: he makes the world's fastest lorries.'

Though the original 3 litre was on the road by the end of 1919 and even road tested by *The Autocar* in January 1920, the fastidious W.O. did not allow the first 3 litre to be delivered to its owner until September 1921. By then a car had been entered at Brooklands and won, while another, sent to compete in the Indianapolis 500 Miles, finished 13th. But it was only after production was under way and money was pouring in that the company was able to launch the racing programme W.O. considered so essential for stimulating goodwill and technical development. W.O. himself was the driver of one of the team cars which won the Ards T.T., while Duff and Clement scored the first of five Bentley victories at Le Mans in 1924.

In 1931, when endless financial problems halted the production of Bentley-designed automobiles, and brought the take-over by Rolls-Royce, 3 litres accounted for more than half of all the cars made by Bentley Motors.

HISPANO-SUIZA H6B

1919

Vincenzo Lancia's fame as a racing driver for Fiat helped to inspire confidence in his products when he started manufacturing cars in 1908, and undoubtedly pre-war products such as the Theta were practically indestructible save by a professional car-breaker. But Lancia's first great contribution to motoring was the revolutionary Lambda shown at the 1922 Paris Salon. For one thing, it introduced Lancia's concept of a short, stiff monoblock Vee engine that with variations – ranging from the 24° of the Dilambda to the narrow 10°14' of the Appia – was to power practically all the factory's products right up to the Fulvia. Yet this was not all; the Lambda had four-wheel brakes that really worked, and sliding pillar independent front-wheel suspension which gave outstanding road adherence, along with steering of almost surgical precision (qualities the works driver used to demonstrate by driving up and down the sidewalk pavestones at high speed, scattering startled pedestrians in all directions). And furthermore it was the first car endowed with integral construction, using deep pressed steel side members which also formed the structure of the open four-seater bodywork. None of these features was actually invented by Lancia, of course. But he was the first manufacturer to combine them in one car, and his unconventional approach to engineering matters, together with an obsession with quality rather than cost, characterised all the firm's products long after its founder's untimely death in 1937 (just as Vincenzo's last personal masterpiece, the brilliant little Aprilia, was being launched). Indeed, when examining a 1967 Flavia, one senior Rolls-Royce man conceded that of all the European manufacturers, only Lancia showed the same lofty contempt for cost-accounting as Crewe – which may explain why this great marque was fated to become the badge for an up-market Fiat. Be this as it may, the Lambda was the first of an exciting new breed that continued for fifty years, and if by today's standards its steering would no longer be considered as feather-light, nor the engine quite so smooth and silent, its road-holding qualities would still meet with approval.

In England too, a number of manufacturers had been forced to cut prices in that bleak autumn, but William Morris — who is usually credited with having started the price war — hung fire until the writing was clearly on the wall. In February 1921 he reduced the Morris Cowley by £100, and lopped a further £81 off in July. Sales of the car, now priced under £350, rose dramatically and contributed to the feeling within the industry that production should be concentrated on economical family cars. Several companies (like Bean, Clyno and Swift) all had plans for cornering a hefty slice of this market, but it was Bill Morris and Herbert Austin who proved to have greater vision than their rivals.

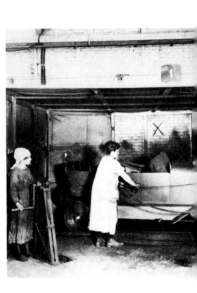

First steps in volume production. *Above:* 'Sliding' production line for the Singer Saloon in 1928. Singer, the third-largest manufacturers in Britain at the time, made heavy investments in plant and premises in the late 1920s but sadly failed to make any real impact on the mass market. Morris, on the other hand *(above right,* the 'Bullnose' in production at Cowley in 1925), continued to capitalise on their good fortune not to have ceased car production during the war. By diligent application of American production methods, by fierce competitiveness and brave advertising, Morris emerged as one of Britain's top three in the 1930s.

From the moment he started up W.R.M. Motors in Longwall opposite the side entrance of Magdalen College, Oxford, and made his first Morris Oxford, William Morris had modelled his business on the American pattern. Back in 1914 he had visited the States and concluded deals to buy Continental engines and other components at very competitive prices, so that although not many people realised it, the endearingly British Bullnose was largely made with American parts. When the McKenna duties were extended after the war to include components, he arranged for the U.S. Continental engine to be built by the Hotchkiss Coventry plant, and following Ford's dictum that one should control one's suppliers, bought a radiator factory in 1919 and the Hotchkiss factory in 1922. When the Budd Corporation had demonstrated the advantages of body shells built entirely from pressed steel panels with chassis frames incorporated in the body, Morris got together with Budd to found the Pressed Steel Company along the road from his assembly lines in Cowley. In this way he was able to produce sound (if rather dull) cars at less cost than his competitors, and sales rose from 16,000 Morris cars in 1923 to well over 63,000 by 1929.

Herbert Austin (who was ten years older than Morris and in the pioneering days had steered the Wolseley Sheep Shearing Company into the largest British car producer before starting his own firm in 1905) had the same objective. To test his conviction that really cheap motoring was the answer, he planned to produce a miniature car that, in his own words, 'would knock the motorcycle and sidecar into a cocked hat'. The result was the Austin Seven (see profile on page 110).

Produced basically unaltered until 1937, the Baby Austin brought about the same revolution on British roads as the Lizzie had done in the States – and was the butt of just as many jokes. It was manufactured abroad first by Dixi, and then by BMW in Germany, by Rosengart in France, by Bantam in the United States, and it started Datsun on their way in Japan. It also hastened the arrival of other small Fours, such as the Morris Minor, the Singer Nine, Triumph Super Seven and the Standard Nine. An influential model indeed.

But individual craftsmanship persisted in many firms. *Above:* These De Dion-Boutons lined up in the tailors' shop are being fitted with hand-stitched upholstery in an English coachmaker's in 1923, and *(center)* ABC sports models get individual attention in the paint preparation bay in 1921. Small – and sadly short-lived – backyard firms like ABC could incorporate unorthodox features in design quite cheaply, but were ultimately unable to compete in the mass market-place. The early Citro-ën *(above left)* gets its finish in a somewhat primitive spray-shop at the hands of two ladies – a tangible result of their wartime employment in car factories.

By now the chassis was a frame of braced channel-section steel carried on semi- (or quarter-) elliptic springs with adjustable shock absorbers. Four-wheel brakes, 'advertised' by a red triangle on the back of the car, were becoming general; while standard specification included electric lighting and self-starters. Bodies and windscreens might be uncompromisingly upright, but they were getting roomier and more comfortable, and offered better weather protection. By the end of the decade saloons and drop head coupes were current, and there was a vogue for Weymann bodies in which leather cloth was tightly stretched over a wooden frame with metal pieces inserted to eliminate the squeaks – though it soon became apparent that fabric bodies could not stand the test of time.

The influence of the United States in this development was clear. By 1920 some 9 million Americans were on the road and the automobile industry was the largest in the country, employing over a quarter of a million people directly. Even during the recession that year, passenger car output alone reached an impressive 1.9 million units – rising to 5.3 million in 1929, or ten times as many as the rest of the world put together. These staggering figures could only be achieved by rationalised production and assembly procedures, using standardised machining tolerances to ensure that all individual items and sub-assemblies were interchangeable. Ultimately it meant that U.S. manufacturers were turning out enormous quantities of more or less identical vehicles, and that apart from a few non-

AUSTIN SEVEN
1922

It was at a critical moment for his firm (whose Twelve and Twenty saloons were not selling at all well) that Herbert Austin decided to produce a miniature car which, while retailing at roughly the same price as a cyclecar or indeed a motor-cycle and

sidecar combination (both of which he abominated), would offer the man-in-the-street greater value and better motoring. And when his co-directors voiced their doubts, he worked out the design on the billiard table at home with the help of a draughtsman.

As it turned out, the Austin Seven – first exhibited at Olympia in 1922 – was one of the most important cars in British motoring

history. With its four-cylinder water-cooled engine, three-speed gearbox, four-wheel brakes and four seats, this cheeky little baby was a scaled down real car, yet at £165, including all-weather equipment and spare wheel, was firmly priced in the cyclecar bracket. Admittedly the body was very elementary and the whippy crankshaft set up a sympathetic vibration in the starting handle, so that one rattled along ringing like an electric bell; and with the pedal operating the front brakes and the handbrake the rear ones, the less said about stopping the better. Who was it who commented that if you applied the brakes in Surrey, you would avoid falling off the cliff in Sussex?

For all this, the Seven was exceptionably durable, and belied its pram-like appearance by scoring many racing successes in tuned-up form. During the next fifteen years it changed the shape of motoring in England, inspired many other small economy four-cylinder models, and lived on, in spirit as well as name, in the Issigonis-designed Mini of the sixties.

Ettore Bugatti was born in Milan into a family of artists and craftsmen. He wanted to become a goldsmith like his father – until the day he got his hands on a motor tricycle and took it apart.

After an apprenticeship whith a car-maker in Milan, he designed and built his own automobile, and raced it himself with

immediate success. He went on to design cars for De Dietrich, Mathis and Deutz before founding his own company in the then German Alsace, settling in Molsheim in 1909.

He was convinced that most cars were unnecessarily heavy, and the first model bearing his name, the Type 13, was a small 1,300 cc car boasting a beautifully clean four-cylinder o.h.c. engine able to outperform almost anything on the road. This he proved in many racing events. During the First War, Bugatti fled to France

and took French nationality – as did Alsace as soon as peace was restored. Production soon resumed in Molsheim.

Bugatti was probably the first manufacturer in the world making racing cars as part of his normal programme, but his great breakthrough came on the occasion of the 1924 French Grand Prix where his new Type 35 stole the show. With their narrow, horse-shoe shaped radiator, their elegant and businesslike polished steel tubular front axle, their cast aluminium wheels with integral brake drums and their narrow, pointed tail body finished in French racing blue, his were the most elegant cars ever seen on a racing circuit. They set the pattern for all Bugattis for the next 15 years. Their straight-eight, 2 litre engine was as much a joy to behold as the car itself. True, on that occasion, the Type 35 was less successful in meeting the Alfa-Romeo challenge than in attracting the photographers, but this was soon remedied when a supercharger was added to make the Type 35 C or the even more famous 35 B which was stroked to increase the engine capacity to 2.3 litres. In 1926 alone, the various types 35 won no less than 12 major Grands Prix, and many of the Type 35's victories were scored by private owners. Altogether, probably around 1,000 Type 35 and derivatives were made, surely a record for a full racing car even today.

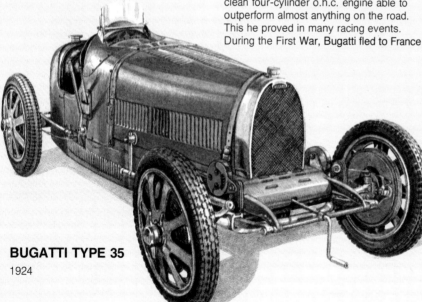

BUGATTI TYPE 35
1924

CHRYSLER SIX

1924

After a meteoric rise to the vice-presidency of General Motors, Walter P. Chrysler took over the ailing Maxwell Company.
He longed to produce a moderately priced automobile featuring a six-cylinder high compression engine for better efficiency.

The model he unveiled in January 1924 had that and much more: aluminium pistons, full pressure lubrication, oil filter, air cleaner, four-wheel hydraulic brakes, hydraulic shock absorbers, a beautifully designed tubular front axle – features that certainly had never yet been combined in a medium priced car. To top it all, the Chrysler Six, exhibited in open tourer style, had beautifully clean and well-balanced lines.

That year (1924) saw 32,000 Chryslers sold through Maxwell dealers, a record for a first production year at the time.
Just over a year later, Chrysler announced a four-cylinder car which, thanks to a three bearing crankshaft and flexible engine mountings, was probably the smoothest running American 'four' of the period. From it, in 1928, the first Plymouth was derived. The soundness of Chrysler engineering was demonstrated when only four years after the announcement of the first Chrysler Six, Chryslers finished third and fourth at Le Mans.

Although the first M-type Midgets were nothing more than rebodied Morris Minors, enthusiasts soon tuned the tiny 847 cc engine to phenomenal levels with the aid of supercharging. In February 1931 George Eyston took the World Class H record at 103 mph on a modified single-seater, and later that year the racing C-types, which were developed from the M-type, secured the first five places in the Brooklands Double-Twelve race (on handicap, of course). From that moment onwards, MGs were continually in the news, and in 1938 'Goldie' Gardner notched up 203.5 mph on the German autobahn with a specially

streamlined machine based on a modified K3 chassis and 1,100 cc engine. Such exploits boosted the MG image, to be sure, but it was the 1932–33 J.2 (along with the Singer Le Mans and the Riley Imp) that epitomised the sports car of the thirties with its tautly-styled two seater body, characterised by rampant headlamps, deeply cut-away doors and wire-spoked spare wheel strapped to the back of the big slab petrol tank. To snarl around country lanes with the windscreen flat, behind twin aero screens, a Bluemel 'sprung' steering

wheel, fly-off hand-brake, huge dials, knobs galore and with an elegant girl friend in the left hand seat: what more could any young man have wished for – even if it ran out of puff at 70 mph? The later T-series Midgets with their short-stroke 1,250 cc engines had better performance, and provided many Americans with their first taste of an English sports car after World War II. MG offered a special, exhilarating form of popular motoring; and it is sad that after 50 years the factory was shut down in 1980.

MG MIDGET

1932

conformists like Cord, Duesenberg and Stutz (who failed to survive), American cars tended to be similar in concept and layout, with a disturbingly made-in-Detroit look.

Against this the Americans introduced a flow of refinements which added greatly to the convenience of motoring. Longer-lasting, low-pressure balloon tyres were pioneered by Firestone and first featured as standard equipment on the Chrysler 70. Du Pont developed 'Duco' spray-on cellulose, which was first standardised by General Motors in 1924 on the Oakland. Safety glass was fitted to Stutz and Rickenbacker windscreens in 1926, and Trico introduced electric wipers which eventually banished

The girls from the garage: brandishing trophies and togged up like racing drivers the Fiat girls of 1925 *(above)* pose for the camera during the launch of the new Fiat 509 (which doesn't get much of a look in!). The Italian firm was one of the most aggressive advertisers, gearing much of its early promotion towards women drivers.

the frustrating suction-operated wipers, whose unendearing trick was to go slower as the car went faster and sometimes stop entirely! Cadillac unveiled the syncromesh gearbox; chromium first replaced nickel-plating on some 1925 models.

Visiting Detroit, Giovanni Agnelli freely acknowledged the debt that European manufacturers owed to the States. Yet if Europe was happy enough to copy American production techniques, it continued to evolve designs over a far wider spectrum. As American cars got bigger, those across the Atlantic shrank in size as manufacturers sought to cater for the individual needs of each country. Take Italy: Fiat had made its name through racing with some truly formidable machinery, like the great monsters that Nazzaro had driven so brilliantly in the Kaiser-preis, the Targa Florio and the Grand Prix of 1907.

But in 1919 Fiat moved tentatively into volume production with the 1½ litre Tipo 501 (rather on the lines of the Citroën A7), but real mass-production came with the smaller 509 of which over 90,000 were sold between

1925 and 1929 — a result that was undoubtedly helped by the introduction of hire-purchase, but nevertheless represented over half the cars registered in the entire country. The paradox is that while the Italians were late to get thoroughly motorised, they were the most creative and intuitive engineers. Alfa Romeo won the very first Grande Epreuve they ever entered when Campari was victorious in the 1924 French Grand Prix, and in 1925 they were declared world champions. Vittorio Jano's lovely 6C Sport must stand as a classic for all time; Lancia's most personal masterpiece, the Lambda, was joined by the bigger Dilambda with the same narrow-V engine layout and surgically precise steering that made it a match for most

sports cars. Both were created by men who could design a whole car as an entity, like a work of art.

Of that other Italian genius, who lived most of his life in France and who built some of the most soul-stirring cars ever seen, Ronald Barker has written: 'Bugatti was inventive, ingenious and intuitive....Above all, he was an artist and his cars disclose an aesthetic flair even more pronounced than his mechanical aptitude.' Of his fifty or so different models the Type 35 may not have been his best, but it was surely his masterpiece (see profile, page 110). An over-the-counter racing car that an amateur could buy, it handled so well that between 1924 and 1927 alone it won 1,851 races. Maybe the age of artistry in car design has indeed passed, but the great conceptions of this period (that came to maturity in the thirties) forged a *pur-sang* tradition that was to inspire Ferrari, Maserati and Porsche.

Competitive events — such as the Scottish Six Days trial *(above*, with a 1922 Citroën on one of the hill climbs) — afforded manufacturers scope for testing and development. And maintenance facilities improved too, with firms opening up their own service centres.

IMAGES OF A DECADE

Brave new worlds. *Left:* 1920s style, the Bright Young Things of the Jazz Age discovering the liberation of the car in the film *Our Modern Maidens. Right:* 1930s style: a Ford motor show of the mid-thirties takes as its theme some Wellsian concept of the future (with orchestral backing), aligning the car with the latest in technological development – triplanes, radio and skyscrapers with built-in landing strips.

Cars carry around with them two sets of images. One is a composite image, an overall view of the car as an inescapable part of our lives: it is a view that tends to change from one generation to another and vary according to whether you are an enthusiast or an environmentalist, a speed-cop or a salesman. The other image is more specific to each model and make of car, the label that distinguishes one from the other: it is of course created almost entirely by advertising. In the 1920s accelerating mass-production demanded high-pressure selling, new market research techniques and blanket advertising. If it was the advertising industry that helped to empty the showrooms in the twenties, equally it was the car business that helped to revolutionise the advertising industry. Just after the war, car advertisements in America counted for 20 percent of all full-page insertions in general periodicals and by 1927 this had doubled: two pages of adverts out of every five were for automobiles. The pressure, to find new angles and create more eye-catching copy, was growing each year.

In the early days of motoring, car-makers had never been reticent about describing their products as perfect. As early as 1899 one manufacturer

had assured his readers that 'no better car will be made. Time cannot improve it.' It was in fact only when automobiles approached being perfected that the adjective 'perfect' was dropped from the vocabulary. It was too absolute and all-embracing a superlative, and it left people wondering why a manufacturer therefore bothered to bring out a new model when he had already produced the 'perfect' car a year or two earlier. So even before the war, producers had begun to invest their vehicles with some kind of distinguishing image, though in fact the same images recurred time and again: particular favourites being Ascot and Monte Carlo, the opera and Fifth Avenue department stores.

Window shopping 1925: the window display of a Morris agent's showroom in London conjures up the pastoral pleasures of motoring – even if Dad at the wheel does look like he's lost. The middle-class family has been provided with all the correct equipment for a do-it-yourself picnic.

The war scarcely touched this brand of advertising: in 1919 the élite were still riding their limousines to the hunt or through the gates of some château in the advertising pages of the glossies, and Winton was still plugging 'the closed car, so necessary to a successful social season'. At the top end of the market indeed, throughout the inter-war years, you would swear life hadn't changed for the owners of Cunninghams, Cadillacs and Hispano-Suizas but for the discreet intrusions of airplanes (the one futuristic symbol the top people's admen permitted themselves) and golf clubs (the society bible *Car Illustrated* went so far as to change its title to *Car and Golf* in the mid-twenties). The Rolls-Royce advertisements remained a classic of the genre with their mandatory stately homes, Rolls-trained chauffeurs moulded to the front seat and looking nowhere but straight ahead, and pillared porticoes designed solely to offset the Phantom II. Motor-cars were apparently reserved for a narrow circle of well-heeled consumers.

Then as the twenties started to roar, advertisers began to discern a substratum of society to whom the car meant something else. These were the Bright Young Things — sometimes known on the distaff side as flappers — who were determined at all costs to be gay. They embraced the motor-car, just as they embraced the Black Bottom and the Eton Crop, as a symbol of their liberation. All-night joyriding after the night club was a great sport, and clue-hunting point-to-points a fashionable craze. In 1924, Hon. Lois Sturt appeared before the magistrates for driving round Regent's Park on the wrong side at over 50 mph: it transpired there was a clue-hunt in progress around London. For their benefit, and in spite of the statutory 20

mph speed limit in Britain, the sportier manufacturers (like Lea Francis and Lagonda) emphasised speed and performance in their adverts — which at least made a refreshing change from the pages of static gleaming monsters, aesthetically parked.

But in the great world outside a far more important market lay untapped. In Europe the motoring 'revolution' did not gather momentum until late in the 1920s, but in America it spanned the decade. The nine million cars on the road in 1920 had leapt to over 27 million by 1929, reflecting the precarious boom that was making sunshine playgrounds in Florida and California and keeping the barometer of Wall Street rising steadily. Like Sister Bessie, the preacher-lady from Georgia in Erskine Caldwell's *Tobacco Road*, who spent every last cent of her dead husband's insurance on a new Ford, it became everyone's ambition to own an automobile. For Bessie the car was the key to getting herself a new husband and escaping the

Picnic and parasol at Brooklands' Whitsun meeting in 1922. The back seat of an AC sporting tourer makes an excellent grandstand; the car cushions are super for elegant reclining.

share-cropping, but not before she had prayed over the embarrassed sales-men: 'Dear God, we poor sinners kneel down in this garage to pray for a blessing on this new automobile trade...and these two men here who sold the new car to us need your blessing too, so they can sell automobiles for the best good'! The car of course could work no miracles for Bessie, but in-stead was gradually transformed into a crumpled, scavenged, rattling shell to match the other debris of the sharecroppers' world.

Nevertheless the automobile remained the highest aspiration for millions, especially in rural America. When interviewed as to why they had bought a car when they didn't even own a bath-tub, one farmer's wife replied that

Cairo that way. By the 1920s, when this advert *(right)* was published, Rolls-Royce spanned the Empire – finding favour in particular with ma-harajahs and other Indian nobility who imported some of the most opu-lent models ever seen.

The rhythm of the road: the automo-bile has been celebrated in music and song throughout its career. The first issue of *The Car* gave away cop-ies of 'The Car Carol' and a special 'Motor Fanfare' was composed for the exhibition at the Imperial Institute in 1896. The best-seller of them all was Maurice Abraham's 'He'd Have to Get Under' *(above)* which contin-ued to be revived in the thirties – unlike some of the more ephemeral ditties *(above right)*.

you couldn't drive to town in a bath-tub. It was reckoned that a man earn-ing $35 a week would spend one week's earnings each month paying for his car, and that this was commonplace. In Robert and Helen Lynd's famous cultural study of a small American town in the twenties, *Middletown,* they discovered that even by 1923 two out of every three families owned a car. Not a few had mortgaged their homes to buy it, and others clearly regarded it as the major priority in the family budget. 'We'd rather do without clothes than give up the car', said one woman. 'No matter how the children look, we just poke them in the car and take 'em along.' 'I'll go without food before I'll see us give up the car', said another.

Some of the inhabitants justified their investment on the ground that the automobile brought the family together just as the Overland adverts pro-mised: 'Some sunny Sunday just drive an Overland up to your door – tell the family to hurry the packing and get aboard – and be off with smiles down the nearest road, free, loose and happy.' Others regarded it as a so-cial disability not to own a car – again a response the advertisers had antic-ipated: 'Designed to appeal to people who are distinguished from the masses by higher ideals', promised the Moon Car company, while the Earl

Somewhere West of Laramie

SOMEWHERE west of Laramie there's a broncho-busting, steer-roping girl who knows what I'm talking about. She can tell what a sassy pony, that's a cross between greased lightning and the place where it hits, can do with eleven hundred pounds of steel and action when he's going high, wide and handsome.

The truth is—the Playboy was built for her.

Built for the lass whose face is brown with the sun when the day is done of revel and romp and race.

She loves the cross of the wild and the tame.

There's a savor of links about that car—of laughter and lilt and light—a hint of old loves—and saddle and quirt. It's a brawny thing—yet a graceful thing for the sweep o' the Avenue.

Step into the Playboy when the hour grows dull with things gone dead and stale.

Then start for the land of real living with the spirit of the lass who rides, lean and rangy, into the red horizon of a Wyoming twilight.

JORDAN MOTOR CAR COMPANY, Inc., Cleveland, Ohio

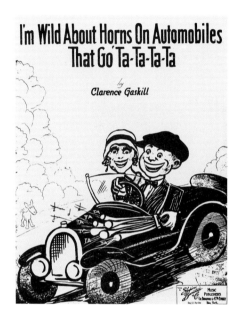

Selling status. *Above left:* One of Jordan's famous series of ads (1920–24), investing the car with an aura and selling the customer – notably the emancipated lady – rather than mechanics. This advertising approach was considered such a breakthrough that one agency required new executives to learn the copy by heart. *Above:* Fancy horns had long been status-enhancers. By the 1920s even little runabouts could boast mutli-tone hooters.

was for those 'who take an honest pride in their belongings, who seek to rise above the commonplace in their homes'.

It was probably no accident that in Middletown so many of the questions about motoring were answered by women. Women were now a challenging target for sales, not just according to the current dictum that 'men buy cars, women choose them', but as car-drivers in their own right (since the self-starter had removed the one major obstacle to the woman-driver). Automobile advertisements began regularly to appear in women's magazines, with ladies at the wheel rather than being assisted into the back seat. Companies on both sides of the Atlantic – Fiat were particularly aggressive in their feminine sales-pitch – started to designate their colour options as if they were fashion accessories, 'egg-shell blue' suddenly vying with 'South Sea turquoise'. Chevrolet, with an eye for the two-car family as early as 1921, asked the men almost accusingly, 'Is your wife marooned during the day?' and offered them their coupe to avert a marital crisis. But it was the Jordan company that really took copy-writing to Parnassian heights, not by advertising their car (which they called the Playboy and sold to girls), but by advertising the customer:

Right: Les Dames du Bois de Boulogne – a French 'art study' of 1925 demonstrating (depending on your point of view) the car's avant-garde appeal, its versatility, or its threat to moral standards.

No hint of impropriety in Morris' advert for the new Minor – a family saloon but clearly for the family that could afford a substantial detached and gabled property in one of the better-class suburbs. In fact, when Morris introduced their cheaper 'austerity' Minor a few years later, sales proved very slow.

'Somewhere west of Laramie there's a bronco-busting, steer-roping girl who knows what I'm talking about. She can tell what a sassy pony, that's a cross between greased lightning and the place where it hits, can do with 1100 lbs of steel and action when he's going high, wide and handsome.

'The truth is – the Playboy was built for her. Built for the lass whose face is brown with the sun when the day is done of revel and romp and race.

'Step into the Playboy when the hour grows dull with things gone dead and stale. Then start for the land of real living with the spirit of the lass who rides, lean and rangy, into the red horizon of a Wyoming twilight.'

If the reader ever puzzled it out, she may not have known anything about the Playboy (which was something of a blur in the advert) but she sure would have liked to be the girl in the ad.

In this fashion Jordan had neatly side-stepped the constant problem facing most manufacturers – how, in a market where the products were becoming increasingly similar, could you tell the public that your car was different? It was partly under pressure from advertising and sales departments that some companies adopted the policy of annual model changes, of offering newer and 'better' packages by juggling with design features, accessories or engine parts. General Motors, with their Chevy in particular, were masters at producing some new selling-points with each succeeding Motor Show (and in doing so contributed to the philosophy of planned obsolescence). Almost alone in the U.S. car industry, Henry Ford had resisted this quixotic approach, as indeed he could afford to when half the cars on American roads were Model T's.

But even by 1926 there were signs that the Model T was at last becoming regarded as archaic: Ford's sales were down 25 percent, Chevrolet's up 40 percent. The jokes which Ford had once encouraged were taking on a more trenchant tone. Then, on 25 May 1927, newspapers round the country carried the announcement that production of the immortal T would be discontinued. For seven months the lines were shut while a gigantic retooling operation was carried out, and speculation about the Lizzie's successor became a national sport. Half a million people paid deposits on the new Ford without knowing what it would look like or cost. When the Model A was finally released in December 1927, 10 million people are said to have inspected the new car in its first thirty-six hours on display. What they saw was a typical Detroit product in which the only vestiges of the T were the Ford emblem and the transverse springs. The new four-cylinder engine developed nearly twice as much power, and was fitted with a normal three-speed gearbox.

'Henry's made a Lady out of Lizzie', went the popular song of the day, and indeed the new offspring underlined precisely how out of tune with the times Lizzie had become. More important, Ford had now committed themselves to playing the game of mutations and the pattern for the future of the popular car market was firmly established. In Europe, where the markets ironically were rather more conservative, the customer was confronted with a kaleidoscopic range of choice. But this sprang rather from the legions of small firms that blossomed immediately after the war, only to wither, many of them, within a few years. Although 'motoring for the millions' was the watchword of the mini-boom of 1919-20, mass motoring

By giving teenagers a new mobility, the automobile revolutionised the rituals of courtship in the 1920s. John Held Jnr's cartoon *(left)* satirised the new contortions, bared thighs and insouciant driving.

did not come to Britain until 1930 when the number of private cars on the road passed one million (a figure that was not achieved in France or Germany till after the Second World War). Indeed the annual increase of cars in use between 1920 and 1930 remained fairly constant, between 80,000 and 100,000 new cars each year, reflecting not a popular revolution but a steady if gradual increase in the standard of living among the professional classes. It was, in effect, an era of middle-class motoring, of what was termed the 'owner-driver'.

The road to heaven... a pastor posing with his mobile Model T chapel, complete with harmonium, steeple and stained glass. The automobile era's version of the itinerant preacher, hoping perhaps you *could* get to heaven in an old Ford car!

A practical demonstration, if one was needed, of where car-ownership was centred in the mid-twenties occurred with the General Strike of 1926. Though few consciously intended it to be, it was nevertheless a class confrontation, with Oxford undergraduates selling tickets on buses and peers of the realm driving trains to beat the strikers. The trade unions had effective control of communications — the railways, road transport, buses — and shut them down from the very first day of the strike. It could have been a paralysing blow to business: the fact that it wasn't rested largely on the massive turn-out of private cars which, though they caused monumental traffic jams, succeeded in ferrying large numbers of people into the cities and delivering essential goods. The unions for their part had immense difficulty in assembling the vehicles necessary, for instance, for the circulation of their strike newspaper. It was hardly surprising in view of a report issued by the Motor Traders that same year, which estimated that nobody could hope to maintain a car if his income was less than £450 a year: that was more than twice what a print-worker earned and three times the wages of an engineer (both of whom were better-off than many). Britain's first £100 car appeared in 1930, but by then many industrial wages had fallen. Predictably, therefore, the middle-class manufacturers adorned their advertisements with middle-class aspirations: tennis parties and mock-Tudor

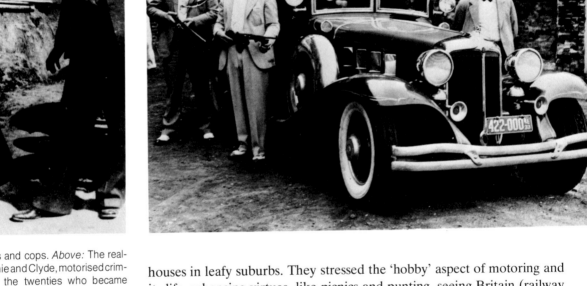

Robbers and cops. *Above:* The real-life Bonnie and Clyde, motorised criminals of the twenties who became film heroes for a later generation. *Right:* Chicago detectives posing with their 1933 Chrysler Imperial, which was used to pick up the gunman Frank Zimmerman. The machine has been specially fitted with armour plating and gun ports in the windscreen.

houses in leafy suburbs. They stressed the 'hobby' aspect of motoring and its life-enhancing virtues, like picnics and punting, seeing Britain (railway posters also began retailing the same temptation, to which the motor trade responded with the slogan 'Buy a car, own your own railway'!), healthy fresh air and the romance of the road. For the most part these allurements were mainly visual, but sometimes even the staid British motor manufactur-

The last journey: mafia capos could go out in style in this somewhat baroque 1928 Fiat hearse. In fact the result looks an uneasy compromise between the car and the old-fashioned horse-drawn funeral car.

er could dabble in a little lyricism. Jowett, who produced a small, austere but increasingly popular car (and who incidentally featured one of the first examples of knocking copy, when one of their ads showed a Jowett unceremoniously dragging a Ford out of a ditch), advised their clients to listen to the song of the Jowett Seven, which went: 'Step on the pedal, my master; the town's behind, the steep hill ahead. We've broken bounds, we're free!' Who could resist the charm of this purring, obedient servant, this 'symphony of comradeship'? Well, plenty of people it seemed. The blandishments of publicity departments were all very well, if you were well-disposed towards the automobile in the first place: but there were those who looked

upon the popularisation of motoring as a miasma spreading over the land. Their objections were not that cars were dirty, noisy or frightening — but that they were too comfortable, too convenient and too seductive. In a way it was the modern version of the puritan ethic that could countenance a horse modestly trotting but not flagrantly racing. In their book fast meant loose, and you only had to look at the declining moral standards of the

Carnage: popular films like Howard Hawks' *Scarface* in 1930 *(above)* recreating the anarchy of Chicago's streets during the Prohibition years, taught cinema audiences the more sinister meaning of 'taking someone for a ride'.

Almost dwarfed by his custom-built roadster *(left)*, James Cagney was one of the earliest exponents of the gangster car-chase that became staple fare for cinema-goers.

young to see. 'The automobile', fulminated one American judge in 1925, 'has become a house of prostitution on wheels', and parents could see for themselves that the car the boyfriend arrived in to take their daughter out on a date could, and surely would, whisk them away from the community and its social restraints. In Middletown it was a cause for local concern that in 1924 two-thirds of the girls (the survey didn't mention boys) who were charged with sex offences had committed the said offence in an automobile. Perhaps it was tough on the car that its maturity coincided with a loosening of sexual conventions, but the fact remained that it was easier to 'go all the way' after spooning in the back of a Chevy than after petting

The Keystone Kops *(above)* off on another of their manic chases. None of the silent movie comedy stars like Laurel and Hardy *(right)* or Harold Lloyd *(below)* ever seemed quite to master the mysteries of the automobile – fortunately.

on the porch or in a horsedrawn buggy. So the car got the blame, and so did the car-makers. It was time, said the head of the International Reform Bureau, that Henry Ford 'frame legislation that will stop the use of the motor-car for immoral purposes'! Even Henry didn't have an answer to that.

In much the same vein, the car was also seen as a threat to religion. Sermons were frequently delivered denouncing the increasingly prevalent habit of motoring on a Sunday instead of coming to church — empty words if the backsliders were by then a hundred miles away on the open road. But 'Sunday drivers' (still a faintly reprehensible term) were now a fact of life, and on the other hand there was an increasing regiment of car-borne evangelists, with their mobile chapels on Model T chassis, in hot pursuit.

Where the moralists had a more tangible target was in the shocking increase in motorised crime. By 1930, reported a commission in the United States, 'crime was inflicting a tax of a thousand million dollars yearly on the people of the United States. Nearly half that enormous sum is due to motor-car crime.' Nor was it just in America that villains had discovered the efficacy of a sharp set of wheels. Even before the First World War Paris had been terrorised by a gang of 'motor bandits' (as the press put it),

whose coups were organised with the aid of stolen cars and master-minded
− characteristically for that era − by an anarchist called Bonnot. Their ne-
mesis, which made headlines all round the world, came in May 1912 in a
dramatic shoot-out with the Sûreté at a garage in Choisy-le-Roi. In Britain,
Scotland Yard's 'flying squad' was organised in 1921, equipped with
extra-fast cars, two-way radios and (a few years later) egg-bombs filled
with green and white paint to hurl at fugitives' cars.
But it was Mr. Hoover's great social experiment that gave the automobile
its most infamous hour. Prohibition, of course, had existed in some American states in the horse-and-buggy era, with what some might have consid-

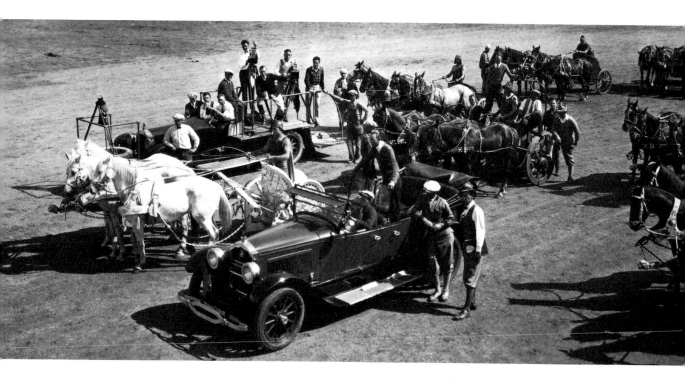

ered an acceptable level of graft. But the nation-wide prohibition, which
came into effect at the beginning of 1920, spawned a nation-wide army
of motorised bootleggers whose budget for automobiles far outstripped
that of the Prohibition Commission. Enforcement agents had their successes, busting the speakeasies and illicit stills from time to time, but a con-
signment of moonshine once it was on the road was guaranteed to out-run
the law. Even for straightforward robberies the heavier and more powerful cars were favoured for the getaway, Locomobiles, Hudsons and Buicks,
all of which carried the essential running-boards in those days. Al Ca-
pone himself favoured a Cadillac, armour-plated of course, with bullet-
proof windows, and what amounted to a machine-gun turret at the back.
John Dillinger spoke very highly of Fords in his line of business and once
wrote to Henry Ford himself saying so.
Outside Cicero, Illinois, to be sure, the nearest the public usually came to
a gangster's machine was on the silver screen (whence they came to learn
the more sinister meaning of 'taking someone for a ride'). The movies,
which had grown up almost in step with the automobile, had been present-
ing exciting images of the automobile to cinema-goers since the early years
of the century. In silent days, with the picture-house honky-tonk doing its

Behind the scenes in Holywood the
automobile also helped to create
new techniques of filming. *Above:*
Film crews on MGM studio cars with
cameras mounted back and front
prepare to shoot the famous chariot
scene from the original (1926) version of *Ben Hur.*

125

Right: Greta Garbo in soft focus alone with the moonlight, the ocean, a chauffeur and her car in the movie *Single Standard.* All the ingredients for a helping of Holywood romantic drama.

Betty Compson

Loretta Young

Richard Arlen

best to sound like a pulsating car-engine, the Keystone Kops and Harold Lloyd, Pearl White and Laurel and Hardy would regularly find themselves in a runaway automobile, on a life-and-death mission, or in a hair-raising pursuit. Their cranked-up, split-second shaves at crossroads and railroad crossings, and their inevitable collisions with market-stalls and shop windows were staple fare for years at the nickelodeon. (Why was it they always missed the moving targets but invariably hit the stationary objects?)

With the talkies the automobile widened its repertoire to include melodrama, light comedy and romance. Garbo would never have looked the same on the back of a tandem, nor Cagney have come to such a satisfying end as after a thrilling car chase, nor the images of the Depression haunt us quite so vividly without that decrepit, hung-about Hudson in *The Grapes of Wrath.* The real apotheosis of the car in movies has, in fact, come rather more recently, with automobiles taking top billing and actors coming a poor second: from the queens of nostalgia like Genevieve and the Yellow Rolls-Royce we have progressed to a whole series of bionic stars, which include the magic Gnome-mobile, the rather intelligent Herbie, and the flying, floating Chitty Chitty Bang Bang. Animals and children beware.

For film stars an expensive car with custom coachwork was an essential status symbol: their publicity packs invariably contained the statutory auto-pose. A random selection of car-borne Hollywood immortals appear below and on the page opposite.

Marlene Dietrich

Jean Harlow

Outside the studios the movie-stars too discovered the image-enhancing properties of the automobile, plunging into orgies of conspicuous consumption that F. Scott Fitzgerald parodied in *The Diamond as Big as the Ritz:* 'Its body was of gleaming metal richer than nickel and lighter than silver, and the hubs of the wheels were studded with iridescent geometric figures of green and yellow... the upholstery consisted of a thousand minute and exquisite tapestries of silk, woven with jewels and embroideries, and set upon a background of cloth of gold.'

Even MGM's budget may not have stretched to one of them, but the boulevards of Hollywood were a showcase for the finest custom coachwork the millionaire marques could produce, from Clara Bow nipping down the Strip in her open Kissel with seven red chow dogs to match her hair, to Gary Cooper dwarfed by a gigantic green-and-yellow Duesenberg Tourer. These were the ostentatious symbols of success, as indispensable as the ornate mansions that were springing up in Beverly Hills. They confirmed the status of the owner: in time, and with a little help from Madison Avenue, the car was going to confer it over the next few years on ordinary mortals as well.

Errol Flynn

NEW HORIZONS

Between the wars the Good Roads Movement in America initiated a dramatic transformation in the nation's highways. But in the meantime folks in their flivvers *(above)* got along the best way they could.

It would be a slight exaggeration to claim that for the owner-driver in the twenties going out for a spin on the whim of the moment was one of the novel pleasures of the motoring revolution. The prudent motorist, rather than place an unnecessary burden on his self-starter, would 'free' the engine first with a few turns of the handle; he would naturally let it warm up for a few minutes before starting off; he would anxiously scan the skies, debating whether to put up the hood and proceed with flapping canvas that seemed to be emulating a square-rigged schooner, or risk getting soaked to the skin trying to erect it when it actually came on to rain. (And yet, when the enclosed car became commonplace by the end of the 1920s, the first thing people clamoured for was the 'sunshine roof'!)

But these, after all, were mere details. For Sinclair Lewis – himself the very image of one of his sagebrush tourists in *Free Air,* 'pasteboard suitcases lashed to the running-board, frying pans and canvas water-bottles dangling' – motor touring was an impromptu adventure. As he told the readers of the *Saturday Evening Post:* 'A respectable citizen with a second-hand flivver, who has never driven any car for more than a hundred miles, can start on twenty minutes' notice – ten for his wife to buy a hairnet, ten to tell the maid what she mustn't let the baby do – and with safety and not much trouble hike from Miami to Seattle. He will find repairmen every five miles most of the distance; lingerie can be washed in roadside brooks; and from corner to corner of the country run through trails with markers on telephone poles at every turn.'

And millions followed his example. Within a few years of the war's end the Tin Can Tourist Association, whose trademark was a tin can hung on the radiator, numbered over 200,000 motorists and was already sowing the seeds of a vast vacation industry. When Iowa held a State Picnic for former

The determined tourist in 1920 was undeterred even by the most ramshackle of conveyances. *Right:* Disembarking from the ferry at Ryde on the Isle of Wight, doubtless with some relief.

residents of the state, 70,000 people turned up, the vast majority of them conveyed thither in automobiles.

One of the first prerequisites for these large-scale migrations was an acceptable network of highways, and here each country faced its own special problems. In Britain, where not much more than one percent of road work was actually on new roads during the twenties, the priority was to surface the existing 175,000 miles of dubious-looking highway. In France, whose roads had once been the ornament of Europe, the war had wrought havoc. Crossing the Channel in 1924, S.F. Edge was dismayed by the state of the roads: 'In some portions there were potholes 4 or 5 inches deep and 3 feet square and this continued for 10-20 km at a time. In other places lorries had torn the surface up to such an extent that there were loose stones all over the road almost as if it had been laid with stones to be rolled in.... France is trying to repair her roads, but I should imagine that she will require at least five years of very hard and serious work to put the main roads into the condition that they were when I knew them before the war.' He was impressed by the inroads Citroën and Renault had made with their cheap cars among the provincial French businessmen, and reassured that along the Riviera at least 'an immense number of Rolls-Royce cars were to be met, all of which seemed to be performing splendidly'.

In America it was a case of more or less building a road system from scratch. The Good Roads Movement, inspired largely by the cyclists in the 1890s and adopted by motorists, had little effect on government with their campaigns. (Good Roads Sunday was one of their favourite ploys, a day on which the aid of clergymen all over the country was enlisted to call the attention of their congregations to 'the relations between good roads and right living, and good roads and Christian progress'!) But this changed abruptly

Congestion in a narrow Sussex lane, when the Mothers Union charabanc met the rural traffic, sometime in the 1920s when millions in Britain took to the road with this form of excursion or on organised 'mystery tours'.

in 1921 with the passing of the Federal Highway Bill, which virtually over-night turned road development in the States into a billion-dollar industry. The elegant Parkways, landscaped and florally manicured roadways with which cities in the east had been endowed, often by private initiative, gave way to more strategic projects spanning the continent. By the end of the decade more than 300,000 miles of road had been constructed, much of it qualifying for the shield of a U.S. Highway and long stretches being re-markable feats of engineering — like the Columbia River Highway with its maximum 5 percent grade and towering bridges, and the Tamiami Trail plunging unerringly through the Everglades.

Competition at the pump: this South London service station in 1921 offered all the extras with its petrol – including free air from the latest in portable pressure pumps. The years after the war were marked by great rivalry between the oil companies and the new benzole firms trying to capture a share of the market.

With amazing speed the landscape of a continent was altered. Searching around in the late 1920s for a characteristically American symbol, a contributor to *Harper's* dismissed the Pullman smoker and Coney Island and opted for the American Gas Station: 'Each is the product of a national art, perfected and unchanging. There is the low shelter with its gabled roof. There is the custodian in khaki trousers and a slightly perceptible scorn for anything which lacks eight cylinders. There are the two great pumps outside his door, precisely like all other pumps at every other station: consistently of the same height, the same diameter, the same cheery shade of red. There is the half-circle of cement driveway which makes an arc between these siphons, from the road outside. At one end of this cement is painted the white letters IN. At the other end is painted the white letters OUT. Not once in years, in this conformist nation, does it occur to any traveler to mutiny at these designations and attempt the OUT end for his IN.'

It also fulfilled, he went on, a new social function as the nucleus of a new inter-city life, like the caravansaries of old. 'Here is a richer, creamier

The Backfire. *Left:* H.M. Bateman's charabanc outing. Chilly, cramped and (clearly) prone to sudden eruptions, these democratic vehicles opened up many of the parts of Britain beyond the reach of railways.

cross-section of America than is to be found on any Main Street: for the reason that many Main Streets have poured their quotas into it. On the heels of a Rolls from upper Fifth Avenue, making time on its way to Saratoga, come six Alabama negroes in a rebuilt Ford. Ten cars in a row may bear the plates of five different states....The filling station is a rare spot, in a country of magnificent distances, for the cross-pollination of ideas.' Petrol stations with their panoramas of tin placards were mushrooming in Europe too, but their potential for democratising was rather more limited. The working class did not own cars (they drove trucks, of course, and in Britain there evolved that grand institution called the 'pull-in', which until the food guides discovered them relatively recently, remained even more exclusive than the French *routiers)*. Nevertheless they did participate in the great return to the road by means of the charabanc, a species of open motor-bus which survives only in faded photographs in family albums. They were intimate, these 28-seaters, especially when forty or more were packed into them; they were precarious to climb into – usually by means of a ladder – and they could be hellishly chilly. But between the wars they created a whole new pattern of leisure for the working man.

In those days no special licence was required to run a bus service, and during the twenties bus companies in Britain leapt from a few hundred to nearly four thousand. Many offered regular outings by charabanc, includ-

Splendid example of the species, a Nottingham charabanc *(below)* with terraced seating and rudimentary protection from the elements. Members of a church outing pose for the obligatory photograph, with one lady looking very proprietorial at the wheel of the bus!

131

ing such exotic excursions as 'mystery' tours or 'sealed order' tours where even the driver didn't know where they were going. Alternatively charabancs could be hired by the day for a company outing, which invariably would include a number of halts at the road-houses that were springing up to cater for the new carriage trade. These four-square redbrick descendants of the coaching inn are still distinguishable on the main coast routes (though usually displaying, ironically, a sign saying 'No coaches'). During August in England, commented *The Times* in the mid-1930s, 'a fever of mobility' seemed to seize the population, but its effects were healthy enough. Together the motor-car and the bus opened up new vistas and cul-

A pioneer caravan *(left)* fitted onto a Ford chassis, with a distinctly homespun appearance. Loosely based on the gypsy tradition, the plain exteriors of many early caravans belied their lavishly-fitted interiors, which only too often made the vehicles hard to manoeuvre.

tural experiences, as stately homes and historic monuments were opened up to the public, seaside resorts shed their bath-chair images, and villages were brought closer to the towns. (Huxley considered that the motor-bus had contributed more to the disappearance of the village idiot than all the lectures on eugenics.)

If J.B. Priestley's thesis, articulated in his *English Journey*, that the bus had 'annihilated the old distinction between rich and poor travellers by offering luxury to all' is correct, it is a curious thing that the more affluent car-owners should simultaneously be gripped by a passion for roughing it. 'The day of the motor caravan', announced *The Motor* in 1920, 'has dawned with promising brilliancy' though not, it had to be admitted, without a few false starts. With only the nomadic architecture of the gipsy to go on, the early designers had a penchant for fitting out their caravans with mahogany panelling, brass fittings and kitchen dressers, with the result that their unwieldy creations sank to their axles in the slightest mud. Others produced flimsy folding boxes that opened out sideways to produce bunks, over which a canvas awning was slung and which required an equal distribution of weight inside to prevent them toppling over. But so what? It was better, as *The Motor* went on to point out, than leading 'humdrum, monotonous lives in a small house, stuffy flat or insanitary basement, with no hope of ever changing one's wearisome, dull, grey existence'. So many people in fact responded to this and similar clarion calls to the great outdoor life that

Mobile music: a homemade aerial and receiver (ca. 1922) mounted on what looks like a homemade car. He didn't, we hope, drive and listen at the same time.

in 1925 the RAC felt it necessary to institute a Caravan Department. If Americans failed to acquire the caravanning or 'trailer' habit with such fervour, it was because for them there already existed a static form of the caravan, known in its early days in California as a 'tourist cabin'. Spartan in the extreme, these cabins were little more than glorified camp-sites (certainly few of them could boast a bed). But as the tide of tourism swelled, so did the cabins – into motor-courts and thence into motor hotels, with canopies for the car and names like Dreamland or Autopia which belied the thinness of the dividing walls. Situated with comforting predictability on the semi-rural fringes of most towns, and with an immutable policy of payment in advance these 'motels' (the word first appeared in 1925) offered the motorist the freedom to come and go as privately as he liked. They also offered the same facility to couples without suitcases (in the darker days of the Depression even the fussier proprietors stopped putting up signs that said 'out-of-country licences only'), and to members of the underworld waiting for the heat to cool, as J. Edgar Hoover was later to remark bitterly. Whatever the clientele, however, the motel industry prospered like no other in America even in the long years of recession for, as Charles Merz concluded in 1930, 'the roving spirit is robust in us. If we cannot rove for the purpose of settling a continent, we shall at least rove, daily or nightly, for the pleasure of seeing something, anything, or seeing nothing and merely having been.'

As trailers became light enough to be towed by the smaller family car *(above left)*, caravan holidays grew rapidly in popularity during the twenties – though the holidaymakers rarely aspired to the social elegance of A.B. Marty's 1929 picture for the October issue of *L'Illustration* *(above)*.

TOWN AND COUNTRYSIDE

In the 1930s – slumps and recessions notwithstanding – car-ownership in some European countries could be numbered in millions, in America in tens of millions. The automobile was beginning to change the face of towns and countryside, spawning new roads and resorts, suburbs and service-stations. As the cars proliferated, so came the dawning awareness of the social problems they were creating. Along with the roads came roadside hoardings and an accelerating accident-rate, and with the suburbs appeared a new form of 'ribbon' development and rush-hour congestion. The sporadic efforts in town and country to come to terms with the new mass mobility were not, it must be said, very successful. But for the motorist driving was still an adventure, whether it was the family buying their first 'baby' Austin, or the enthusiast tucked into his sports car and given the freedom of the open road. On the racing circuits and the sands of Daytona Beach, speed was more than ever a matter of national prestige.

AFTER THE BOOM

When You
BUY an AUTOMOBILE
You GIVE
3 Months' Work
to Someone

Which
Allows
Him to
BUY
OTHER PRODUCTS

BUY A CAR NOW—HELP BRING BACK PROSPERITY

A cornerstone of capitalism: by the 1930s automobile production in America was inextricably locked into the national economy – as this Detroit poster *(above)* spelled out to consumers during the Depression.

Anyone who had invested $10,000 in General Motors in 1919 would, in the summer of 1929, have been worth over $1.5 million. The inexorable rise in General Motors shares had been one of the eternal verities of Wall Street, an undentable indicator of the success of America and the booming car industry in particular. Then, in just three days in that Black October, GM shares joined all the other high-flyers in sinking to the floor of the Stock Exchange, and for the next eighteen months the market (in the dealers' own words) was deader than a doornail. The thirties were not the happiest decade for the motor industry: the commercial glitter of the New Era had disguised many of the industrial problems, not least the conditions under which cars were produced. Visiting one of the vast Detroit factories in his parish, the pastor Reinhold Niebuhr was horrified at what he saw: 'The heat was terrific. The men seemed weary. Here manual labour is a drudgery and toil is slavery. The men cannot possibly find any satisfaction in their work. Their sweat and their dull pain are part of the price paid for the fine cars we run.' In the course of the decade Detroit was to see violent labour unrest – with pitched battles between unions and strike-breakers at both General Motors and Ford in 1937. Many car firms, small and

$100 WILL BUY THIS CAR MUST HAVE CASH LOST ALL ON THE STOCK MARKET

Sign of the times: a casualty of the Wall Street crash in 1929 *(right)*. Auto industry shares had spearheaded the phenomenal boom of the twenties, and were among the first to plunge when the day of reckoning came.

WORLD'S HIGHEST STANDARD OF LIVING

There's no way like the American Way

large, in Europe as well as America, were destined to shut their gates and swell the rising tide of the unemployed.

But industrial problems apart, and in spite of what diehards of vintage persuasion may say, the thirties were a golden age of motoring. The proposition that no decent car was built after 31 December 1930, when vintage machines are considered abruptly to have ended with the demise of the Cricklewood Bentley, is all the more curious since this was the precise moment when the motor-car blossomed in a flowering which it had never attained before, and in many ways has never matched since. In performance, in elegance of line, in comfort and in sheer joy of driving, the aristocrats that were made between 1930 and 1939 were superior to their predecessors, and had a distinction that would never be recaptured. They included cars like the V12 Hispano-Suiza, the Type 50 and 57 'surbaissé' Bugattis, the DS8 Delage, the 150SS Talbot-Lago, the 540K Mercedes, the Twin Six Packard, the Fleetwood Cadillacs, the Duesenberg SJ.

Since most upper-crust manufacturers supplied rolling chassis only – Rolls-Royce, for example, never built a complete car before the Standard Steel Mark VI and Silver Dawn – this crowning period of the petrol-driven car was greatly enhanced through the artistry of the great coach builders. One thinks of Hooper and Barker, Gurney Nutting, Mulliner or Thrupp & Maberly, who knew precisely how to clothe a Rolls-Royce; of Chapron and Saoutchic and Figoni, who gave logical yet exquisitely extravagant shapes

This public service message that appeared on the billboards in 1937 summed up the contradictions of the Depression years. The dream was epitomised by the car and family togetherness; the reality below was altogether more pedestrian.

to continental thoroughbreds; of Darrin and Le Baron who brought both glamorously formal and compulsively rakish lines to American production cars. The idiom of each period, the car's morphology if you like, decrees that changes must be gradual: too rapid a departure from the tenor of the times is unacceptable, as the Chrysler Airflow and the Tatra 77 (both based on Paul Jaray's Zeppelin tear-shape) were clearly to show.

Conservative taste had required that lines should be vertical. Certain proportions had to be observed, it was felt, by anyone setting out to design a beautiful car. For instance, the line of the radiator should be set slightly behind the front axle, to give an air of lightness. The windscreen should rise

The Great Depression takes to the road. The crash, and the hardships that followed, did not mean that car production halted, or that the automobile disappeared from the landscape. When poor American families in the 1930s had to move on, they often did so by motor-car — or jalopy, as here – taking all their possessions. Here such a family is seen on an impromptu picnic beside the road.

vertically at a point precisely halfway between the axles. On a drophead coupe the hood, after sloping upwards from the windscreen for one third of its length, should then slope gently backwards, accentuated by the tumble of the chromed hood-irons, and drop precisely to the centre of the rear wheel. Behind a massive trunk came the spare, and flanking the radiator were two enormous headlights. When it came to limousines, the passenger compartment continued behind the rear axle, and finished in a vertical drop that curved demurely inwards above the tail of the rear mudguard, while a luggage rack hid the petrol tank. The passengers were seated as far back as possible over the rear axle, which gave plenty of leg-room and a sickeningly bumpy ride.

But now in the thirties, changing tastes and underslung chassis brought cars and their occupants nearer the ground. Designers began to understand

that to give a lithe and powerful appearance a car had to sit down behind its front, as a ship steams from its prow; and though the classic rules
continued to be observed – the windscreen exactly at half-point between
the axles, the roof tumble exactly over the rear axle – vertical lines made
way for a more horizontal emphasis, curving downwards towards the back.
While the radiator gave the car a character that was instantly recognisable,
like a human being his face, the lines began to flow in a horizontal sweep
and harmonious curves. Given a lower centre of gravity, better specific output, improved suspension, and synchromesh gearboxes, motor-cars became not only sleeker but more fun to drive. The low snort of a Delahaye,

the snore of a Hotchkiss, the knife-through-butter gearchange of a Bentley,
the wuffle of a 540K Mercedes-Benz before you engaged the supercharger
(which made a noise like an air-raid siren and projected the car forwards as
if it had been released by a spring) and of course that special eight-cylinder
Bugatti whine which sounded like 8,000 mosquitoes – all these were truly
heady stuff. But such cars were extravagantly expensive. Plenty of fun was
to be had from the new breed of volume-produced sports cars, which were
relatively inexpensive.

A great deal of ink has been used, and many epigrams coined, to define
what a sports car is, yet in those days no one had any doubt: a sports car was
a machine you drove for fun rather than convenience. It had a longish bonnet with a strap, Rudge Whitworth knock-on wire wheels, a windscreen
that folded flat with aero-screens behind to keep the midges out of your

A contrasting style: the other face of
the 1930s is reflected in this car-side
picnic complete with hamper and
china service. All was not depression
in those years, and in fact for the
automobile the thirties were a golden
decade which saw the production of
many superlative models.

Self-service coin-in-the-slot machines *(below)* had first appeared on the forecourts of Britain in the twenties. By 1930 even in Aberdeen *(bottom)* your Armstrong-Siddeley could be filled up from an automatic 'multiple' pump, dispensing a whole range of petrol grades.

eyes, deeply cut-away doors that exactly fitted the elbow, leather covered bucket seats behind a raked steering column that allowed a horizontal driving position with the legs well stretched, a 15 gallon slab-shaped petrol tank with a quick-release filler and a couple of spares aft, a dashboard with a large speedometer and rev counter, a chrome handgrip for the passenger, and a minimal hood you hardly ever put up. A sports car was light, with brisk acceleration, nimble steering and better performance and roadholding than a top-heavy family saloon. Without leaning over much you could touch the road. And that was the point; in a sports car you were in contact with the surroundings and had a sense of participation that no saloon could give. You were part of the living stretch of ribbon ahead, be it Alpine pass, narrow tree-lined *route nationale,* or sinuous country lane. You felt the temperature, the humidity, the wind: you experienced the road as if on a thoroughbred hunter.

To enthusiasts in the thirties, the sporting machine meant a P Type MG, a Singer Le Mans, a Morgan 4/4, a Riley Sprite, an SS 100, a Frazer Nash, an Ulster Aston Martin, and maybe even a Fiat Balilla or an Adler Trumpf — though not really, because the sports car of the thirties was an intensely British device.

In the 1930s the pattern of the modern car was evolved. A widening market pushed the threshold of motoring downwards; while there were fewer than a million cars on British roads before 1930, by 1939 this figure had doubled, and more than half Britain's cars were Eights and Tens. At the beginning of the decade Morris and Austin controlled more than half the market. Yet despite their wide selection of models they were progressively challenged by other aggressive contenders. Ford introduced the Y model Eight, and General Motors, who had acquired Vauxhall in 1927 (after an offer to buy up Austin had been rebuffed), pioneered synchromesh in 1932

and unit-constructed bodies in 1937. John Black achieved a remarkable turn-around at Standard, lifting production from 7,000 cars in 1930 to 53,000 in 1939. But the most astonishing progress was made by the Rootes Brothers.

William and Reginald Rootes began as dealers in Kent, and their first big gamble was to rent imposing showrooms at Devonshire House, Piccadilly. Next they took over the ailing Hillman-Humber concerns, whose factories were next door to each other in Coventry, and before long had swallowed up the remnants of the STD combine. This put them in the upper class market, though within a short time all traces of the old products had vanished and both Humbers and Sunbeam-Talbots were virtually Hillmans, or simply tunes played on a basic Rootes theme. But the Hillman Minx was an excellent little car, and brilliant salesmanship from their headquarters opposite the Ritz and the Berkeley enabled Rootes to become the biggest success story of this period, and to push their way into the 'Big Six'.

For this was the age of the tycoons, who ran their empires like renaissance *condottieri* and became legends in their time. Bill Morris, later Viscount Nuffield, was a pernickety tyrant, who once bought a golf course near his home in order to become a member. His enormous personal fortune was substantially increased by floating his company's shares at an inflated price, and rather than re-invest the money in the firm (which might have avoided the BMC debacle later) he gave millions to charity and founded Nuffield College at Oxford. Lord Austin never allowed a visitor to enter the Longbridge works if he was not driving an Austin, but made generous gifts to Cambridge University. Lord Rootes owned several large estates, raised thoroughbred cattle and had a weakness (or maybe a gift?) for choosing his aides from members of the peerage. John Black was a complete dictator at his Canley works, but a genial host in the Bahamas.

It was a measure of the enormous personality of these men, like their continental counterparts (Louis Renault with his castle on a lonely island eight miles out at sea off Mont Saint-Michel; Giovanni Agnelli, Ettore Bugatti, André Citroën and Commendatore Bianchi playing for huge stakes in the 'royal corner' of the Palace at St. Moritz) that by sheer individuality and dictatorial power they succeeded in forging their concerns into the giants of the motoring world. There were others who achieved a less flamboyant success. Spencer Wilks, the most courteous of men, quietly took over the derelict Rover factory in 1932, and converted a very mediocre product into the beautifully made and delightfully understated car of the late thirties. His marketing policy was simple; if he had 11,000 orders he built 10,000 cars, with the result that there was a queue at every Rover dealer, and resale values remained high.

But perhaps the motoring personality of the decade, since he started a new marque from scratch and bucked all the trends, was William Lyons. Back in 1922 he and his partner, William Walmsley, made motorcycle sidecars at Blackpool before progressing to rather smart special bodies for small cars like the Austin Seven and Standard Nine. In 1928 Swallow Bodies moved to Coventry, and on 9 October 1931, during the depth of the Depression, the SS 1 was unveiled on Stand 72 at Olympia. It was a striking low coupe with a Bentley-style radiator, an enormously long bonnet and a diminutive cockpit behind. These rakish looks concealed straightforward mechanical components supplied by the Standard Motor Company, but the advertise-

The 1930s were the heyday of the sports car, which gave the driver an exhilarating sense of contact with his surroundings. In this instance *(above)* the surroundings were particularly sticky, and a Morris needs a few helping hands up a hill in an Abingdon car club trial.

ments proclaimed: 'In appearance it was a £1,000 car', but the price was a modest £310. Not surprisingly, sales raced ahead of production. The Jaguar was launched in 1936 (after Lyons had browsed through a list of bird and animal names) as a handsome four-door sports saloon with a 2.7 litre o.h.v. engine. It was a triumph of economy production for, although the Jaguar was never by absolute standards a cheap car, it was never by comparative standards anything but a cheap car, so that whatever you expected from it, you could not actually demand it.

Over the channel, Peugeot, Renault and Citroën were firmly established as the 'Big Three'. In 1927 Peugeot acquired its old rival De Dion-Bouton,

Fiat's poster (right) proclaiming the elegant 'feminine' lines of its new Balilla in 1934 failed to impress the Vatican. It wasn't the car's chassis they were worried about, but the lady's – more especially the curve of her posterior and the way in which her clinging skirt appeared to exaggerate it. After protests the poster was withdrawn by Fiat and the offending part of her anatomy remodelled to everyone's satisfaction.

Above: Illustration from the Mercedes Benz catalogue for 1939. Since the First World War, car advertisers had exploited the fascination for airplanes to enhance the image of their own terrestrial products – though here the plane seems, almost prophetically, to have taken over.

now suffering from hardening of the arteries. The Sochaux firm continued making its bread-and-butter 201, but the big change came in 1936 with the 402: this had an o.h.v. 2.1 litre four-cylinder engine, dashboard gearchange, and a bulbous, but supposedly aerodynamic body, in which not only the headlamps but also the battery were housed between the rounded grille and the radiator. In 1938 Peugeot produced a small 1100 cc saloon of similar shape, whose remarkably low price, the equivalent of £117, took them within a year into second place behind Citroën. André Citroën had been a trend-setter since the 5 cv clover leaf, and in 1934 he produced another revolutionary model in the shape of the 7 hcv *Traction Avant*. This opened new horizons by having front-wheel drive, an o.h.v. wet-liner 1.6 litre engine, unitary construction of chassis and body, all-round torsionbar independent suspension, and an umbrella gear change on the dash (a device that found favour in France, but not elsewhere).

In Italy Fiat was producing the Balilla, by 1934 a four-door pillarless saloon that formed the basis for Simca and also the Polski-Fiats made in Warsaw up to World War II. The legendary 'Topolino', which appeared for the first time in 1936, had a roll-top convertible body with a tiny 570 cc engine right up front ahead of the radiator, and independent suspension. It

FIAT
La nuova BALILLA
per tutti
eleganza
della Signora
M- DUDOVICH

was followed by the Millecento,which was revived after the war, updated in 1966, and had a good deal of influence on both the 128 and the Ritmo. Alfa Romeo was nationalised in 1933, but continued to make high prestige sports cars that won practically every Mille Miglia. Lancia, always the car for the connoisseur, as opposed to Alfa who catered for the sportsman (and Fiat for the masses!), was now concentrating on the 1,200 cc Augusta and the 1,500 cc Aprilia, both with unusual swept-back saloon bodies and V4 engines, which delighted the *cognoscenti* at the time and are now collector's items if the rust has not ruined them.

Since the Kaiser's war little of interest had come from Germany, although forty-six factories had exhibited at the Berlin Motor Show of 1921, which was restricted to home products. While Benz, Adler, Mercedes, Opel, Dixi and NAG showed a range of sound and solid pre-war designs, there were a host of cheap runabouts with engaging names such as Bob, Koco and Peter-und -Moritz. But galloping inflation hit Germany in 1922, and only the strongest firms survived. Once the dust had settled, Opel went in for American-style production with a two-seater named the 'Laubfrosch', or tree toad. (This was so similar to the 5 cv Citroën that the French company sued unsuccessfully for licence infringement.) By 1927 some 39,000 of these little cars had been built before General Motors bought the Russelsheim firm, and made it the centre of their European operations. But by far the biggest news was the amalgamation of the two great pioneer marques, Benz and Mercedes, merging together on 29 June 1926 to form Daimler-Benz AG.

It was on Hitler's order that German cars came back into Grand Prix racing with Mercedes' legendary Silver Arrows and the astonishing 16-cylinder rear-engined P-wagons designed by Ferdinand Porsche, and made by a consortium of letter manufacturers — Audi, DKW, Horch and Wanderer — who established the new Auto Union marque. The engine-behind-driver layout was in due course to become commonplace, but it caused a good deal of head-shaking in the thirties, when no one knew that these magnificent unorthodoxies would bear fruit in the design of the KdF, or Volkswagen.

These fearsome machines made their first appearance outside the fatherland in the 1934 French Grand Prix at Montlhéry, where Louis Chiron held off the German attack with an old-style P3 Alfa Romeo. Next year, in the German Grand Prix, Nuvolari's Alfa again dashed Hitler's hopes. But with government support and unlimited funds at their disposal, Mercedes responded with the most powerful Grand Prix car ever built — the amazing W125 with a top speed of 185 mph. Laurence Pomeroy called 1937 'the year of the titans' because of such 'incredibly high performance factors', and the spectacle of Caracciola, Lang, von Brauchitsch and Dick Seaman duelling around the circuits against Rosemeyer, Fagioli and Stuck in their enlarged Auto Unions was one of the most memorable moments of motor racing.

During the years of the New Deal the shape of the American car changed out of all recognition, even if much of the same ironware lurked in the engine room. The old square-bodied sedans became streamlined, with restrained and graceful lines. This trend began with V-shaped radiators and swept tails; by 1936 the first notch-backs were appearing, and General Motors featured split-V windscreens. The following year Fords were wearing alligator bonnets and built-in headlights. Big brother in the shape of a

A brief revival in 1929 for the electric motor. This curious Red Bug *(above)* driven by a 16 volt battery was imported from America and demonstrated with little success in London. Its top speed was 12 mph.

slashing new fastback V12 Lincoln Zephyr made its bow; by 1940 it was longer, lower and even sleeker. Buicks discarded their running boards and gained a built-in trunk; their shapely Fisher-built bodies were refined each year until they had evolved into the lovely 1940 Century series, matched only by the similar but even more patrician elegance of the Fleetwood Cadillac and La Salle. By the time war came the American car had made its most convincing statement. It was still as rugged as ever, but it had a much silkier, more sophisticated ride. The old roadster with its rumble seat had grown into the convertible; radios were an optional extra, gear shifts were up on the steering column, automatic drive was available. Whitewall tyres were in fashion, and chromium was still used with discretion.

The battle for leadership among the 'Big Three' was so fierce that many classic cars such as Auburn, Cord and Stutz were forced out of business. To make up for this loss, the 1940 offerings from General Motors, the Lincoln Continental and the 1941 Packard Clipper were as sensuously beautiful as any American car that had been seen before or would be seen again. For having achieved a brief moment of perfection, the stylists in Detroit were already busy with an airpump and a stockpile of chromium, turning these desirable machines into Arabs' delights.

The effects of the automobile revolution plainly visible in this holiday view at Nantasket Beach, Massachusetts – taken sometime in the 1920s. From Miami to California the car created new holiday resorts and the foundations of a vast tourist industry.

THE GOLDEN AGE OF RACING

The years between the World Wars saw a remarkable growth in motor-car racing on both sides of the Atlantic. Most prestigious were the Grand Prix events sponsored by such countries as Italy, France and Germany. A driver with an impressive record for quality and durability was Hermann Lang, seen here in his

For two years after the armistice an official ban was imposed on motor racing in Europe. Only the Targa Florio was run in November 1919, despite the ban (and a snowstorm); the first off was Enzo Ferrari, driving his maiden race. He was followed by Ascari, whose Fiat landed thirty metres down a ravine. André Boillot's gyroscopic instincts helped him survive half a dozen such potential apocalypses, but ten yards from the end he crashed into a grandstand, spun violently, and crossed the finishing line back-

Mercedes in an Austrian event in 1939, the year he won seven GP victories. Lang, who had started as a Mercedes mechanic, was able to continue his racing career after the war until 1954.

wards. His Peugeot was manhandled round, and as the chequered flag fell, Boillot collapsed over the wheel crying: 'C'est pour la France!' – a piece of bravura which showed that, whatever else had happened, the spirit of romance was happily not dead.

Indeed, once the shackles were lifted, motor sport resumed with ebullient fervour. The first postwar Grand Prix, run at Le Mans in 1921 under the 3 litre formula, proved a classic. In terms of sheer power there was little to choose between the Ballots, the French Talbot-Darracqs and the Duesenbergs. But the beautifully turned out cars from the States had hydraulically operated four-wheel brakes, which gave them an advantage over their competitors. And although Jimmy Murphy crashed during practice and broke three ribs, he took the lead in what was described as 'a damned rock-hewing contest' over the narrow, unpaved country roads from which stones exploded like shrapnel, and finally brought the blue-and-white Duesenberg across the finishing line with two flat tyres and water boiling out of the holed radiator. He had to be lifted out of his seat, but for the first time an American car driven by an American driver had captured the highest European prize.

In 1922 the new 2 litre formula came into being, and for the next four seasons the Italians were the cars to beat. By developing an efficient small engine and then supercharging it, Fiat sparked off an Italian renaissance: In the first Italian Grand Prix to be run on the newly-constructed autodrome at Monza, Bordino and Nazzaro gave Fiat a one-two win. The Fiats that were confidently driven over the Alps for the 1923 French national event were the first GP machines to be fitted with superchargers. But though this initial outing ended in retirement, as grit and road metal were sucked into their unshielded Wittig superchargers, they pulverised the opposition – including twin o.h.v. straight-eight Millers and Dr Rumpler's rear-engined

Left: The drama of the Le Mans 24 hours rally is evoked in this painting by G. Hamm, 'Refuelling at Night, Le Mans', from the French magazine *L'Illustration,* 1933.

Britain's foremost racing centre, Brooklands, Surrey, offered an elegant atmosphere *(above)* along with its spirit of connoisseurship. Here Grand Prix cars (on handicap) could be seen pitted against tourers, standard cars and some bizarre hybrids (such as aero engines mounted on Mercedes chassis).

Benz *Tropfenwagen* at Monza three months later. All the same, 'Tours 1923' has a special place in British racing lore, since Henry Segrave drove his Sunbeam to victory, slipping clutch and all.

Sunbeam, in fact, came in first, second and fourth. Designed by Vincenzo Bertarione, they so closely resembled the Italian pattern that they were practically 'Fiats in green paint'. But they were green all the same and gave victory to a British driver in a British car, a 'double' repeated in Spain in 1924, but not seen again until Tony Brooks won the Syracuse GP in 1955 on a Connaught. Possibly it was because so many of his top designers were being lured away to plagiarise (and often improve upon) the Fiat expertise

Wheel of fate: a spot of bother for a Type 13 Bugatti as it negotiates a bend on a hill climb in 1920. The 13 was Ettore Bugatti's first car, which immediately gained considerable success in club events.

that Agnelli decided to withdraw from racing. Yet even as Fiat bowed out, a splendid new successor was waiting in the wings.

Nicola Romeo had taken over the old Alfa plant in 1915, and renamed it Alfa Romeo. With Enzo Ferrari directing operations, and Vittorio Jano (from Fiat) as chief designer, an eight-cylinder double o.h.c. 2-litre supercharged model known as the P2 appeared for the 1924 season. This was a vintage year, culminating in a spectacular French Grand Prix at Lyons. For their last GP appearance there, the Fiat supercharged 805s were again driven by Nazzaro and Bordino, while the Alfa Romeo P2s made their debut in the hands of Ascari, Campari and Wagner. The new generation of V12 Delages designed by Planchon were driven by Divo, Benoist and Thomas. And, having scrapped barrel bodies and tanks, Ettore Bugatti brought his classic aluminium wheel Type 35, one of the most beautiful GP cars of all

time, to its first *grande épreuve*. Five drivers and three marques led at various stages of the thirty-five laps. Ascari's P2 blew up while ahead only three laps from the end, leaving the way open for Divo's Delage; but French hopes were dashed as Campari's Alfa Romeo took the flag just ahead of the blue machine after seven gruelling hours.

Alfa Romeo's ascendancy was confirmed when they swept the board at Monza in October, and opened the 1925 season with a win at Spa. What is more, they were all set to repeat their victory in the French Grand Prix at Montlhéry when Ascari, who was in the lead, crashed into a brick wall and was killed. As a result of this tragedy the team was withdrawn, and Benoist's Delage went on to take the flag. But Count Brilli-Peri's victory at Monza ensured the title of world champion for the Lombard firm (who thereafter added the laurel leaf surround to their radiator badges).

The view from the bank. *Above:* punting parties on the River Wey in 1937 get a free view of the race at Brooklands. The race, on the outer circuit, was a club event involving an Amilcar, a Riley, Brookes Special and a Bentley.

By now preoccupation with safety factors had already prompted a ruling by which riding mechanics were banned, and to combat ever-increasing speeds, the formula was reduced to 1½ litres for 1926. This discouraged constructors like Alfa Romeo and Sunbeam, though it inspired some brilliant machinery in France. Bugatti swept the board with his blown version of the Type 35, and in 1927 the supercharged double o.h.c. Delage straight-eights carried all before them. But the truth is that the new small formula downgraded the *grandes épreuves* to the level of a contained, glyptic exercise – tame in comparison with the new long distance sports-car races such as the 24 hours of Le Mans, with its extravagant relationship between

The classic sprint start at Le Mans was introduced in 1925. *At left*, the start of the 1931 twenty-four-hours. For four years previously the race had been dominated by the Bentley team who had won on each occasion (in 1929 they came in 1–2–3–4). But in 1931 financial problems forced the works team to withdraw from the racing scene – thus opening the door for a series of Alfa-Romeo victories.

speed and endurance, the RAC Tourist Trophy at Ards, and the Mille Miglia (which for Italians was to become a headlong plunge of almost mystical recklessness around the backbone of their land).

For the British, Le Mans had a special mystique from the time Duff and Clement won the 1924 race in a 3 litre Bentley, and Sammy Davis brought his battered 'Old Number 7' safely into first place after the entire Bentley team had crashed into each other during the night at White House Corner in 1927. From then onwards it was Bentleys versus the rest at Le Mans, and a hat-trick of resounding Bentley triumphs between 1928 and 1930 gave substance to the legend.

No less of an international test of speed and endurance was the Alpine Rally, whose origins stretched back to the pre-war Austrian Alpine Trials, and which was revived in 1928 by a consortium of national motor-clubs. Intended, in the words of the *Autocar,* to be 'the trial of trials, fulfilling the double object of testing both man and his car to the full', the Alpine was run over a route that varied from year to year, but always included the highest passes in the Alps and the Dolomites. And testing it was: cars had to be standard production models, while certain parts, such as radiator caps, were sealed so that even topping up with water en route was barred. To win a coveted Coupe des Alpes you had to dice for a week over some of the most hazardous roads in the world, and complete the course without loss of marks.

If this smacks of Bulldog Drummond (then the hero of all schoolboys),

there was a whiff of Dornford Yates about the cars and equipages that set off, silver flasks and all, for the great winter adventure of the Monte Carlo Rally; and it is sobering to reflect that in the wicked old days it was quite normal to start from Tallin in Estonia, passing through Riga, Kaunas, Koenigsberg and Berlin – which provided the winners in 1933 – or Bucharest (via Cluj, Kosice, Olomonc and Prague). The magic, of course, lay in battling through all that snow for a place in the sun, and originally merely to reach Monaco from one of the starting points was test enough. Not until 1931 did anyone get through from Athens, and only then were enough competitors coming through unpenalised for it to become necessary to hold special tests to decide the winner.

For the tightly-knit circle of British racing enthusiasts Brooklands was the hub of the universe. Tucked away in the green of Surrey, Brooklands was a smart country club where Grand Prix cars mixed, on a handicap basis, with fast Tourist Trophy type tourers and standard cars tuned by enthusiasts who raced for fun and didn't much care whether they won or lost. Often it was a battle against the handicappers, whose ideal was that all races should finish in a mass dead heat. Giants and eccentrics abounded at Brooklands: Malcolm Campbell, Segrave, Archie Frazer-Nash and Kenelm Lee Guinness, who set up a Land Speed record in the 350 hp V12 Sunbeam which now rests in the Montagu Museum. Count Zborowski had a penchant for fitting aero-engines into pre-war Mercedes chassis. One of these 'specials' had a 23 litre airship engine with an exhaust that rumbled

Brooklands was the epicentre of British motor racing between the wars. The great variety of its events attracted the whole spectrum of drivers and sports cars (on a handicap basis), from GP cars to tuned-up standard models. One of the most popular was the Double Twelve Hour race *(above)* organised by the Junior Car Club, later to become the British Automobile Racing Club.

The German 'silver torpedoes' of Mercedes and Auto Union – backed up by chauvinistic inducements from the government – dominated Grand Prix racing in the second half of

the 1930s. By 1937 their titanic machines were sweeping the board in the hands of Rosemeyer, Caracciola, Nuvolari and others. Even when a new GP formula was introduced in 1938, the smaller 3-litre Auto Unions *(above and right)* continued to match their former speeds and successes.

softly: 'chitty-chitty-bang-bang'; it was known as Chitty I. The appeal of such exotica was understandable, for new cars were still expensive, and surplus aero-engines and pre-war chassis were readily available. One young hopeful built a machine around a 20 litre Clerget aero-engine and promptly killed himself.

Alongside these aero-engined bangers (the precursors of today's dragsters?) were the sophisticated machinery of the 'Bentley Boys', the backyard ingenuity of the early GNs and Morgans, the sporting flair of 'half-size' racers such as Calthorpes, Hillmans, side-valve Aston Martins, chain-driven Frazer Nashes; and the almost dainty French Amilcars and Salmsons. If Louis Coatalen's brilliant little 1½ litre Talbot Darracqs were reputed never to lose a race (except against the handicapper), innumerable sporting successes were recorded by Gordon England's racing Austin Sevens, which prompted Cecil Kimber to breathe heavily on a bull-nosed Morris Cowley and produce the first MG; later he turned a Minor into the earliest of the Midgets. Thus Austin and Morris not only brought motoring to the millions, but motor sport too.

Across the Atlantic there were plenty of circuits, but Indianapolis remained the fastest and richest venue in America. Indeed, once European domination of the '500' had been ended in 1920 by Gaston Chevrolet on a Montroe-Frontenac, European and American racing went their own ways – the one to road events and the other to the oval track. Designers like the Duesenberg brothers and Harry Armenius Miller (who 'admitted to an inexplicable occult insipirion', says Setright, 'his ideas seemed to come without any real working out') concentrated on how to travel ever faster round a geometrical strip to such good effect that the Brickyard became exclusively their domain. Even the great mass producers in Detroit stopped fielding factory teams when they found that they could not compete successfully with the specialised products of the Duesenbergs, Miller and Louis Chevrolet. Though to Europeans it seemed as exhilarating as staring at a record player with the sound turned off.

By contrast, speed in a straight line was almost entirely a British preserve. After Kenelm Lee Guinness had taken his 350 hp Sunbeam out onto the railway straight at Brooklands in May 1922 and notched up a new Land

Speed record of 133.75 mph (215.25 kph), it developed into a three-cornered contest between Henry Segrave, Malcolm Campbell and Parry Thomas (who tragically lost his life in the attempt at Pendine Sands in Wales, in 1927). An American challenge was mounted in 1928 by Frank Lockhart – sadly killed when his Black Hawk somersaulted at over 200 mph – and by Ray Keech, whose fearsome Triplex with its three Liberty engines raised the record briefly to just over 207 mph. But the spectacle that absorbed the world was between Segrave's Golden Arrow and Campbell's Bluebird, both powered by Napier Lion engines. In 1929 Segrave, to the ecstacy of all **Britons**, regained the record before 100,000 people on Daytona Beach (at 231.45 mph), announced his retirement and was promptly knighted. Campbell persisted and by the age of forty-six had broken the LSR five times, yet still he did not retire. 'When I reach the 300 mph mark I shall leave the arena', he vowed, and the annual trek to Daytona continued. Finally, in 1935, Campbell achieved his ambition, and

Nürburgring was built in 1929 and remains the longest and most testing of all the great circuits. In the thirties it was the scene of repeated duels between the monster Mercedes and

hung up his helmet at last – only to start attacking the water speed record.

Yet the British quest for the ultimate motoring prize continued. Behind guarded doors in the Bean works at Tipton, Captain George Eyston's 'Thunderbolt' was being built. It had three axles, eight wheels and two supercharged Rolls-Royce Schneider Trophy engines with a staggering capacity of 73 litres. And at Thomson and Taylor's shops at Brooklands, Reid Railton was producing a brilliantly unconventional machine for John Cobb, in which Napier Lion engines at different angles drove all four wheels, and the driver was placed right up in the streamlined nose. The duel between these two splendid machines lifted the LSR over 350 mph, and very nearly reached the 600 kph mark. Just a week before World War II, Cobb rocketted down the sand at Utah at 369.70 mph (591.7 kph) to ring down the curtain on the thirties – 'A last rare English gesture', as *L'Auto* called it, 'before the blackness of war fell upon the world.'

rear-engined Auto Unions. *Above:* The start of the 1936 German Grand Prix, won by Rosemeyer in his 6.1 litre C Type Auto Union.

THE MENACE OF THE CAR

The value of a split second. *Above and below:* Illustrations from a 1920s driving manual, which set out to edu-

cate drivers to the higher speeds and performances of the post-war cars.

In 1928 Stirling Taylor thought the time had come to deliver a strong polemic against the way the motor-car was being driven. 'At the present moment', he wrote, 'the new petrol-driven transport vehicle has not yet found its balanced place in the social system. The car is being used in the same reckless, unbalanced way that charwomen used gin in the eighteenth century....The motor-car is the most fashionable modern drug for restless nerves.' In particular he attacked the arrogance of the motorist, who appeared to undergo some sort of Jekyll-and-Hyde transformation as soon as he settled behind a steering-wheel.

'If the individual is allowed to hoot (or, in other words, yell) at any fellow-being who dares to use the road when he, the hooter, wishes to use it, then it will not be long before he begins to believe that the rest of existence can be conducted on the principle that the highway of life is for the man who can push most people out of the way....To suggest to thousands of thoughtless creatures who drive cars that their responsibilities to their fellow-citizens can be discharged by pressing a horn bulb with their thumb or foot is a licence to take risks.'

Doubtless he had before him the example of countless magistrates whose view of the automobile had mellowed remarkably, by the fact of their being motorists themselves. 'Had the driver sounded his horn?' they would enquire when investigating an accident. If he had done so then he had done, so it seemed, everything that could reasonably be expected of him.

Attitudes – official or otherwise – towards road safety were amazingly haphazard. Safety First campaigns were mounted throughout the 1920s, but too often concerned with such injuctions to the pedestrian as 'Do not cross the road while reading a newspaper.' There were no driving tests, indeed you could take a car straight from a showroom out onto the public road without ever having been in the driving seat before in your life. (Like the – probably apocryphal – story of the lady who drove her new Austin out of the dealer's and into a dead-end road. Having no idea that cars could reverse, she had to pay passers-by to lift the car bodily and turn it around!) There was no compulsory insurance (except in the state of Massachusetts) and no highway code. Safety accessories, such as bumpers and brake-lights, were left entirely to the whim of the manufacturer and were usually omitted. In fact the Minister of Transport in Britain in 1924 declined to make driving mirrors compulsory on the grounds that he was 'not satisfied that the universal adoption of mirrors to enable drivers to see overtaking traffic would generally assist in the prevention of accidents'. Well-meaning private firms that offered the motorist safety equipment did so without any practical research on their bright ideas. One marketed a direction indicator, to be attached to the rear of a vehicle, which reported

The fruits of progress: no progress at all along Oxford Street, London, in 1938. By then there were approaching two million private vehicles on the roads of Britain, while new roadbuilding had remained almost static and traffic control in cities was embryonic.

to the car behind that the driver was intending to go 'straight ahead'! Another – attempting to come to grips with the problem of headlight dazzle at night – produced a system which actually switched off the front headlights when another car approached and automatically switched on rear headlights. The idea of this brainwave was that your path would be illuminated by the lights of the on-coming car: no-one explained how you could fail to dazzle any car that happened to be following you.

An intriguing sidelight on the motoring conventions of the time can be gleaned from a little book that was reprinted regularly in the 1920s, *How to Drive a Motorcar*. This publication – to be fair to it – does proffer some very sound advice on driving techniques, but also includes sub-sections whose titles fall very oddly on a modern ear: 'Passing on the wrong side', 'The art of skidding', 'Coasting'. This last was a much-discussed topic, especially when some cars appeared in 1930 equipped for 'free-wheeling'. A control under the dashboard allowed the car to coast, the engine picking up again without a jolt when you pressed the throttle. Did it, or did it not, save fuel? Running through the book also is the, no doubt unconscious, assumption that the motorist was the master of the road. In the section dealing with what to do about pedestrians who dithered in the middle of the road as they were about to be run down, the authors recommended the use of 'the commanding eye', that is to say a look from the driver which would freeze the jaywalker in his tracks and thus enable the car to swerve safely. This was only a marginal improvement on the 'pedestrian-sweeper' of the pre-war era, a contraption attached to the front of the car which caught stray walkers instead of running them over.

In almost every country there were speed limits in force, but most of them dated back to the days of the horseless carriage (or shortly afterwards), were totally impracticable for the powerful contemporary cars, universally ignored, and increasingly hard to enforce. Indeed the 1930 Road Traffic Act in Britain faced up to the anarchic state of affairs by abolishing all speed limits, with the approval of the motoring organisations, the police, even the National Safety First Association. It was, as it turned out, a disastrous piece of legislation. Road casualties which had totalled 185,000 in 1930 leapt up to almost 240,000 in 1934 (a total that was not to be exceeded until 1955) including 7,343 deaths. By then the Minister of Transport was describing road-deaths as 'a hideous and growing blot on our national life', and so many children were being killed that in some areas parents went on strike and refused to send them to school until safety measures were taken. In 1934 the government had to go into reverse and brought in a new bill, establishing a 30 mph speed limit for all built-up areas, driving tests for all new drivers, and a ban on sounding the horn in London at night. Motoring organisations were up in arms at the new speed limit. Their attitude had been epitomised by an editorial in *The Motor:* 'Nobody who drives a motor vehicle in the streets of London can fail to be astounded at the folly of which pedestrians are capable. Considering what traffic is today, the risks taken appal the man at the wheel of a motor-car who...is constantly saving the lives of walkers.'

But it was an argument that sounded increasingly unconvincing when road-deaths fell by over 10 percent the following year and (in spite of an increase of half a million vehicles on the road) stayed at that level until the war.

In America in 1934 there were 882,000 accidents with more than 36,000 people killed. (That year also saw an outcry against the number of sea-turtles being slaughtered on the boulevards, as they crawled laboriously from the sea at Miami Beach to lay their eggs inland!) The conclusions culled from various state inquiries were unanimous in indicting speed as the biggest killer: California recorded that the majority of slain motorists were driving in excess of 45 mph, while Michigan maintained that the chances there of killing someone were five times as great over 50 mph as they were at a rate under 20 mph. Many states in the course of the decade lowered their speed limits, and instituted speed patrols equipped with two-way radios. New York even flirted briefly with a system of lights 'moving' along the sidewalk at 30 mph and fining any motorist who drove faster. In the absence of government or federal guidance on the subject of traffic control, increasingly congested cities had to make their own experiments. In Paris – where the Prefect of Police in 1925 had called the traffic problem 'insoluble' – a wholesale 'gyratory system' (of one-way streets) and parking restrictions were imposed in the late twenties with modest results. But their new, clearly-marked pedestrian crossings prompted the British transport minister, Hore-Belisha, to introduce them to London and signal their presence with his famous orange flashing globes. They became popular targets for drunken marksmen on Boat Race night and *The Spectator* complained that they made the city look as if it were 'preparing for a fifth-rate carnival', but the Belisha beacon remains to this day an urban landmark in Britain.

Walking traffic lights *(above)*. New York traffic cops being fitted up with illuminated waistcoats in 1921. Point duty must have been one of the less popular assignments!

These Swiss trams in 1929 appear to have devoured a motorist who strayed into their path. Today the trams of Zurich still enjoy their own rules of the road.

Traffic signals achieved their consummation as winking red, green and amber lights in the latter half of the decade, evolving over ten years or so from rudimentary hand-held Stop/Go placards. In due course these were transmuted into red and green placards, a colour combination known previously only to engine-drivers. Semaphore signs had their day too – a particularly engaging variation of these was the umbrella issued to traffic cops in Syracuse, N.Y., in 1921, which was crowned by a Stop/Go weather vane and which had to be twirled appropriately by the policeman. More sophisticated was the clock-face traffic signal pioneered in Berlin, with a hand that revolved slowly from red segments to green segments: at least with

these you could tell how fast you needed to go to beat the signals. The first traffic lights to appear in New York were actually mounted onto waistcoats and worn by the cops themselves.

Many of the experiments of the inter-war years have become familiar features in the geography of our modern streets: round-abouts, white lines, parking-meters (the world's first parking-meter sprouted in Oklahoma City in 1935). Other ventures which looked promising at the time have faded into oblivion. Maybe the activities of the mobile vigilantes in Germany, whose cars were fitted with automatic signs warning other drivers of their misdemeanours, smacked too much of officiousness. But Lancashire's 'courtesy cop' scheme, which ran throughout 1938, produced impressive results. On the assumption that accidents would be reduced not by rigid enforcement of the law, but rather by advice and example, the county's police force was concentrated in black spot areas and their cars fitted with loudspeakers, which would boom their polite admonitions all the way down the street. Offenders were spoken to rather than booked, and then sent letters requesting their future co-operation. Undoubtedly a new spirit betweeen public and police was created, and total casualties that year fell by 44 percent. In contrast, in Peking – never a place for wishy-washy experimentation – the penalty for speeding was death.

One concept that was endlessly debated was that of segregating the automobile, either wholly or partly, from pedestrians, which meant in effect building limited-access highways. Proposals and plans for such roads had

Taking the law into their own hands. *Left:* A patent pedestrian-catcher, from an era when motoring was rather more leisurely. Even though the idea mercifully never got off the ground, the motorist's attitude towards walking people persisted. *Above:* Auto-vigilantes on parade in Berlin in the 1930s. Speeding motorists were overtaken by a vehicle of the 'Auto-watch' and cautioned by signals to keep their speed down to 35 kph!

been regularly put forward since the early years of the century, and been opposed on grounds of cost and (in the words of one British MP) that it would be 'taking the motorist and placing him on the heights of fame with a special road to himself'. However, by the time an international congress on roads was held in Seville in 1923 there was widespread enthusiasm for the idea, and a vision emerged of wide new motor roads, landscaped and forested, crossed only by fly overs or underpasses. Within the year this ideal was in fact realised in a stretch of road opened between Milan and Varese in Italy. It was examined, admired, envied by delegates from many countries, but the will to emulate it was lacking. Ten years later Lewis

New roads for the Third Reich: Germany was the first country to embark on an integrated network of national motorways – designed, as the propaganda poster *(right)* suggests, to link up the furthest outposts of German-speaking people. In their technical design, construction and landscaping, autobahns were a model for all future motorway building. *Above:* Officers being briefed on a scale-model of a clover leaf intersection on the Berlin-Munich motorway in 1936.

Mumford, one of the chief advocates of 'townless highways', was complaining:

'There is a scorching ugliness of badly planned and laid out concrete roads peppered with impudent billboards; there is the vast, spreading metropolitan slum of multiple gas stations and hot-dog stands; and on the through highways there is the conflict between speed, safety and pleasure.' It was to be another five years before America's first expressway, the Pennsylvania Turnpike, was to be opened; by then the damage had been done.

Unlike the railways which tended to concentrate population around the stations (themselves never far from the centre of a town), roads were great scatterers. Easy access to a main road became the ambition of car-owners; 'on a convenient bus route' became the estate agents' great selling-point. The resulting aberration, as towns sent out their lengthening tentacles of mass-produced houses and bungalows, was termed ribbon development. Not only was it unsightly (and nowhere more so than in America, where this urban sprawl consisted largely of commercial enterprises), it was dangerous for residents, and it was the beginning of an irreversible disintegration of the cultural and social life of towns – 'no centre, no sense, no communal spirit...composed of little more than individual motor-cars come to rest' was how the historian A.J.P. Taylor described them. The extent to which it became a matter of public concern in Britain can be guaged from

the fact that, belatedly in 1935, Parliament was obliged to pass a Restriction of Ribbon Development Act – which didn't in the end prove very restrictive, and was totally impotent to check the march of the giant hoardings that were leaving their indelible imprint on the roadsides of many other countries as well.

It was not entirely surprising – given the political climate of the times – that when Germany's first *Reichsautobahn* came into service between Frankfurt and Darmstadt in 1935, it should have been greeted with suspicion. As the network spread, joining up the fringes of the German-speaking peoples, foreigners talked darkly of its being a 'military' undertaking (after all, hadn't all the best roads from Babylon to Napoleon been the instruments of conquest?). Doubtless it was, but the more the planners scrutinised it, the clearer it became that none of the problems that afflicted their own roads were visible. A huge British delegation numbering over two hundred officials returned from an inspection in 1937 virtually unanimous in its approval of the motorways' 'sense of safety and security, aesthetic quality, and the absence of any feature arising from the works which would cause disfigurement or destroy the beauty of the countryside'. For a moment in 1939 it looked as if Whitehall's procrastination might be crumbling. But by then the armoured columns were already moving up the autobahn towards Poland.

Surrounded by the full panoply of Nazi pomp, the Fuehrer opens the new Frankfurt-Darmstadt motorway in 1935. The martial band and military processions attending the ceremony confirmed many observers' suspicions that Germany's road-building programme was for strategic reasons.

WAR ON WHEELS

Seasoned exponents of the hit-and-run type of warfare, in which the jeep played such an important part, were the British Special Air Service *(above,* looking suitably brigand-like). With machine-guns mounted on their vehicles and extra fuel cans they made lightning raids on depots and airfields behind the Axis lines in North Africa.

The second world conflict of the century was a war conducted, for the first time in history, on wheels or at least on tracks: only the poor bloody infantry continued to use their feet. The top brass travelled everywhere in staff cars – Mercedes for the Germans, Humbers for the Allies – and even officers who did not qualify for four wheels were given instruction on how to ride pillion on a motor-cycle. As in the first war, all car production except for military vehicles was suspended as the car plants in Britain were turned over to war supplies (in America the last cars for the duration came off the assembly lines in February 1942). The volume and variety of armed machinery assembled by the car factories was prodigious: one major development was in the waterproofing of engines and the resulting amphibious vehicles which played vital roles on the Normandy beaches and Guadalcanal. The Allies had their Landing Vehicle Tracked (LVT), and their DUKWs which predictably were christened 'ducks', the Germans their Volkswagen 166 designed by Ferdinand Porsche. There were gun-carriers, and self-propelled guns, track-laying vehicles and armoured personnel carriers, half-tracks and turretless tanks. By the end of the war there were even light tanks that could be carried in gliders – indeed some were landed in France on D-Day – and others that could swim by means of flotation screens. Of the heavy tanks the German Pz's, Panthers and Tigers, had far the more awesome fire-power; the British Churchill and the American Sherman were deployed more often as infantry support.

The crowning success of the war, however, was the Jeep – an elision, it is supposed, of GPV which in turn stood for general purpose vehicle. Developed by Willys-Overland in response to a competition launched by the U.S.

Tanks – especially the feared panzer divisions *(right,* in the Brenner Pass) – added a new dimension to military strategy. Even staff-cars *(left)* could be transformed into mock-tanks with the aid of some cardboard scenery, to fool enemy spotters!

The new face of war: the armoured column (with its highly mobile artillery, *left*) became the spearhead of Second World War offensives. *Below:* A German convoy in the Balkan campaign passing the remnants of a shattered Serbian unit. But in Russia *(bottom)* after a rapid advance, the military columns got bogged down when the weather turned and supply lines became stretched.

161

Private motoring was completely curtailed in Britain after 1942, and severe shortages of petrol after the war meant the imposition of a very meagre ration. When that was abolished in 1947 the chances of the motorist getting a fair share fell still further, and gave rise to protests *(above)* backed strongly by the RAC and AA.

Army for a four-wheel-drive cross-country vehicle, it was produced in vast quantities and became the backbone of all Allied military transport. (In fact the contract was originally awarded to a prototype submitted by Bantam, but Willys designed and paid for their own version outside the rules of the competition and ultimately underbid the luckless Bantam.) This plucky little machine seemed willing to go anywhere, do anything, and came to be regarded with great affection by the troops. The motoring writer Sammy Davis held his Jeep ('Fi-Fi') in great esteem: 'We had great fun together, that car and I. While most staff cars, saloon jobs, pretty high in the air and heavy, had got themselves into dire trouble up trees or in ditches, my Jeep careered along happily enough because the exceedingly high-geared steering let one control skids to an inch. Put the thing into four-wheel drive and it appeared able, even willing, to climb up houses.' His only complaint was that it was left-hand drive, because that was the side that German snipers instinctively shot at!

On the home front the motoring scene was bleak. Within three weeks of the declaration of war, Britain introduced petrol rationing (according to horse-power) and replaced branded fuel with the decidedly inferior 'pool petrol'. Americans experienced their first gas coupons in December 1942, and thereafter displayed stickers proclaiming which category of motorist they were: some people wondered how you earned an X sticker which entitled you to unlimited petrol, and felt it was a bit of a slur to have to wear an A sticker which publicised you as 'non-essential'. Still they put up with it, and at least so long as your car held together and your tyres survived, you could carry on motoring after a fashion.

That was a luxury that didn't last long in Britain. You could get extra coupons for 'helping your neighbour' by giving lifts to work, but the black market was shaky since all military and commercial petrol had been dyed red (although it was not a particularly well-guarded secret that the dye could be removed by filtering the stuff through gas-masks). Familiar strictures about 'pleasure motoring' were heard and photographs of car-parks at race meetings were produced. But wisely the government refused to get embroiled in this controversy, as it had done in 1916 (in the States a ban on pleasure motoring *was* imposed in 1943, but proved too hard to enforce fairly and was lifted after nine months). In any event, after July 1942 it became academic, for that month even the basic ration was withdrawn. From then on drivers had to prove their journey was essential, a regulation that was rigidly enforced: the composer Ivor Novello was jailed for a month for driving to his home in the country from the London theatre where one of his plays was on. In an effort to stay legally on the road some cars were fitted, once again, with those monstrous gas-bags that came in all shapes and sizes. But the weight of the extra equipment meant that a fully-inflated bag held only the equivalent of one gallon of petrol, so that after twenty miles or so the car had to find, or be pushed to, one of the gas-stations that had been set up around London. Many motorists decided it just wasn't worth it, and laid up their cars for the duration.

For those who remained on the road, driving could be a nightmare. There were no signposts, since they had been removed very early in anticipation of a German invasion. Headlamps had to be masked by an official device that looked like a slatted tin-lid, and which threw only the smallest trace of light on the road ahead. Driving in the blackout, there was some assistance

for the eagle-eyed in the newly-painted white lines on the road and the compulsory white bumpers on other vehicles. But pedestrians were invisible, and road-deaths increased so appallingly that a 20 mph speed limit was introduced in 1940. Even so, accidents did not decrease at all until after the end of the basic ration. The horse made a dramatic comeback on the streets, pulling milk-floats and carrying doctors on their rounds, and the buses for all their impromptu diversions around bomb-craters were invariably full to overflowing. Indeed the orderly bus queue, which replaced the traditional melee around the bus-stops, survived into peacetime. Cycling became the only means of transport for many, and they were the healthier for it. But however much they must have enjoyed the rare pleasure of pedalling down roads utterly empty of cars for the first time in thirty years, they must have admitted at times that the combustion engine did have something to be said for it.

The last stand: like a line of ghost sentries, these battered jalopies *(above)* were brought out of the knacker's yard in 1940 to defend the fields of southern Britain against the airborne landings that were daily expected after the fall of Dunkirk.

FORD V8 STATION WAGON
1935

Initially the station wagon was just what its name implies: a hack car for use on private estates, to carry staff and guns and dogs, and indeed fetch people from the station. It was an American concept, and though Durant came out with the first production station wagon, those with long memories will best recall the 'Woody', as Ford's T-Model estate car was affectionately known – a miniature charabanc that had three rows of seats and a hand-finished wooden body with a flat roof and open sides. In those days station wagons were rattly, rudimentary devices and of course their

image was hardly improved by Chevrolet's all-steel wagon which appeared in 1935 and looked like a baker's van with some extra windows and seats. Nobody wanted to be seen driving a machine like that. In contrast, Plymouth's Westchester Suburban with its elegant four-door wood framed body and 'chair-height' seats, the first non-utilitarian estate car, set a fashion that culminated in the 1946 Chrysler 'Town and Country' – an attractive (though most incongruous) combination of station wagon and sports coupe styling that had white ash and mahogany panels attached to the steel

body. By now most U.S. manufacturers were offering an estate car option, and in England Harold Radford even carried out conversions on the Mark VI Bentley, complete with silver flasks and crystal glasses. Yet for chapter-and-verse on the surge in popularity of the station wagon, we must look to Ford – who from 1935 onwards produced a practical, good-looking machine powered by the V8 engine that set the pace for American cars for decades. It was functional, robust, and it went like the clappers; it met the needs of people all over the world.

WILLYS JEEP
1940

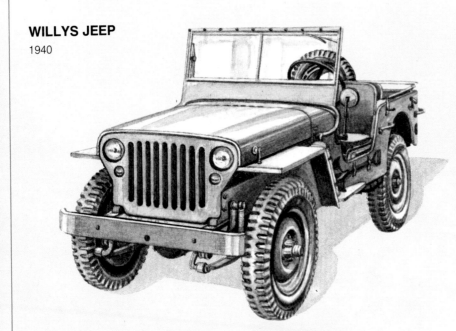

Though some like to trace the Jeep's ancestry back to the 1921 Overland roadster, the first batch of 4×4 scout cars known as 'Jeeps' was initially designed by Captain Robert G. Howie of the U.S. Army in association with Bantam Cars (makers of

the American Austin Seven) for Army trials. The Defense Department had invited a large number of manufacturers to tender for a light cross-country vehicle designated 'Truck, quarter-ton, 4×4', but only Bantam and Willys-Overland produced prototypes,

which were tested during manoeuvres staged in Louisiana under the direction of a colonel called Dwight D. Eisenhower. As it happened, Bantam secured the contract on a technicality, but since they could not keep up with the orders, Willys and Ford were brought into the act to produce Jeeps of the Willys-Overland design. Powered by a 72 hp four-cylinder Willys engine, their four-wheel drive enabled them to operate in sand, mud or snow, to climb a 69 percent gradient, and even – when fitted with special canvas sides and a snorkel – to cross streams six feet deep. When World War II ended, large quantities of army-disposal Jeeps were sold off cheap, and they became a cult with cross-country-minded folk. Willys themselves continued to produce Jeeps for the civilian market, along with a station wagon version and a curious four-seater hybrid called the Jeepster. In England, too, the Rover Company began to make the Land Rover. ('Always a bad sign, that sort of thing', commented a top Nuffield executive at the time.) But BMC itself was soon producing the Austin Champ, and once the vogue for cross-country vehicles caught on, Land Rovers and Jeeps sold better and better. In fact, the Range Rover has become a sort of status symbol today.

FIAT 508C

1936

When Giovanni Agnelli founded Fiat in 1899 with a group of Torinese aristocrats, he made it clear that he was not really interested in originality or innovation in design. 'I don't want inventions – just mechanism and methods that have already been tested', he told his staff. In a land of craftsmen, he was the apostle of series production, yet at the same time endowed with a sense of human concern that enabled him to view his factory as 'a Co-operative Society of man'.

The Type 508, known as the Balilla, which appeared in 1932, was indeed a car for the people – compact, utilitarian and economical. But its specifications included hydraulic brakes and dampers, 12 volt electrics and a short piston stroke for high cruising speeds. Designed by Tranquillo Zerbi, it was followed by the more luxurious 1500 in 1935 and the delightful Giacosa-designed little 500 cc Topolino in 1936. Indeed when updated that same year, the 508C looked

like a cross between the two, with independent front suspension, overhead valves, cylinder bores enlarged to raise the capacity to 1,089 cc, and a pillarless saloon body with a downswept bonnet that gave low drag coefficient. The Millecento, as it became known, continued in one shape

and another for thirty years, and although certainly less exciting than its more expensive rival, the Lancia Aprilia, nevertheless offered quite exceptional road-holding and performance at that time. When all is said and done, it was the first popular European car that was also a driver's car.

VOLKSWAGEN

1938–47

The task of designing the Third Reich's 'People's Car', and of getting the prototypes made, was assigned to Ferdinand Porsche Sr, whose Stuttgart design organization had already produced several intriguing small car prototypes for the Zündapp and

NSU companies and had won worldwide acclaim for the V16 engined Grand Prix racer it designed and developed for the Auto-Union Group. From 1938 on, production was under way in the rather depressed area of Wolfsburg, and millions of Germans began paying their monthly instalments. A firm believer that better racing cars breed better road cars, Porsche designed the VW very much along the lines of the Auto-Union

Grand Prix model. The engine and the entire transmission, both largely made of light alloy castings, were built as a single unit driving the rear wheels, while the all-independent suspensions were virtually identical with those of the Auto-Union racer. Further innovations: the chassis, of backbone construction, was clad in an aerodynamic body. To save space and reduce maintenance, the 995 cc engine was an air-cooled flat-four, increased to 1,131 cc before production began.

But by then Hitler had other ideas. The monthly instalments had gone to finance the manufacture of tanks, aircraft and ammunition, and the Wolfsburg factory, scarcely finished, was soon turning out VWs of less aerodynamic shape – which were among General Rommel's main assets during the African campaign. A tougher development and testing programme could hardly be imagined.

After the war, the British chose not to transfer the production works to England – finding the car too crude, seeing little future for it. So the company was left to the Germans, who proceeded to make 20 million Beetles, an all-time record, in factories all over the world – with more still being made in Brazil and Mexico. No car ever had a longer production life.

THE TRIUMPH OF TECHNOLOGY

The problems of the automobile age which had inevitably been shelved during the war very soon re-asserted themselves in peace-time. The car finally broke through the class barrier and on every level became the normal means of transport. It began to dictate patterns of living and working, creating a new mass species – the car commuter – with consequent effects on public transport systems. For many years the automobile was considered to be one of the cornerstones of economic progress, and efforts were made to accommodate it rather than control it. Pressure to buy cars – and to change them frequently for newer and more expensive models – increased as the motor-car was promoted as a tangible token of status in an affluent consumer society. Yet at the same time mass production methods made it increasingly difficult to tell one make from another! True status could only be acquired from driving the élite examples of consummate engineering and design that were sold at the top end of the market. Ironically as standards of speed and performance were raised, the opportunities to exploit them decreased.

CITROËN 2 CV

1948

The 2 CV – Deux Chevaux, or Two Horses – also called 'an umbrella over four wheels', was intended as the ideal car for the masses. A few prototypes were built before World War II started, but the finished car was first shown at the Paris Salon of 1948. Throughout the show it proved to be – as it has been ever since – the butt of countless jokes.

It would be hard to imagine anything more basic. But it was practical as well: from the top of the windscreen to the rear bumper (well, that's what they called it), the car was covered by a single sheet of canvas which could be rolled up for an open roof, or completely removed to carry bulky items placed in back, with the detachable rear seat removed. The seats themselves were just tubes carrying rubber bands covered by a bit of fabric, under which bags and odds and ends could be carried. There was ample room for four, each passenger having his own door. Electricity was kept to an absolute minimum, even the windscreen wiper being powered by the speedometer cable. Only one finish was offered: dull grey – so that dirt would not show, and washing could be infrequent.

But the mechanical units reflected first-class engineering. A 375 cc flat-twin o.h.v. air-cooled engine drove the front wheels via a four-speed all-synchromesh gearbox and huge inboard drum brakes. Its all-independent suspension with the front and rear wheels interconnected, was extraordinarily soft and scantily damped. All bumps were efficiently absorbed, but the car was also subject to a continuous bouncing movement. Nor was it immune from jerks, caused by turning the steering to full lock, whereby the ordinary (non-homokinetic) driveshaft

universals transmitted an irregular movement to the front wheels. The effect was not without humour. The engine could not produce more than 9 bhp: and it was pretty much up to the number of passengers and the direction of the wind, whether 40 mph could be reached or not. At the slightest suggestion of a headwind or a slope, you shifted immediately into third gear. But the 2 CV was economical, required virtually no servicing, could be driven cross-country and through woods, was nearly indestructible and could be put to a great variety of uses.

CITROËN DS

1955

Nobody believed that André Citroën would succeed when he started making his own cars in the old Mors works in 1919, but the Type A proved critics wrong and within a few years his jaunty little yellow 'Clover-Leaf' had become part of the folk-lore of France. By then Citroën had begun a dialogue with Budd, culminating in the 'Traction Avant' of 1934 which had an all-steel body and front-wheel drive. Despite early gearbox troubles, this proved to be one of the most advanced and long-lived cars in Europe, until after

twenty years it was replaced by the astonishing shark-like DS. Characteristically unorthodox, here was an architect's car that many people found unacceptable; an engineer's machine spoilt by a chattery engine – for the long awaited V6 never materialised. But above all its aerodynamic shape gave an exceptionally low-drag coefficient, its fibreglass roof made plastics respectable, and its exotic hydraulic system – operating brakes, steering, clutch, gearbox and suspension – seemed to isolate the

occupants from the world outside. Perhaps it was a car that only French logic could have conceived, with Gallic disregard for conventions; certainly it gave other manufacturers plenty of food for thought. The CX that followed has a slippier, more pleasing silhouette and a space-age interior: who knows, this could be the shape of things to come.

JAGUAR XK 120

1949

William Lyons came to automobile production by way of motorcycles, having co-founded at the tender age of twenty the Swallow Sidecar and Coachbuilding Company in Blackpool, England. After producing special sporting bodies for Austin Sevens (beginning in 1927) and others, he designed his first car: a startlingly low-built two-seater fixed head coupé with two very, very occasional rear seats. The first 'SS' – Standard-Swallow, or Swallow-Standard, no-one knows for sure – was probably the most striking, lowest-built closed car made up to that time. A year later, in 1932, the SS, made in two sizes, had evolved into a real four-seater (also made as an open tourer), which would become the most copied car in the world. Only the performance of the side-valve four- and six-cylinder engines did not quite measure up to the car's looks.

This was remedied when, at the Olympia Show of 1935, Lyons launched the Jaguar line – a car that resembled the Bentley, but at a quarter the price, and one that very nearly matched the Bentley performance. By the end of World War II, Lyons (having, for obvious reasons, dropped the SS label and renamed his company), scored a new

coup: a magnificent-looking streamlined two-seater powered by a breathtaking twin o.h.c. six-cylinder engine with a capacity of 3,442 cc, guaranteed to do 120 mph and retailing at £998, excluding purchase tax. Even the most incredulous were convinced

when this model (known by the internal code name XK 120) racked up an official speed of 132.596 mph. An aero-screen replaced the standard windscreen. Bill Heynes' basic six-cylinder engine, which he first designed more than 30 years ago, still powers the Jaguar XJ-6, mainstay of today's Jaguar production.

MORRIS MINI-MINOR/
AUSTIN SEVEN

1959

The Mini gave a new word to the language, and a new concept to motoring. It was conceived as BMC's answer to the bubble cars of the fifties; a British response to the Beetle and the 2 CV. A stark roller-skate for

those who couldn't really afford to run a car. Yet, as things turned out, it was BMC's last truly original design – which many of the world's leading manufacturers have paid the compliment of following.
Never mind the body leaks, the ignition system that got drowned when it rained, the sliding windows, the exposed door hinges that broke off, and the speedometer that was so cleverly hidden from the driver's vision by the steering wheel. The

Mini was a star in the history of motoring because it was a personal car which, while reducing things to essentials, to minimum mobility if you like, fitted four people into a tiny space more comfortably than in many larger cars and which, when tuned, could outperform many sports cars. For instance, when the 1,071cc Mini-Coopers made their first appearance in the 1963 Alpine Rally (which they won), it was enlightening to see them tear down a rubble road and stop precisely in front of the control point, whereas others slid all over the place; it was equally surprising to note how at the end they only needed a wash to put them back into showroom condition, in contrast to so many other competitors which looked ready for the scrapheap.
Now, after 22 years and nearly 5 million units produced, the Mini is beginning to show its age. But it remains a moving testimonial to the genius of Alec Issigonis, and a reminder that a single-minded spirit, doodling away on the back of envelopes and menu-cards, can (when given the right conditions) design something better than a hundred-strong committee. Even with the help of the Japanese, will BL produce anything else as good?

THE NEW COMMUTERS

New patterns of travel and employment brought increasingly high tides of traffic into the large cities after the war, creating congestion problems on an unprecedented scale. In an effort to control it, serried ranks of parking meters *(above)* sprouted on the kerbs and the traffic warden, or meter-maid, became the figure motorists loved to hate.

The immediate problem for the car industry after the war – at least for those firms who didn't have to rebuild their factories out of the rubble – was not selling cars but building them fast enough. In the States car prices had to be pegged to their 1942 level to prevent inflation, but many customers were happy to do under-the-counter deals, desperate to get their hands on anything that was not five years old. In Europe, in spite of petrol rationing and war-ravaged roads, the second-hand car market went berserk creating a new brand of entrepreneur, the 'wheeler-dealer' with his unenviable reputation. Whatever else a war-weary world was short of – and that was almost everything – what it seemed to want above all else was a car. The austerity years were to linger on in Europe for longer than expected, with petrol only finally de-rationed in 1950 and the wartime 'pool spirit' surviving even longer. What with chronic steel shortages and the government's insistence on export quotas, it took nearly five years for car-ownership in Britain to reach its pre-war figure. But as the restraints were removed in the early fifties the car-makers began to read the omens eagerly. By the end of the decade there were more than 5½ million private cars running in the over-crowded island, but more significant still was the fact that the motor-car had undoubtedly broken the class barrier. Half the country's hire-purchase debt had been incurred in the payment for cars, and the greatest part of this sales-explosion was accounted for by new owners among the manual workers and lower-paid white collar workers. (Much the same was happening in France where, over the same period, car-ownership had trebled as the 2CV penetrated where other brands could not hope to reach.) In retrospect it was the first solid indicator of the approaching 'age of affluence' but it was also the result of a new social mobility imposed by post-war planning.

Among the major priorities after the war was the re-settlement of families who had been blitzed out of their homes in the large cities. Inevitably this meant shifting huge numbers of people to the periphery of cities, if not further. In London for instance, where 1 million people were scheduled to be moved from the centre, the limits of the metropolis had been prescribed by a five-mile-wide 'green belt' (in an effort to curtail the ribbon development that the car had helped to create). So eight 'new towns' beyond the green belt were sanctioned and took shape with commendable speed. It had been planned that the new inhabitants would find employment in their new towns but, predictably perhaps, London remained the magnet drawing in a new wave of commuters. Most of these had to rely on cars in the absence of established public transport, or at least on car-sharing – a practice that Ford even managed to make into a selling-point for their Zephyr, showing six bowler-hatted city gents getting aboard for the office: 'Takes

six in style for less per mile.' Indeed when Harlow New Town was in the blueprint stage, the designers had planned on one garage for every ten houses. By the time the town was half built they had been obliged to alter the ratio to one garage to every two homes.

During the 1950s the volume of traffic passing into and around London doubled, and towards the end of the decade the city's traffic speeds were the lowest on record. This depressingly familiar pattern was repeated in city after city: In Paris, where Haussmann's *grands boulevards* incited on-street parking but were subject to severe thrombosis at their *rond-points*, police struggled incessantly to impose their *zones bleues* on the unruly Parisians; in Tokyo an alarming increase in car-commuters jostled for access to streets that occupied a meagre 10 percent of the city space (as compared, say, with 35 percent in New York). City authorities attempted to deal with the snarl-ups in their own ways. In the fifties London kept trying to press more and more traffic through the existing road-system, till it was obliged in the sixties to resort to restrictive measures and appeals to motorists to use public services. If they fell on deaf ears, perhaps it is because the commuter in fact cherishes the privacy his car gives him, the sense of freedom for a while from family or work which can transcend even the frustrations of daily traffic jams? Some American cities – like New York with its Cross-Bronx Expressway, and Boston with its Central Artery – took the radical and extremely expensive step of building urban highways that disgorged commuters right in the heart of the city. Such projects displaced huge numbers of people, usually the less well-off, who took refuge in suburbs.

Off to work in the morning: pin-stripe commuters *(above)* embarking for the City, while one of their wives gives the car a last-minute brush-up. Car-sharing was a popular form of commuting in the early days, but as families acquired their own vehicles, one occupant per car became the norm, throwing an increasing burden on inadequate roads.

Overleaf: A congregation of cars at a drive-in-movie-theatre in South Dakota, assembled to see Moses receiving the ten commandments. What the car occupants were doing is another matter.

Cause and effect? As the automobile took over the city centre *(below,* the morning rush hour in Berlin), so families preferred to move out into quieter newly-built suburbs. By 1953 the trend in America was well established. *Right:* A mass moving-in into a Los Angeles development. The

vicious spiral began, with more cars pouring into towns and centres becoming urban wastelands.

But these refugees were not the sole reason why America's suburbs mushroomed so phenomenally in the post-war years. By 1950 car ownership had already passed the 50 million mark, and at the end of the decade it had reached 75 million, which meant more or less that the entire country could fit into the front seat of their automobiles. With such a total commitment to the car, abandoning the city and its problems was easy, and attractive when the network of federal-funded Interstate Highways (41,000 miles of them) began to splice the continent after 1956. The new suburbs were car-oriented from the start, creating a way of life that was epitomised by the gigantic 'shopping-centres' that burgeoned in the fifties surrounding themselves with acres of car-park and containing every conceivable form of merchandise under one roof. These emporia were the logical (and least objectionable) outcome of the auto-inspired movement which had started in the 1930s and was to find a sort of grisly perfection in the fifties: the drive-in.

Gas stations on the highway, as we have seen, had often developed into social centres where you could fill the tank, then have the car washed while you snatched a bite to eat or played pinball. The bother of it all was that you had to get out of your car. But not for long. The first drive-in movie theatre was opened in New Jersey in 1933, the earliest of the drive-in restaurants not long after. After the war all kinds of other enterprises opened up their drive-in branches – banks, libraries, laundries. Nor were the spiritual requirements of the motorist neglected: time came when you could get married by car, pay your last respects to granny in her drive-in funeral parlour, and worship your creator at a drive-in church (with the tempting option of switching off the plug-in loudspeaker if the sermon was boring?). With the automobile already serving as an alternative bedroom and (with the arrival of radio-telephones) an office, if it weren't for the calls of nature it might be hard to think of any reason ever to leave it.

Clearly man's relationship with his car went far deeper than simply regarding it as a conveyance. In the old days, when each car had had its own identity, it had been easy to recognise the symbolism of wealth and social standing; but now that they had acquired a certain uniformity and each motor was duplicated by a hundred thousand others, it was a much more complex matter altogether. Simple observation of the rituals that had come to attend car-ownership suggested that the automobile was an expression of some human desire. Did it not get put to bed each night in its own room? Was it not tenderly washed, possibly more often than a man's own offspring? And hung with more trinkets and ornaments than his wife?

On such speculations a regiment of motivational researchers began to wax prosperous in the fifties and sixties. Car manufacturers urgently required to know the nature of this relationship, so that they could design cars to nurture it, and their advertising agencies also needed the information to direct their campaigns towards it. Early in the 1940s psychologists like Ernest Dichter had come up with some intriguing theories. A man looked on his convertible, he suggested, as his mistress and on a saloon as his wife. It followed therefore that he would use a completely different set of criteria for choosing one or the other (and, as a corollary, he would display brand loyalty when changing it for fear of punishment for 'unfaithfulness'). For a long time advertisers, aware of how the car had changed the patterns of courtship, had offered their customers hope of fulfilment by showing their products being driven by happy, laughing couples. But the new sexology of

174

the car was more sophisticated, unearthing reactions that were not perhaps immediately apparent. Automobiles, it turned out, confirmed virility and were a means of compensating for growing old. Owners endowed their cars with personalities ('steering is like holding hands with another person'). Cars were an extension of the owner, or as Paul Wilson put it more vividly in *Chrome Dreams:* 'like an aborigine donning a horned and lurid ceremonial mask, the henpecked husband of suburbia happily climbed behind the wheel of his new 1950 Buick and set out to terrorize the populace' – and indeed it is hard to think of the Buick's enormous fanged grille serving any other purpose. Firms that ignored these tenets did so at their peril – as

Ultimate apotheosis of the automobile, when churches and even cathedrals *(below and right)* are built for in-car worship. But perhaps it was

no more than the inevitable conclusion of the motor-age, when even 'farm-fresh' milk can be delivered to your car in a drive-in grocery store *(bottom)*.

Ford discovered in 1956 when they concentrated on selling the new safety features of their models, only to watch their share of the market plummet. But for the most part advertisers were happy to fill their space with phallic symbols and exotic ladies. For years at the British motor show, scantily-clad models were to be seen adorning one rakish brand of car. With each visitation they seemed to be wearing less; then, one year, there was nothing left to take off.

Perhaps a more potent sales thrust came through exploiting what Vance Packard called the 'upgrading urge', which the researchers discovered was a specially powerful incentive in suburbia, where people bought a more expensive car than they could afford just to show they could afford it. Driving was like life – so this philosophy went – and the car was a tangible symbol of success. 'Why come second when you could be first?' enquired one typical advert. 'They'll know you've arrived when you drive up in an Edsel' promised another (in fact they would have known you'd made a ghastly mistake, since the Edsel was one of the all-time flops in motoring history, but no matter). Disgruntled by it all, E.B. White of *The New Yorker* wrote: 'From reading the auto ads you would think that the primary function of the motor-car in America was to carry its owner first into a higher social stratum, then into an exquisite delirium of high adventure.' By harping constantly on the theme of status, manufacturers hoped to engender a permanent state of discontent with motorists' current model, and that when they traded it in they would move one rung higher up the hierarchy of models (a pecking-order that was also firmly established in the allocation of company cars, thus reinforcing people's preconceptions about status). By and large, more prestigious meant bigger, though few of the consumers interviewed on the question would ever admit it: they usually hankered after a bigger car because it was 'safer'. Campaigns were sustained on variations of both the psycho-sexual and the status-enhancement themes through most of the sixties, to the benefit of U.S. big car manufacturers, the sportier European firms and, curiously, the oil companies whose virtually identical products offered to make you one of the 'getaway people' and 'put a tiger in your tank'. In the seventies a new set of priorities were to appear. It was perhaps no accident that the post-war generation should have embraced the motor-car with an almost fanatical fervour: much the same reaction had occurred after the first war, if on a different social level. In the fifties these tremulous pleasures were open to a far wider range of kids from the campus. In their hotted-up jalopies they would congregate at some local drive-in, then spend the evening racing each other up and down the street (the ever-growing sport of drag-racing owes its origins to organised efforts to channel these street races onto safer territory). Or else they would just cruise, eyeing the talent and trying to look like James Dean, who by a tragic irony was killed in an automobile accident in 1955 at the age of twenty-four. Nancy Friday, the novelist, recalled these cruising manœuvres of her youth, when carfuls of girls would haunt the streets in the hope, and expectation, of getting chased by carfuls of boys. 'The cars', she says, 'brought us together, but also kept us separate and intact.' It was only when one ventured into a car alone with a boy that a sense of anxiety asserted itself. 'There was an awful lot of weighty decision-making in those cars.... Even now when I get in a car with another man – not the man to whom I'm married – I still feel a certain zing inside at the thunk of the door.' Maybe the motivational psychologists did have a point.

Familiar feature of the motorscape, the motel *(below)* which developed from the tourist cabins of the 1920s into a full flowering of 'autopias'.

Above: Fast food at a drive-in restaurant, where the waitress hangs your table on the window and settles your check before you can accelerate away!

177

EXPORTS AND MERGERS

Dunlop's dawning of the new era: their 1945 advertisements *(above)* still projected a tough wartime image. By 1946 *(below)* they were celebrating the promise of spring and a return to the old pleasures of pre-war motoring.

By the time hostilities ended, some $30 billion worth of military equipment had been made, but no passenger cars had left the lines in England for five years, or since 1942 in the States. There was little option, therefore, but for factories on both sides of the Atlantic to get busy making the same models as they had been building before. By August 1946 a million postwar cars had been put together in America, most of them based on 1942 styling with an extra slosh of chrome, which hardly improved their looks – though worse was to come. In England the 'Big Six' brought back their pre-war range of models, a large proportion of which were exported on the government's insistence and were welcomed by a car-hungry world, though whether they enhanced the image of the British car in unfamiliar surroundings is quite another matter.

Since it takes between three and five years for a new model to grow from a twinkle in the designer's eye to manufactured metal on the showroom floor, the first generation of post-war cars really appeared in 1949. The new Chevrolet was 2½ inches lower on a one-inch-shorter wheelbase. The front mudguards were now flush with the bonnet: there was a larger grille and a curved split windscreen. A million and a half were sold, which made it the front runner. Ford also had a longer and lower silhouette in the three-box idiom, with mudguards integrated into the body, giving it a lighter but tinnier feel. Buicks were more bulbous, with a huge chromium grille and 'portholes' in the mudguards.

In England the Morris Minor appeared along with its big sister, the Oxford. The Minor's rotund shape sprang from the fact that Alec Issigonis had intended to use a flat-four engine rather than the old Morris side-valve unit which was eventually fitted, and also (it is said) because when the pundits at Cowley complained that the car was too narrow he sawed it down the middle and put another slice in. But its rack and pinion steering and torsion-bar suspension gave far better roadholding than its predecessors, and set a pattern for the opposition. The Standard Motor Company, who had acquired Triumph in 1945 as a prestige label, were among the first to produce a wholly new car. The 1800 Triumph saloon had smartly tailored razor-edged lines, and unfortunately looked better than it performed – just the opposite of the roly-poly Standard Vanguard, designed to spearhead Britain's export drive to far-flung places.

Notable newcomers were the 1½ litre Riley saloon with pleasingly swept lines of a pre-war vintage, and the Jowett Javelin, with a flat-four engine and a smooth fastback body. But the car that smote the motoring world with awe and admiration was the XK Jaguar, for its breathtakingly beautiful shape had performance to match from the new 3.4 litre o.h.c. six-cylinder engine.

At about the same time a very different, but just as revolutionary, car was being born after a long and complicated pregnancy. Back in 1934 Hitler had announced that a *Volksauto* would be built, and invited Ferdinand Porsche to Berlin, where the two men discussed their ideas in the Kaiserhof Hotel. But although the Third Reich collected a large number of down payments, no vehicles reached the public. In 1948 the British Control Commission offered the plant to the British motor industry for £3 million, but no one was interested. Lord Nuffield considered the idea of taking over the facilities to produce the Minor in Europe, though he scorned the Volkswagen itself. It was, declared his general manager, 'the most God-awful design I ever saw – all the wrong way round!' Far better give it back to the Germans. Which is precisely what happened. From 1949 onwards production was stepped up, and as the years passed the Beetle became accepted throughout the world as the most practical and best-made form of everyday down-to-earth motoring.

Inevitably, many of the continental manufacturers had a rough passage during the war. Fiat had to open an entirely new plant at Mirafiori after their works at Lingotto (like Alfa Romeo's at Portello) had been blown to bits by Allied bombers. In France, the Ford and Peugeot plants were almost totally destroyed, to say nothing of Bugatti at Molsheim. Renault came to grief with a self-inflicted wound – for, suspected of collaboration with the Nazis, Louis Renault died somewhat mysteriously while imprisoned at Fresnes – and the firm was nationalised. But in Germany the Daimler-Benz and Opel factories had to be rebuilt virtually from scratch. Less privileged were BMW in Eisenach and Auto Union in Zwickau, both of which fell under Soviet control and were fated to produce different products under new names.

If the years after the war did not, as in 1919, generate a crush of entrepreneurs hustling to fill the commercial vacuum, there was still room for the

Beetle in captivity: in 1946 the Volkswagen plant was administered by the British Occupation Force *(above, a scene from the VW calendar for that year)*. Short-sightedly the British motor industry disregarded the brainchild of Prof. Ferdinand Porsche (standing, *below*) as a commercial proposition – only to watch production booming and the company handed back to the Germans in 1949.

rugged individualist who had something positive to offer. In 1948 the first cars appeared bearing the already illustrious name of Ferdinand Porsche. Since he was probably the most versatile genius that the motor world has seen, it is curious that he should have allowed the early post-war Porsche to be devised around a mixture of ideas derived from Mickl, Glockner and Abarth. The tear-shape of the 356 seemed at the time to be the ultimate statement in aerodynamics, even though the handling was so dicey that over-steer became another word for Porsche. His later 911 clung to much the same shape, though less curvacious and considerably more desirable. But both were magic to the fast car lover, and established a cult of their own among afficionados, especially in the United States, who found driving joys in the Porsche that were quite unmatched by other makes. In contrast, the cars of Colin Chapman almost crept onto the scene in the early fifties. His Lotus – initially sold as a kit to which proprietary engines and running gear could be added – moved steadily upmarket, and finally with the Lotus 18 became the fastest machinery in Grand Prix racing. 'Chunky', remarks L.J.K. Setright, 'is a man whose creative processes are marked by an obsessive and almost malignant objectivity; every scrap of superfluous weight, every item that is irrelevant or otiose, every poundsworth that can be replaced by a pennysworth, is pruned away as though Chapman's commercial object were to sell air.'

Elsewhere the drift of the industry was towards mergers and combines. In 1951 Morris joined Austin to form the British Motor Corporation – an uneasy marriage of convenience that grew into a vast, unwieldy bureaucracy, and did no-one much good. The architect of this disaster was Len Lord, though so long as he remained as 'supremo' in his headquarters at Longbridge (aptly known as the Kremlin) the behemoth worked. One of the best things that Lord did was to call Alec Issigonis back from Alvis to design a successor to the Morris Minor. 'Those God-damned bubble-cars', he fumed, 'we must drive them out of the streets by designing a proper miniature car.' This, recalls Issigonis, is how the Mini started – as an answer to the Frisky, the Isetta, the Heinkel, and the Goggomobile. (See profile of the Mini, page 169.)

During the third quarter of this century there were some exciting developments. Rover, Renault and Chrysler built several experimental cars with gas turbine engines: the Wankel rotary combustion engine took shape un-

Those Saturday afternoons at Brooklands are not quite so far off. And, when they do return, Ford motoring will be back again too, adding to your pleasure with greater *comforts* and *economies* than those you enjoyed in the past.

FORD will continue to make history

False optimism: Ford's cheerful promise of racing at Brooklands in their 1945 advert (above) was never fulfilled. A victim of war production, the course was bought by Vickers Armstrong after the war and all racing ceased.

Nostalgic names from the past: bustling scene at a post-war Earl's Court Motor Show, displaying stands for many famous makes now sadly deceased – Wolseley and Humber, Hudson and Armstrong-Siddeley among others. The show lives on, though now held at Birmingham.

Transatlantic challengers. *Left:* Ford's British range displayed on the front cover of a 1955 issue of *The Autocar,* with its appropriate background of village cricket underlining

der the guidance of NSU. In the United States, Curtiss-Wright produced various twin-rotor Wankel RC engines: Mercedes-Benz equipped their experimental C111 sports coupe with a fuel-injected three-rotor Wankel unit, and Toyo Kogyo of Japan came out with a series of Wankel-powered sports cars. Technically, the rotary engine was a logical development, but it turned out to be thirstier than expected, and there were sealing problems. In the end, neither the gas turbine nor the rotary engine were able to displace the well-tried piston unit; and car design as a whole continued to be a question of steadily refining the orthodox to provide higher standards of performance, road-holding and general comfort. By the mid-seventies an ordinary small car of, say, 1100 cc could reach 90 mph, handle as well as a sports car once did, and be endowed with such creature comforts as good heating, demisting and stereophonic radio. Yet in this process, the notion of what was orthodox went through a number of permutations.

In 1950, for example, most mass-produced cars were still built on the old Panhard layout of engine, clutch, gearbox and drive to the rear wheels. But then came a grown-up version of the 4CV in the shape of the Renault Dauphine, which sold enormously well in the States until the market for it suddenly collapsed in 1960. In the top-selling league, Fiat followed suit with a rear-engined 600 and 500, though they retained the classic front engine – rear drive layout in their larger models before settling on front engine – front wheel drive for the 128, 127 and subsequently the Ritmo. This east-west formula, which was first popularised by the Mini, became accepted as the most suitable small car layout with the advent of a new generation of VWs in 1974, and has now been adopted by nearly all major manufac-

the company's policy at that time that these cars should be recognisably British and designed primarily for the home market. The sporty British image of the MG *(above,* advertised in 1953), on the other hand, was what put this model in the vanguard of the sports car invasion of the States in the 1950s and early '60s.

turers, even if they have retained a preference for rear-wheel-push rather than front-wheel-pull in their larger models.

Gear-shifts came down off the steering wheel, where they never should have been, except in American cars built to seat three in front – and which soon moved over to two-pedal drive anyway. Yet whereas 90 percent of U.S. cars featured automatic drive (General Motors, for instance, made all their cars automatic, so that manual shift was a piece of optional equipment that had to be specially ordered), the opposite was the case in Europe, with its smaller engines that lacked the power to stir away at hydraulic fluids up mountainous roads. Some manufacturers offered

Industrial illness: under the effects of stop/go economic policies, automation, weak management or militant unions, the European car industry has had more than its share of labour unrest in the past 25 years.

automatic boxes as an alternative, but Europe has never been convinced by two-pedal driving, particularly Italy, whose citizens like to nip around *con brio*, and consider that to remove a man's gear shift is tantamount to depriving him of his political rights (or his masculinity?).

As performance increased, suspension and steering improved. There was some clever and innovative design by Alec Moulton, first with hydro-elastic and then with compressed nitrogen gas, as seen on the Allegro; Citroën produced some sumptuously complicated hydraulics on the DS and GS; but on the whole manufacturers continued to flex lengths of steel in torsion or coil, and progressively achieved that elusive compromise between comfortable ride and handling ability. The MacPherson strut front suspension was generally adopted, while rack-and-pinion steering replaced the recirculating ball and other systems. Radial tyres, with higher ratings for speed, showed their advantage over the old cross-ply. Disc brakes, so long scorned by Rolls-Royce, spread from competition cars into the most mundane saloons. Development rather than innovation was the watchword, for the enormous cost of tooling up meant that innovative risks could not lightly be taken. Even such immensely applauded essays in individuality as the DS Citroën were financially unrewarding, and it is said that when Ford took a Mini to pieces and costed each item, they came to the conclusion that there was no way in which it could be made at a profit – as British Leyland found to their chagrin.

Once they had consolidated their home markets, the big prize for European firms lay across the Atlantic – for though Americans might total only 5.7 percent of the earth's population, they owned 46 percent of the world's cars. Following the expeditionary force of sports cars (MGs, Triumphs, Porches and Jaguars which sallied forth like Davids to harass the home-grown Goliaths, like the Mustang and Barracuda which were selling increasingly well), the foreign invasion of the States was spearheaded by Renault, VW and Fiat. Within a comparatively short time Beetles and Dauphines, and a few open Friskies, were nipping between the yellow taxis in Manhattan. That it was a tough marketing proposition Renault quickly discovered

when some 60,000 Dauphines stood around in open-air parking sites slowly decomposing; nevertheless more than 400,000 foreign cars were imported in 1963 when the boom really began to get under way, and by 1967 one out of every fifteen American buyers chose a foreign-made vehicle.

Familiar sights were lockouts *(far left,* at Dagenham in 1956), empty shop floors *(centre,* Ford's assembly line at a standstill in 1962) and protest marches *(above,* by Renault workers in 1960).

Their reasons for choosing them varied, but chiefly it was to save on running costs. Multi-car families discovered that an inexpensive but reliable small car was an attractive proposition in city traffic. It was a new trend which only American Motors with their Rambler series, among the domestic manufacturers, took to heart. The big league, who had always tended to equate price with size and power, dealt rather summarily with the matter by rushing some not very convincing compacts into production, such as Chevrolet's aluminium, air-cooled, rear-engined Corvair (which was something of a disaster), the Ford Falcon and the Plymouth Valiant. In their eyes the small car – or sub-compact as they called it – was a passing phase. The immediate demand they met by making arrangements for such models to be built for them abroad: a new form of badge engineering known as captive imports. Meanwhile Volkswagen were notching up huge sales figures on their very doorstep, and continued to breed even more prolifically after the introduction of their Rabbit (surely a rare piece of teutonic humour there?). But by then, as we shall see, the dinosaurs of the road were facing an evolutionary crisis.

THE CAR AS ART

Bulbous baroque: in fact, one of the more sedate examples of Detroit styling, this Cadillac coupe of 1951 *(above),* though still awash with chrome and curious protuberances. In due course grilles were to grow even more ferocious and rear ends sprout huge fishtail fins.

Until mid-century, cars had maintained a national identity. Britain still clung nostalgically (at least at the top end of the market) to the tradition of craftsmanship and *ancien régime* elegance, with leather upholstery, walnut dashboards and P100 headlamps but the end was in sight for the traditional concept of coach-building. The post-war generation wanted something quite different, and neither Coventry nor Cowley knew quite how to provide it. Nor, it seemed, did the French: while lacking the charm of classical proportions, their cars still had an old-fashioned look. And the early post-war offerings from Germany were uninspiring too. Clearly the moment for the stylist had come, and at the time there were two distinct schools to choose from: Detroit and Turin. Harley Earl, chief of General Motors' styling section, writing in 1954, called automobile design 'an elusive task'.

Too elusive perhaps, for the transatlantic line had degenerated from the purity of 1940 into a bulbous baroque: one recalls those huge horizontal grilles filled with chromium dentures, the almost floral Pre-Raphaelite strips down the side, the three-colour paint jobs, the fake air-intakes on the rear fenders of the Cadillac, Buick's portholes, the whitewall tyres. 'I have been deeply affected by airplanes', confessed Harley Earl. 'I was so excited by the P-38 Lockheed Lightning when I first saw it that I contrived a viewing for members of my staff. That viewing blossomed out in the Cadillac fishtail fenders.' They caught on with the public, he added, because 'owners realised that it gave them an extra receipt for their money in the form of a visible prestige marking for an expensive car'. And there, in that slightly curious reasoning, lay the key to Detroit's philosophy of styling. Whether it was a response to the marketing department, the engineers or the motivational psychologists, styling ultimately boiled down to the aggregate of 'features', ideally ones that at a glance yelled luxury.

The Italians for their part, though well grounded in engineering, preferred to approach the whole business from an aesthetic point of view and to aim for unity of design. Their cars consequently were sleeker, smoother, more sculptured. Piero Dusio's Cisitalia (with bodywork by Pininfarina) is generally regarded as having initiated the Italian 'new look' in 1947: an example of this masterpiece is now preserved in New York's Museum of

Modern Art as 'one of the eight most important cars in the world'. And Bertone's BAT (short for Berlinetta Aerodinamica Tecnica), far-fetched though it was, was a stunningly beautiful exercise showing just what could be done. Both Giovanni Bertone and G.B. Pinin Farina (his names got elided in due course) had begun as specialist coach-builders before the war and then moved up into series production. Bertone had become internationally recognised for his work on Alfa Romeo's Giulietta Sprint coupe, Pinin Farina for the aerodynamic fixed head coupe (one of his favourite themes) on the 1937 Aprilia chassis and the open Alfa Romeo 2900C, which was surely one of the loveliest cars of its day.

The Cisitalia Coupe focussed attention on Turin and soon executives from much of the motoring world were catching a plane to Caselle airport. Pi-

Classic Cisitalia: the initiator of the Italian 'new look' which was to have a profound effect on world car design, Piero Dusio's 1947 Cisitalia Coupe *(above)* with bodywork by G.B. Pininfarina *(below)*. As his drawings *(left)* illustrate, he approached design problems from an aesthetic point of view.

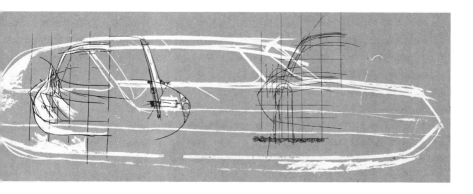

Cool lady, enigmatic driver: Lichten-stein's 1963 comic-strip parody *In the Car (right)*. An even cooler lady appears in Kit Williams' *'Distress Call' (below)*. Has the Morris Minor broken down, or has she deliberately chosen this unfortunate spot to sun-bathe?

These shoes are made for driving: 150 soles – not to mention countless ceramics, seashells, buttons, ash-trays, combs and hair brushes – went into the adornment of Don Palwell's customised car, photo-graphed here in San Francisco in 1975.

ninfarina began collaborating with major manufacturers: he designed the 1952 Nash-Healey, the 1950 Lancia Aurelia (which, though the front didn't match the back, became the saloon that everyone wanted to emu-late), various Alfa Romeo and Fiat coupes and almost all Ferraris, and beginning with the 403 all Peugeots. BMC followed suit with the Austin Cambridge and the A40, a clever design that anticipated the hatch-back solution. The Cadillac Eldorado coupe was yet another of Pininfarina's efforts.

But since there was a limit to the capacity of any single firm, and foreign manufacturers were pressing to sign national exclusivity contracts, the net had to be cast wider. Chrysler came to an arrangement with Ing. Segri of Ghia to build a number of prototypes; other manufacturers sought inspira-tion from Allemano, Vignale, Fissore, Boneschi, Superleggera-Touring, and Viotti. Yet in many cases the designing was being done by one single man. Giovanni Michelotti first gained recognition with the Frisky minicar which was unveiled at the Geneva Motorshow in March 1957. It was, rather significantly, the first attempt to offer a meccano-set mini that could be built in the Third World, designed around a tubular chassis and fibreglass body

that could be constructed on the spot, meaning that only the more sophisticated components had to be brought in from abroad. Since he was both an engineer and an artist, Michelotti's designs were at once functional and beautiful. And he worked very quickly, turning out an average of one new model a day. But he was always punctilious to interpret his clients' instructions, even if he disagreed with their ideas – though after the directors of Standard had approved one of his designs (all very British) destined to replace the Standard Ten, the chief engineer who had stayed behind noticed Michelotti gazing very sceptically at their choice. Risking the sack, he persuaded the designer to draw the car as *he* thought it should be. The car devised in a single afternoon was the Triumph Herald, which introduced a new, Italian sparkle to British family motoring, and still looked up-to-date a dozen years later.

Since the fifties this handful of men in Turin – Pininfarina, Bertone, Michelotti, and later Giorgio Giugiaro of Ital Design – have virtually dictated the outward shape of motoring. Incredible, come to think of it, that cars as different as the BMW and the DAF, the Japanese Hino (which joined Toyota in 1967) and the Triumph TR7 should all have sprung from the same quick-

Good crop of cars: *Cadillac Ranch in Amarillo* is the title of Ant Farm's satirical collage. Doubtless it is quicker, easier and more profitable to produce an automobile than it ever was to raise a good head of beef.

Self-expression *(left)*. Nowadays it requires nothing more sophisticated than an air brush and some acryllic paint – or indeed some strong glue, some fur, foam rubber or assorted sea-shells – to adapt your vehicle to match your personality.

187

moving pencil; that Rolls-Royce, Ferrari and Austin should share the same tailor; that Ford's prestige models should bear the label of Ghia, and that the new generation of VWs (like the Alfasud, the Morris Ital and so many others) should be moulded by Ital Design.

Even as the artists of Turin were attempting to turn the automobile into a work of art and assemble its components into a sculpture, artists elsewhere were creating works of art out of the automobile and fashioning sculptures out of its component parts. The car has fascinated modern artists more than any other ingredient in our consumer-oriented society (and that includes soup cans). Of course art and the automobile have always been closely related, if only because the painter could communicate the chosen image of a model to the public better than a photographer could; between the wars, for example, manufacturers often insisted that any human beings cluttering up an advert should be diminished in scale, so that their car could appear bigger and more dominant. These artists were almost exclusively naturalistic, glorifying the car in loving detail.

In the 1960s a new generation of artists continued to celebrate the car on canvas, but from a variety of new perspectives. The high priests of Pop Art gleefully selected the automobile as one of the gaudy, ephemeral elements of the consumer society with which to make their statement. With his *In the Car*, a parody of a strip cartoon frozen in mid-sequence, Lichtenstein mocks the pretensions of the automobile. Warhol, by repeating a news photograph of a particularly gory crash in *Green Disaster,* underlines how quickly we become immune to the shock of the car's lethal power. Rosenquist's vast close-ups of small sections of the automobile serve to remind us that its glamour is only as deep as a few coats of paint. Other artists found their inspiration in the pseudo-sexual symbolism of the adverts, in the synthetic glitter of roadside car-scapes, or in the metal jungle of automobile graveyards. Indeed the very cars themselves sometimes provided the raw materials for a work of art: an old tyre and a car-door, for instance, for Rauschenberg's *Dylaby,* while the French artist César's own special medium was a giant car crusher – by feeding in different coloured cars, or parts thereof, he would manipulate the tone and texture of the finished metal cube, his sculpture.

While the artists and sculptors were making us stop, look at and think about the bland stereotypes of the motor age, the custom car addicts were

For the housebound motorist, Phil Garner's auto-derivative furniture *(top,* a Chrysler-chimneypiece and *above,* a Chevrolet-couch) must be very comforting. Alternatively the car-bound homelover can transform his van into a chalet *(opposite, far right).* Other ways to express your individuality might be to weld together a 'beetle-bus' *(centre)* or else tile your van and mount a perspex dome on top *(right).*

At its best, customising can combine humour and airbrush artistry, like this exhibit *(left)* at a London custom car show in 1980. On a more basic level

busy in their own backyards chopping and channelling standard models in search of their own brand of individuality. The hybrids thus produced by acetylene torch and arc-welder were eye-catching, and in the hands of the more accomplished customisers they became something of an art-form in their own right, not to be driven on the highway but to be exhibited (as they still are) at custom car rallies. They were known as 'alternative cars', one of the earliest appearances of that all-embracing word in the context of life-styles; but they were not a reaction against Detroit (indeed some manufacturers soon made a point of producing cars that were easy to customise), they were, as Tom Wolfe suggested, a reaction against the Mondrian principle, the geometry that was penetrating so much of contemporary design.

The cult spread like a bush-fire, until 'alternatives' were almost rolling off a production line (not unlike, come to think of it, Pininfarina's 'specials' for Fiat before the war). It is already big business, with thousands of clubs for enthusiasts, monthly magazines, and custom supermarkets. Even on the humblest level a motorist can express himself through his car, even if the racing trim is a transfer, the snappy slogans are someone else's brainwaves, and the stick-on badges are from places he has never heard of.

there are an infinite variety of stickers on sale *(above)* to prove your beetle gets about a bit.

THE SEARCH FOR SPEED

Great names in motor-racing, at the threshold of the sport's last truly dashing decade, the 1950s. The German racer Hans Stuck is seen at the wheel of his Alfa Romeo at the start of the 1949 Monza 1,000 kilometres. Stucks's racing career ran from the 1930s to the year 1960. Alfa Romeo was a consistent winner of championships until 1951. And Monza has been, since 1922, the showplace of countless Grand Prix contests.

Old motor-racing sweats, looking back, still regard the fifties as the last great romantic decade of racing, when hard commercialism was not the final criterion and heavy-money sponsorship was not the guiding principle. It was the age of Farina, Ascari and Juan Manuel Fangio, five times world champion in eight years. The best classroom of all for any racing driver was about two car-lengths behind Fangio, claimed Stirling Moss who, with Mike Hawthorn and Peter Collins, led the vanguard of a new and spectacular generation of British Grand Prix drivers. The world championship was inaugurated in 1950, and that year Alfa Romeo swept all before them as they had done consistently since the war (with the exception of 1949 when they withdrew from racing after the deaths of Wimille and Count Trossi). So too in 1951, but with increasing pressure from an upstart new marque. Enzo Ferrari's cars racing under the insignia of the prancing horse had already had successes in the Targa Florio, Mille Miglia and at Le Mans in 1949, but his heart was set on GP racing and there in the early years the Ferraris seemed always to be chasing Alfas and Maseratis, if not their own tails. But in 1951 at the British Grand Prix at Silverstone, the stranglehold of the supercharger – so long an article of faith in grand prix racing – was broken, and a Ferrari beat the Alfa Romeos, who chose the end of that season to withdraw from racing with their championship record still intact. For the next two years Ferrari became the name to beat, until Mercedes returned to the fray with a new breed of Silver Arrow and bristling efficiency (an astonishing sight was to see the mechanics form up and be marched off the curbside café for their tea-break).

Each year lap records tumbled and average speeds crept upwards, but not without extracting a heavy tithe. In 1955 Le Mans witnessed racing's worst

disaster to date, when Pierre Levegh's Mercedes rocketed into the crowd killing the driver and eighty spectators. That same year racing ended at the Irish road course at Dundrod because of a fatal multiple pile-up; and Alberto Ascari, having nose-dived into the sea during the Monaco Grand Prix virtually unscathed, crashed to his death at Monza only four days later. In 1957 the Marquis de Portago's Ferrari drove into the crowd during the Mille Miglia and killed eleven people, a tragedy that spelled the end of this most romantic of all road races. But speed, as Aldous Huxley remarked, is the only genuinely modern pleasure – and in pursuit of it men continued to drive to the margin and continued to fashion machines in its devotion.

One of the most electrifying newcomers was the Cooper. Father and son, the Coopers had graduated from their 'blacksmith's shop' 500 cc to a rear-engined sports model powered by a Coventry Climax engine, which in turn was developed into a Formula One machine with superb road-holding that enabled the Australian Jack Brabham to walk off with both the 1959 and 1960 world championships. Such was its impact that of the starters that

Another face of the motor-racing sport is seen in this photo of Mike Beuttler taken in more recent years. The stripped-down simplicity of the old days (as in opposite picture) is gone: the sport has become professionalized and commercialized – as can be seen in the ornate, glistening gear, the emblazoning of the driver's name (for television viewers?) and above all the advertising of various products and marques, nowadays so essential to the support of racing.

lined up on the grid for the 1960 Grand Prix at Rheims, no less than ten were mounted on Coopers. Another seven were also on British machines, three BRMs, three Lotus and a Vanwall – and to complement them were three imminent world champions: Phil Hill, the only American to take these laurels (in 1961), Graham Hill (1962) and the unassuming sheep-farmer from Scotland Jim Clark (1963 and 1965), who was also the first foreigner to break the American grip on the Indianapolis 500 for half a century.

Speed was also getting increasingly expensive, as Ford discovered for themselves. Noting the commercial benefit that accrued to Jaguar after five

Sunday Dispatch

151th Year. No. 8,010. 2½d. JUNE 12, 1955. TV & Radio Page 6

The Most Callous Sports Event Ever
70 DIE IN RACE HORROR
But The Le Mans Twenty-Four Hour Car Contest I
Still Continuing

AT least 70 spectators, including many women and children, were killed and 75 injured last night when one of the cars in the Le Mans 24-hour race crashed into the crowd lining the track and burst into flames. But, despite the disaster, the race is still continuing. It will end this afternoon.

The car, a Mercedes driven by Pierre Levegh, who was killed, tried to pass an Austin Healey with 35-year-old Londoner Lance Macklin at the wheel. The cars touched, and the Mercedes heeled across the track and smashed into the protective barrier in front of the stands. Macklin escaped with minor injuries.

The engine and back axle of the Mercedes sliced like a razor through the packed spectators. Some were decapitated, and for 100 yards along the straight the scene was like a bloodstained battlefield.

Wailing men and women tried frantically to find out whether their friends or relations were among the victims.

Police, doctors, nurses, and first-aid men took nearly two hours to remove the dead and injured.

Spectators Faint

Secrets Of The Harem

NOTHING conjures up more fabulous visions of glamour, romance, and riches than the mystic word HAREM. Many people immediately think of

Some of the dead and injured inside the enclosure.

Moment of tragedy *(above):* the camera captures the last split-second for Jean Behra, who was killed when his car spun off the Avers circuit in 1965 and he was thrown into a concrete post.

Motor racing's worst-ever disaster *(right)* occurred at the 1955 Le Mans 24-hour race, when Pierre Levegh's car crashed into spectators.

consecutive wins in the Le Mans 24-hour during the fifties, Henry Ford II decided to break the unofficial arrangement among American manufacturers to abstain from racing, and in 1962 made a bid for Ferrari. It was accepted, but the deal floundered. Then, almost in pique, Ford decided, regardless of expense, to beat Ferrari at his own game and threw down the gauntlet (in the shape of their GT40) to initiate one of the classic duels of the post-war scene. The first two seasons were fiascos, with none of the GT40s staying the course for 24 hours at Le Mans; but in 1966 corporate muscle and computer technology finally ended Ferrari's five-year reign. Mark 2 Fords came in triumphantly 1−2−3, but the effort had cost the company an estimated $15 million.

It proved that money could achieve results, and it also underlined the degree to which motor-racing was becoming big business. Not only was its popularity spreading world-wide (the South African GP became a championship event in 1962, the Tasman Series opened in Australia in 1964), but television was transforming it into a major spectator sport – second in America only to baseball. Nor did this escape the notice of the advertising world. Sponsorship had been rampant at Indianapolis since the fifties, but in the mid-sixties the national emblems which had been *de rigueur* on the circuits of Europe began to give way to advertisements for after-shave, to-

bacco, even in due course contraceptives. Getting the Grand Prix circus on the road cost some £3 million each year, half of which began to come from sponsors' pockets. Accordingly the successful drivers became key elements in this promotion and superstars in their own right, champions like the highly articulate Jackie Stewart, the Brazilian 'bomb' Emerson Fittipaldi, the courageous Nicki Lauda who returned to the track after a near-fatal accident, the debonair James Hunt (once known as 'Hunt the Shunt' for his crashing propensity). The rewards were enormous, but drivers were severely professional in their approach to the modern sport where just a couple of seconds could mean the difference between pole position on the starting grid and barely qualifying, and (through their 'union', the Grand Prix Drivers Association) took a close interest in the improvement of safety measures. Out of 32 drivers who had won Grand Prix in the first twenty years of the world championship, eight had lost their lives; and as Jackie Stewart once pointed out, 'I'm not paid to risk my life. I'm paid to drive a racing car as fast as I can. And to live to drive another day.'

The same technical intensity infused the select band of men who foregathered from time to time at the Bonneville salt flats in Utah, courting the world's land speed record (Daytona had been abandoned in the mid-thirties for erring two inches in a hundred feet, a flaw that could prove fatal as

Another crack-up: Monza, March 1970. Pica's car is seen flipping over, about to leap up into the air, having struck Bianchi (in car at right). Though some drivers may feel attracted to the danger inherent in the sport, others such as Jackie Stewart feel differently: 'I'm not paid to risk my life', says Stewart. 'I'm paid to drive a racing car as fast as I can. And to live to drive another day.'

speeds got more outrageous). In 1947 John Cobb had taken his Railton back to Bonneville in the hope of topping the 400 mph mark; on one run he did so, but had to content himself with a mean of 394.2 mph. And there matters rested, curiously enough, for fifteen years until Donald Campbell lifted it to 403.10 mph in his turbine-powered Bluebird, after four gremlin-ridden years of effort. Even then he was not the fastest man in the world, since the previous year the American Craig Breedlove had averaged 4 mph faster in his Spirit of America: European authorities, however, rather snootily regarded this as the motorcycle record seeing that he had done it on three wheels instead of four.

Breedlove's machine was also jet-powered and – with or without Europe's approval – it was this form of propulsion that was to send the speed record sky-high. Between October 1964 and November 1965 Breedlove, and Art Arfons in his Green Monster (very aptly named except that it was painted red, white and blue), were to lift the record beyond 600 mph and surely out of reach of the petrol engine. Indeed they looked more like aeroplanes on wheel, these creations, with their nose-cones, tail-fins and parachute brakes. Yet even they were to be eclipsed in 1970 when Gary Gabelich (a test astronaut) brought record-hunting into the space age with his rocket-powered Blue Flame. Over the measured mile of salt, in just over eleven seconds there and back, he was timed at an average of 622.41 mph (which meant that the 1,000 kph mark had been passed), and the sound barrier was in sight.

Somewhere between the traditional sport of motor-racing and the calculated dedication to absolute speed, there evolved (from the street racers of the fifties, as we have seen) the ever-growing sport of drag racing in which two machines are matched over a quarter-mile straight, squirting from a standing start with mind-blowing acceleration. To watch is to submit voluntarily to an explosive assault on the senses, as the 1,000 hp engines scream away in a burst of orange flame and all-enveloping smoke. The long, needle-like machines fed on nitro-methane regularly complete the course in six seconds and reach speeds up to 300 mph; the drivers, whose weight is doubled as they are forced back into their special seats, have to be padded, masked and protected against fumes and fire. Accidents, as it happens, are rare, but inasmuch as these machines are neither designed to go round corners nor equipped for anything but sheer acceleration, it is

Stock car racing is a picturesque aspect of the sport of speed racing. In the United States it usually emphasises speed, as in the 'Grand National', with speeds over 200 mph. European circuits (as above) feature outlandish models salvaged from the scrap-heap, which plough into one another at will.

Drag racing drivers (right) need elaborate gear: fireproof clothing and gloves, helmet and breathing mask to protect them from the fumes of the fuel used in their explosive 1,000 hp engines. Racing on a quarter-mile straight, they reach speeds up to 300 mph.

truly a pastime that represents the ultimate deification of the automobile engine.

Stock car racing, on the other hand, is more an offshoot of the mass-production line and a way of life that (in America in the mid-sixties) built over 9 million autos annually and scrapped more than 7½ million. In its several manifestations it can vary from the American-style 'Grand National', where special production cars elbow each other round steeply-banked tracks at speeds in excess of 200 mph, to the souped-up bangers of the European circuits where anything goes. In the latter, the contestants often look as if they should have been on the scrap-heap even before they

reached the starting-line. Of the other forms of motorised sport, go-carting caught on in the late fifties, and continues by virtue of being a cheap and popular way of racing at speeds well over 100 mph; an autocross, a form of cross-country speed-trial against the stop-watch, and the rather lengthier rally-cross now rival the traditional and rather more dignified hillclimbs, and give the ordinary enthusiast his weekly share of 'mud, sweat and cheers.' In contrast, the great international rallies have become highly specialised events: some of the classics have survived – the Acropolis, the Lombard RAC, the East African Safari, the Monte Carlo (though that had to be cancelled during the 1973 oil crisis) – and have been joined by new adventures like the London-Sydney in 1968 and the World Cup rally to Mexico in 1970. These marathons, were wonderful showcases for the successful manufacturers and were undoubtedly the toughest rallies ever devised. But they were also the most expensive, and it is noticeable that in the last ten years no-one has rushed forward to sponsor another one.

Unfamiliar rig-out for a Rolls-Royce Silver Shadow *(above),* competing in the 1970 World Cup rally from London to Mexico. It proved to be perhaps the toughest rally ever devised, over 16,000 miles of testing roads sometimes at an altitude of more than 10,000 feet. Only 23 out of the 96 starters reached Mexico: it was won by Hannu Mikkola in a Ford.

COUNTRIES FIT FOR CARS ?

Approaching the second century of motoring, developed countries have had to face up to the realities of
living with the car, and to the vulnerability of its
source of power – oil. Its benefits are so obvious that
the automobile has become totally ingrained in the
fabric of our lives, but its very pervasiveness has
finally provoked concerted accusations of danger,
pollution and squandering of natural resources –
among other things. Somewhat belatedly governments have been forced to intervene to control its
production and its use. The twentieth century's
'love-affair with the automobile' has passed through
its adolescent passion and settled into a mutual
co-existence that often seems increasingly uneasy.
There is no question of a separation, of course; just
an ordering of priorities. Motor-cars – outside the
sports tracks and custom-car exhibitions – may not
be so much fun as they once were, but they are no
less of a challenge.

Like the bones of cattle that have perished in the parched wastes, the carcasses of abandoned cars litter a desert in California *(below)*. Automobiles have ceased to be cherished possessions for their own sakes: now they can be discarded, at least traded in, annually under the dictates of planned obsolescence. They are stolen too, at a rate of one every few minutes in America — not for their resale value, but simply as an appropriation of the common currency of travel.

LIVING WITH THE CAR

The omnivorous motor-car? In fact a 'miracle car' (called Herbie) made specially for Walt Disney by Volkswagen, which could smile, talk and wink. But whatever the screen image of the motor car, in the seventies western countries were forced to face up to the harsh economic realities of the automobile age.

Modern motoring presents us with a series of paradoxes, none of which have we yet succeeded in resolving. All of them spring from the simple fact that, in an exceptionally short space of time, the automobile has become an indispensable part of our lives. Its development, particularly in the last sixty years, has accelerated so fast that its problems have literally overtaken us before we were fully aware of them. Only in the last decade have we begun — or been forced — to recognise the magnitude of what faces us. From its earliest days the car was recognised as a great 'liberator', an extension of the home, opening up new horizons and promising new ways of life. But while this is certainly true of individual cars, multiplying each one several million times has the opposite effect. For giving us almost unlimited access to the remotest parts of the countryside, for instance, the car has extracted a high price: in Britain considerably more than 1 million acres are now buried, presumably for all time, beneath tarmac or concrete. In America the network of interstate highways alone has devoured 1.75 million acres. And the tendency of all these thousands of miles of highway, ironically, is not to disperse people throughout the countryside but to channel them and concentrate them in certain areas, usually areas of great natural beauty. The car has thus helped to devalue the very amenities it made possible to enjoy.

Just as the railways achieved a peak of expansion in the third quarter of the last century, so there are signs today that the major phase of road-building is passing. Of course there will be roads built in years to come, but some authorities believe that in most western countries the pattern for roads for the future is now set. The gospel of the sixties, that we should build more and more roads to accommodate more and more cars, has few adherents today; and the economic argument, that new roads would be a lifeline for depressed areas by bringing in new industries, is far from being proved. In reality, new roads tend to centralise industry still further and help prosperous centres to extend their business at the expense of others.

Which leads us to yet another paradox. In extending the 'commuting' process begun by the railways, cars have made it possible for more people to choose to live well away from their places of work. New, and often very pleasant, suburbs have been created — with the car as the main link with the city centres. The result is that many urban areas have become de-humanised business centres, with no social or cultural focus or, worse still, grey acres of slums. Those cities which were developed in the pre-automobile era now find themselves strangled by the daily in flux of cars, and until relatively recently there was the added absurdity that the more crowded city streets became, the longer, wider and faster the cars became. Congestion is scarcely a modern problem; nearly two thousand years ago Juve-

Hunks of junk: the end of the road for thousands of obsolescent cars in a graveyard near Berlin. The inevitable outcome of mass production – and national economies depending on the motor industry – is mass destruction.

Carate chop. A miscalculation by a motorist in Tokyo, where the traffic problem is so acute that residents have taken to converting their apartments into parking lots.

nal was complaining bitterly about the traffic jams in Rome. But the modern, and massive, migration of the car is more than an inconvenience, it is an environmental catastrophe. In its wake has come a new science, that of traffic engineering, which seeks primarily to find ways of keeping urban transport on the move, however slowly. Zoning, tidal flows, integrated traffic signals, bus lanes, computerised systems – all are currently in the traffic engineers' armoury, yet no-one would pretend they are doing more than deferring the day of reckoning.

The dilemma is much more fundamental: it is, in crude terms, whether our cities can survive the car. There are those who say they can't, at least not the traditional, high-density, 'vertical' cities like Paris, New York or London, and that the cities of the future will have to be horizontal, low-density, recognising that mobility is the keynote to progress. Such cities exist, of course, of which Los Angeles (where traffic hurtles along some freeways at the rate of 300 vehicles a minute) is the best-known, but by no means the only, example.

This vision, not to mention our experience to date, of the motorised metropolis is not encouraging. There are real practical drawbacks, like automobile smog (of which more later) and the sprawling pollution of commercialism dedicated to servicing cars and their occupants – that Lewis Mumford once described as 'degraded urban tissue' – springing up along our roadsides in what might otherwise be semi-rural areas. But the over-riding problem is that the car dictates a new form of social organisation; at one and the same time it is the instrument that keeps us in touch with

Spaghetti junction, Europe's largest motorway interchange outside Birmingham. It cost more than 40 million, has thirteen miles of elevated highway, and was opened in May 1972.

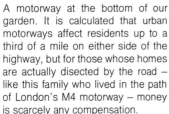

A motorway at the bottom of our garden. It is calculated that urban motorways affect residents up to a third of a mile on either side of the highway, but for those whose homes are actually disected by the road – like this family who lived in the path of London's M4 motorway – money is scarcely any compensation.

other people and other places, and also segregates us. Urban areas become suburbs in search of a city, suburbs become islands stranded on a network of roads, while rural areas simply get eaten up. Not to own an automobile under such circumstances is to be socially deprived, not just because of the distances involved but because basic amenities like shopping areas get concentrated into immense hypermarkets, to which access is primarily by car.

Besides, there is the inescapable fact that the vast majority of people happen to live already in older cities, products of an age when life was conducted at walking pace. These are the cities, it was once argued, that would have to 'adapt' to the car. For those planners, particularly in Western Europe, who had seen huge areas of ancient cities razed to the ground by air raids during the war, it was perfectly credible to bulldoze further areas to provide the new roads that were needed. The post-war years were preoccupied with anxious predictions and ambitious projects: but the predictions were based on two dubious (and in due course discredited) premises: that the growth of car ownership would be in line with economic growth, and that there would be a 'saturation point' beyond which the proportion of cars to population would not increase. Such thinking has now been respectfully interred, but we live with its legacy: there are more cars on our roads than we ever dreamed of. The truth is that new roads simply gener-

'Nothing wrong at all, thank you, officer – its just that I'm a terribly slow reader.'

ate more traffic. This phenomenon was dimly perceived even before the war, but now we can fully appreciate the vicious spiral that this creates: more cars make alternative transport (buses, trains, etc.) less efficient and less economical, which in turn creates a demand for more cars.

Obviously this philosophy of making cities fit for cars was based on the assumption that the car (and other vehicles) was the cornerstone of economic survival. People once said the same about railways, and much the same sort of claim, one suspects, is beginning to be made for the microchip. There are powerful factors – industrial decline, oil crises pollution problems – which are demanding new perspectives on the automobile's place in the scheme of things. But there are also signs that personal attitudes towards the car are changing radically, and in the end it is these that will determine long-term policy and planning.

The received idea of the motorist as a member of some semi-exclusive club no longer applies. In any conflict of interests nowadays the motorist may well find himself on both sides of the argument, since he is also a home-owner and a pedestrian, when he is not driving his car. When surveys began to investigate travel patterns by 'number of journeys' rather than 'distance', walking emerged very high on the lists. In other words the motorist is also a victim of the effects of the car, and this is reflected by a growing concern for the environment. It cannot be pure altruism that prompts 86

So familiar have the visual scars of our contemporary roadsides become that we scarcely notice them any longer, the arrows and the signs and the lights that pre-determine our progress from one place to another, the forests of pillars and posts and parking meters. Even in a small town in Switzerland (Lucerne, where these pictures were taken) efforts to control the motor-car have become a blight on the beauty of the surrounding countryside. No longer is it automatically thought desirable to build more

roads to accommodate more cars: the science of traffic engineering has had to resort to a campaign of containment, attempting like Canute to stem the ever-increasing tide of automobiles.

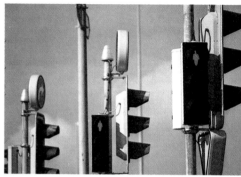

percent of motorists responding to a Gallup survey in Britain to agree that 'limitations on the use of cars in larger towns will be necessary in the future', or 75 percent in another (Metra) survey to declare that 'the use of motor vehicles in towns must be controlled even more in order to protect the environment'. It is easy enough to give virtuous answers to a questionnaire of course, yet when such opinions do percolate through to policymakers, surprising things happen, as the Washington Square Gardens scheme proved. In deference to New Yorkers' protests, a plan to build a super highway through the square was dropped and the existing road actually was closed. Instead of the predicted chaos in adjoining streets, it transpired that many of the surrounding roads experienced a decrease in traffic!

Such examples are rare, however, and we are very far from resolving the environmental issues, whether they be questions of landscaping, noise congestion or danger. Even non-motorists are pre-conditioned to accept the visual scars of the motor era – forests of traffic signs, lights, parking metres, roadmarkings, and hoardings. The cacophony of car-horns in many continental cities seems to be built into the very fabric of life. And even on such basic matters as road safety we have a remarkably ambivalent attitude. Everyone is in favour of it, of course, provided it doesn't interfere with personal liberties (which is the argument put forward against compulsory seatbelts) and provided it doesn't affect the performance of the car (which is the tacit reason why built-in safety features are slow in appearing on the market). The problem anyway is what constitutes an effective safety feature. Considerable research was conducted in the early seventies into the possibility of equipping cars with air bags that would inflate in less than 40 milliseconds when their triggering mechanism sensed a 'crash situation' – the drawback was that the impact of the bag on the passenger was estimated to be five or six times more violent than having a football kicked at you by a professional footballer!

Many other worthy ideas have been tried out, and in response to

Safety campaigns, research programmes and demonstrations (like this one below, organised by the British Safety Council in 1960 to show the effectiveness of seat-belts) have continued throughout the motor-car's career. In the mid-1960s the momentum was increased, partly through the publication of Ralph Nader's book *Unsafe at Any Speed* which maintained that 'potential safety advances are subordinated to other investments, priorities, preferences and themes designed to maximise profit'. Manufacturers disputed some of his findings and conclusions, but public and official awareness of safety problems was increased and led to considerably more stringent safety legislation in many countries.

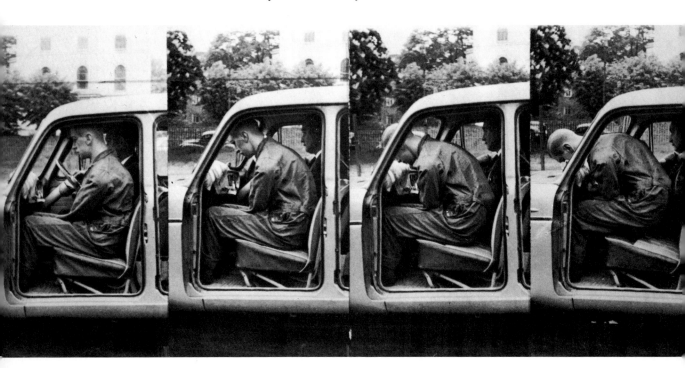

recent safety legislation car bodies are considerably tougher than they once were. But 'survivability' for the occupants of a car that crashes at, say, 50 mph is cold comfort for the pedestrian who gets knocked over at 50 mph. All the safety features in the world cannot compensate for one reckless moment or one incapable driver. Such legislation as has been concerned with fitness to drive (like compulsory driving test and the breathalyser) has always come belatedly, and modern studies on the psychology of driving show there are many questions left unanswered. There is nothing quite like a car for bringing out man's latent aggression, and under the present stressful conditions of the road it can turn all too easily into an offensive weapon. In this respect there is little in our motoring past to offer encouragement: advertising campaigns for cars (and petrol) have consistently played on the competitive instincts of the car-owner, and the machinery of the law – usually by lagging far behind the development of the motor vehicle – has scarcely engendered a respect among motorists for traffic regulations.

Man, it is commonly said, has had a twentieth-century love affair with the automobile, and perhaps it isn't such an inappropriate analogy. There was, after all, a courting period when he got to know and understand it; and a honeymoon period when it could do no wrong. Now, having lived with it for some time (as in all relationships) he is coming to appreciate its faults – even if these are of his own making. There are still times perhaps when the romance flickers and the excitement stirs, but there is a feeling that if he had known how things were going to turn out he might have organised things a bit better. There is no case for a divorce – even if there were a possibility – but only for a measure of independence.

Glamorous beginning, inglorious end: at its launch at the 1971 London Motor Show the new TVR *(above)* gets publicity from two stripped-down models. Less privileged machines, when redundant, simply feed the car-crusher.

COOPER CLIMAX

1960

You may point a finger at Porsche and even Rumpler, but it was the Cooper Climax that changed the whole face of motor-racing by switching the engine from the front to the back. By 1955 the Coopers, father and son, had progressed from their 500 cc 'black-smith's jobs' to produce a rear-engined sports model powered by a Coventry Climax unit, which in its turn was developed (via Formula 2) into a light, whippy Formula 1 machine with a tremendous power-to-weight ratio and superb road-holding. Jack Brabham drove the Type 60 Cooper with such gusto that he walked off with the World Championship in both 1959 and 1960. So electrifying, indeed, was the Cooper revolution – which counterpointed the commercial success of the rear-engined VWs and Porsches – that by 1961 Ferrari, Lotus and BRM had all gone over to the driver in front of engine layout. When Jack Brabham first took his 'funny car' (as the old guard at Indianapolis mockingly dubbed it) to the Brickyard, A.J. Foyt thought the Cooper looked like 'a bunch of pipes lashed up with chicken wire'. But he soon changed his tune when Brabham qualified at 145 mph (233 kph), which was only 2 mph slower than the pole man. Indeed, Cooper's design theories heralded a new technological era, which Lotus, thanks to Colin Chapman's greater science, was able to exploit to the full. But today's Formula 1 cars, no less than the humblest go-carts, find their genesis in the Coopers' basic logistics of driver and engine. Moreover by implementing Kamm's theory of turbulence and chopping off the tail of their sports car, the Coopers initiated the flat posterior school of styling that has been adopted by the Citroën GS and Giagiuro's Alfasud.

VW GOLF

1974

Maybe Farina's Austin A40 pointed the way towards a trend that started with the Primula and Fiat 127. Renault's R5 followed, and when VW finally dropped the Beetle to concentrate their efforts on the Golf (or Rabbit, as it is known in America), the day of the hatchback had come. A sensible, sprightly, economical vehicle for our energy-ridden times. The right formula for crowded roads, parking problems and radar speed-traps. In short, utilitarian transport for a pre-packaged society. An invitation to leave the XJ at home and have fun with superbrats like the GTI, Chevette 2300 or Sunbeam Lotus. The driving enjoyment is still there. What more could one want? Yes, the volume-produced car of today. Maybe it's just mobility for the masses in an impersonal world. Confirmation that the car is now a non-event like a Holiday Inn Hotel or a colour TV. Or simply that motorists have become realists rather than romantics? Of course, there will always be a demand for automobiles that look different, handle better, and have greater performance. There are still Silver Spurs and 924 Carreras for egos who don't mind being slaves of their own exotic machinery. But those of us who would prefer not to be clobbered by OPEC and the taxmen will probably opt for one of the smaller front-drives. Since it first took to the roads in 1974, the VW Golf – though a geometric exercise in Teutonic austerity – is the right sort of car for today. And seven years later, BL has paid it the compliment of turning out a very similar machine.

NSU RO 80

1967

In 1967 the porter of Stuttgart's leading hotel pointed at a svelte new NSU saloon and observed: 'By 1980 the others may have caught up with that.' The Ro80 was equipped with a twin Rotary Combustion engine.

By then, Wankel's revolutionary RC engine had been under development at Neckarsulm for over ten years, and licensees – such as Curtiss-Wright in the United States and Toyo Kogyo in Japan – had evolved various single, twin, three and four rotor units. Indeed NSU's own Spyder, fitted with a single rotor engine, went into production in 1964, followed by the Ro80, Toyo Kogyo's Mazda Cosmo sports car and the R100

coupé in 1969. Mercedes-Benz' experimental C111 sports coupé with a four-rotor engine gave 350 bhp at 7000 rpm, but was never put into production.

At the time, it seemed that an engine which revolved rather than reciprocated was an obvious step forward, particularly as the Wankel was a lot smaller and lighter than an equivalent piston engine. Moreover it was simple to maintain and almost vibrationless, thanks to the low torque fluctuations and absence of reciprocating masses. And if anything its performance potential was

greater up top. On the other hand, there were problems of sealing and exhaust emissions, but above all of uneconomical fuel consumption just at the time that the oil crisis was erupting. By 1980, therefore, the 'Others' had not yet decided to catch up – preferring to concentrate on refining the well-tried piston engine on which such a vast investment was centred. As things turned out, the Ro80 was a gallant failure. All the same, it was a pointer towards what the future may have in store. Let's see how the Mazda RX7 shapes up.

PLYMOUTH RELIANT

1981

Until the oil crunch came, U.S. manufacturers saw very little incentive to build small cars: for reasons of profit and tradition, they continued to turn out the glamorous gas-guzzlers that Americans loved. In fact Big Is Beautiful lasted right up to the end of 1978 (the third-best year in Detroit's history) when buyers suddenly switched their tune and foreign imports claimed 30 percent of the market. In 1980 Japan sold over 2 million cars in the United States, and the Japanese motor industry, still a fledgling only ten years previously, produced more

cars than America. Small Is Super was now the cry.

Against this background, Detroit counterattacked with new smaller models. General Motors brought out their compact X cars; Ford its new Escort and Mercury Lynx. Chrysler's contribution to the New Start was the entirely fresh K-body, 2 feet shorter than the Aspen/Volare it replaced, and powered by a new 2.2 litre four-cylinder engine driving the front wheels. The sharp

razor-edge styling of the Reliant (and even more so the Imperial) harks back to Gurney Nutting, Austin Sheerline, and the 280 SL; its quality, size and handling are an eloquent tribute to the European idiom. In its gamble against disaster, the giant has looked both backwards and forwards; its new generation of economical, sprightly and realistically-priced cars are probably the most sensible piece of technology to have emerged from Detroit.

CRISES AND ALTERNATIVES

Alternative sources of power have been experimented with since the dawn of motoring. Electricity and steam have had their day – gas too, as in this 1936 Chevrolet fitted at the back with a somewhat bulky gas generator. But for the time being, and in spite of the vulnerability of world oil supplies, the petrol engine has no serious competition.

The production of cars – and the driving of them, the maintainance, selling and insurance of them – is the world's biggest business. At a reasonably conservative estimate there are 2 million people engaged in making them, another 3 million turning out components, and perhaps another 20 million around the world whose livelihoods depend on them, from taxi drivers to petrol-pump attendants. With national economies literally hinging on the fate of national car industries, it is hardly surprising that governments can no longer stand aloof from the market-place, after decades of happily allowing manufacturers to boom or bust. In Britain the government has repeatedly baled out British Leyland, the French government imposed a solution on Citroën's problems, and Congress has invaded some of Detroit's most sacred preserves. Now, for the first time in the history of motoring, there is beginning to be some sort of integration of policy among all the disparate elements of the automobile age – roads and environment, safety and resources, unemployment and manufacturing.

One of the first examples of constructive intervention came about over the issue of pollution. You didn't need to be a scientist in Los Angeles in the 1950s to recognise the grey pall that on some days hung over the city, diluting the sunlight. Inhabitants of L.A. took to wearing masks in the street and raised a chorus of complaint. Among the culprits identified by analysis were unburned hydrocarbons from exhausts and lead compounds (to prevent 'knocking' in high-compression engines). California passed its own legislation to combat exhaust pollution in 1959, which was taken up by Congress in 1965 and culminated in 1970 with a far-reaching Clean Air Act. American manufacturers are now required progressively to reduce the contaminants emitted by their cars until – as one commentator wryly put it – cars in the still-polluted areas of California will be 'pumping out cleaner air than they suck in'. Japanese firms planning their export invasion adopted anti-pollution measures early on, and European manufacturers have had to follow suit; but it is an expensive exercise since the current method of breaking down hydrocarbons and carbon monoxide is by a 'catalytic converter' which uses a combination of rare and costly metals.

Then in 1973 an even more penetrating trauma struck the automobile industry. At the height of the Arab-Israeli war that year, some Arab countries announced that they were slapping a huge increase on the price of their oil and customers could take it or leave it, others that they were cutting down production and imposing an embargo on exports to the United States (because of their support of Israel in the conflict). As a political weapon it proved to be remarkably quick-acting: for some motorists it was as if armageddon had been announced. When the shortages began to bite there

were free-for-alls at those few garages that didn't have 'sold out' signs in the forecourt, and queues stretching sometimes for miles. In Holland (also embargoed) weekend motoring was banned; in Britain petrol-hoarders were hauled before the Bench; in some parts of America the diminishing gas was doled out on alternate days according to whether your registration ended in an odd or even number (obliging some desperate drivers – whose legs presumably had long since atrophied – to buy a second car with the appropriate registration number!). In most western countries new speed limits were imposed, which have remained in force and, what do you know, have reduced road fatalities quite substantially; in America some 9,000 per year are estimated to be still alive as a consequence.

Total rationing was narrowly avoided, but the episode demonstrated to the oil-exporting nations what an economic trump they hold, and the price of oil has escalated sharply every year since then. The oil consumers, for their part, have begun to appreciate what a precious and finite resource oil is. As the price of petrol at the pump has grown prohibitive, so the car companies have had to face up to producing economical engines. For the smaller, lighter vehicles of Europe this has been no great hardship (BL's new Metro is proudly advertised as capable of 83 mpg), but it spelled the end for America's leviathan gas-guzzlers. In spite of the qualified success of the new breed of 'sub-compact' like the Pinto and Gremlin (though not the Vega, whose production caused a labour revolt at the plant), the average petrol consumption in the year of the oil embargo was 13.9 mpg, which was an all-time low. Washington has set legal standards that will ensure a minimum of 27.5 mpg by 1985, and a massive shake-up in Detroit.

American motorists have grown familiar with fuel shortages of late, brought on by vacillating relationships with the petroleum exporting countries. This attendant's T-shirt *(above)* summed up the motorists' feelings as they queued up at a Las Vegas service station in 1979, during the oil shortage in the wake of the Iran crisis.

Echoes of war. *Overleaf:* The effects of the first major oil crisis of the 1970s, during the Arab-Israeli conflict in 1973. Although rationing was narrowly avoided, garages ran out of petrol for long periods in many European countries like Britain *(inset)*. In Holland, which suffered an oil embargo, there was the rare sight of utterly deserted motorways during the weekend, when all driving was banned.

Fresh air or fumes? *Above:* An environmentalist in New York in 1970 protesting against pollution of the air by car exhausts. If the situation hadn't been subsequently improved by legislation, cartoonist Hans Stigg had a suggestion *(top)* for a sporty motorists' smog-mask.

A further consequence of OPEC's quadrupling of the price of oil in 1973 was that it opened the flood-gates on a tide of cheap, thrifty Japanese cars. Four centuries ago that old sage Nostradamus predicted a yellow invasion of the world in the 1970s. When his prophecies were republished early in the thirties, it was assumed that he meant a military invasion: no-one thought in terms of cars, for the Japanese motor industry was hardly stirring then. Its speciality was trucks, and even in 1949 when reconstruction was under way, total output amounted to 50,000 trucks and less than 2,000 cars. For the next ten years Japanese cars were constructed under European licences. By 1960, however, industrial expansion was clear of the ground and there was a pent-up demand at home for stylish comfortable cars, so manufacturers scrapped the old licences and launched out on their own, calling in the Italian designers to create new bodies for them. Pininfarina styled the Datsun Bluebird 1200 and the Cedric 2000, and Michelotti the Prince Skyline and the Hino Contessa (during what he called his Japanese period, the Triumph Herald was endowed with slant-eyed headlights!).

In 1961 the Japanese car industry was the sixth biggest in the world; ten years later it was second only to America, and poised to conquer the world. Japanese cars did not suffer from such constraints as sloppy management and self-destructive labour practices which bedevilled so many European firms, particularly the British. They were cheap, efficient, as trustworthy as a rolling-pin and about as imaginative. The Japanese manufacturers had done their homework thoroughly. High productivity and clever marketing did the trick: in 1978, for example, Toyota produced 42.8 units a year per employee, as against 14.9 at Opel, 12.5 at Renault and a bare 6.1 at Alfa Romeo. Their cars came fully equipped with such things as radios and seatbelts included in the price, instead of being loaded on as non-optional extras.

The Japanese export drive was aggressive, almost reckless, and it penetrated the demoralised American market like a Samurai sword through butter, till in 1977 they had scooped up over 11 percent of the new car market. Even before the oil crisis Detroit was staring in the face the realities of 'maturity', that is to say a declining growth rate – from 12 to 13 percent a year (in relatively recent times) to a current 2 to 3 percent. A market has matured when its customers are overwhelmingly those replacing existing cars, rather than first-time buyers. And in California, a weathervane for future market trends, there are already more cars than there are drivers. In the pit of the 1974–1975 recession, U.S. car production fell from 9.6 million a year to 6.7 million, and five out of the six Chrysler plants closed down for a time. Add to this the fact that the motor companies have been compulsorily committed to a multi-billion dollar investment programme just to meet the new pollution, safety and economy regulations, and it is not entirely surprising that Detroit has had to re-think its business policies from scratch. In her book on the decline of the auto-industrial age, Emma Rothschild suggests that, with almost historical inevitability, Detroit is facing the same kind of troubles that afflicted the late-Victorian textile industry. Nevertheless both Ford and General Motors pin considerable hopes on their new concept of 'world-cars', machines that can be made and sold globally – the ultimate rationalisation of their home and foreign operations. In addition, Ford in September 1980 opened a factory in New Jersey that was dedicated exclusively to making small cars.

If the Japanese exporters failed to establish a bridgehead in Europe in the seventies (except in Britain where they already had a toehold), it was because the EEC was protected by discreet but effective tariff barriers. West Germany's incisive management and sensible labour relations have consolidated its industry as the heavyweight of Europe. Even if labour costs in Germany do amount to £20,000 per worker, unions strive to increase productivity rather than slow it down. With a strong home market that can absorb about 2.5 million new registrations a year, German industry has been able to invest heavily in modern plant. And although the strength of the Deutschmark prevented the Germans using low prices as a marketing weapon, the high specification built into many of their models made them attractive abroad. Of course there were some ups and downs. In 1961 BMW would have folded had not local pride prompted the Bavarian authorities to step in with fresh finance; and when Volkswagen were in trouble in 1973, the government had to chip in with the necessary cash to get the successors to the Beetle on the road.

In contrast, Gallic logic decreed that Citroën and Chrysler-Simca-Talbot should come under the Peugeot umbrella, and moreover that all French cars – including those of the highly successful Régie Renault – should share the same three or four engines. Yet this policy of rationalisation enabled French output to increase by some 10 percent in the seventies. In Italy

No place to go: hundreds of new automobiles lying idle at Chrysler's plant in 1974, in the depths of the recession that caused the company to lay off tens of thousands of workers. Meanwhile the Japanese 'invasion' of the U.S. car market (above) gained an important bridgehead.

213

Untouched by human hand: computer technology arrived at British Leyland in the late 1970s for the production of their Metro cars. *Right:* A line of robot welders, which can be reprogrammed for different models. Meanwhile, outside BL continued its saga of sad industrial relations.

'mamma' Fiat contrived to keep the Italian industry's exports steady. But the prima-donna antics of Italian labour following the 'hot summer' of 1969 and an absurdly high record of strikes and absenteeism caused Alfa Romeo a loss of a million lire on every Alfasud produced, and finally provoked the state-owned factory to make a deal with Nissan (which pessimists predict will act as a Trojan horse and open the European market to Japanese cars, when already production capacity is far in excess of demand and there are too many firms chasing too few customers).

If other countries had their problems, Britain was little short of becoming a disaster area. Ever since the amalgam of Austin and Morris the dictum of big-is-best has prevailed, and there have been a flurry of mergers throughout the industry. Jaguar and Rover joined BMC; Leyland, with their record of good management, acquired Standard-Triumph, and then in a reverse takeover of majestic proportions swallowed BMC itself to create the mammoth British Leyland. Billy Rootes, after a successful but financially ruinous confrontation with the engineering unions, sold out to Chrysler, who in turn had to beg £10 million off the British government and eventually disposed of their operation to Peugeot.

All these consolidations were probably inevitable in view of the huge operating costs, but the trouble was that they have turned the giants of the industry into white elephants, at the mercy of their own bureaucracies and hostages to politically motivated unions. After 75 years of building cars, there were now only four major manufacturers in Britain: two were owned by Detroit, one by France, and a majority of the fourth by the government. What is more, over 50 percent of the cars sold in Britain in 1979 were made abroad and BL's loss for the first six months of 1980 was over £100 million. To compound the misery, MG was shut down and BL embarked on a programme to assemble a Japanese car that is apparently more advanced than anything their engineers could design. The future, as Paul Valéry once remarked, 'isn't what it used to be'. But there are still

Returning ohm: research into electric cars continues to generate prototypes (like the 'Stil', *left)* from time to time. One of the most promising experiments was the 'White Car' plan in Amsterdam in 1974. The cars could be hired at special car stations by members of a cooperative. An environmental success, it nevertheless foundered for lack of public support.

silver linings. Firms such as Lucas and Smiths still lead the way in electronic development, and Rolls-Royce have risen magnificently from the ashes of 1971. And, come to think of it, the Royal Automobile Club itself was faced with imminent demise as recently as 1977, yet through energetic management has returned to its former prosperity in just two years, showing a profit of nearly £400,000 on the clubhouses and a trading surplus of some £2.2 million by the associate section. Looming over all the transient declines and rebirths of the industry is the permanent question: what happens when the oil runs out? Every now and then, in the hope of finding a new answer, those venerable competitors to petrol – steam and electric power – get taken off the shelf and dusted down. Steamers, it is almost universally accepted, would be quite unsuitable for mass-production. Electric cars, with their seductive virtues of cleanliness and silence, tend to get much more of an airing. In 1974 a whole fleet of them (called 'white cars') was put onto the streets of Amsterdam for hire by a cooperative: when the scheme finally broke down it was for organisational reasons rather than technical ones. However, without a major breakthrough in the storage capacity of batteries – which looks very far-off at present – the uses of the electric car are severely limited. The most acceptable substitute for petrol, at present, looks likely to be petrol substitute (made perhaps from coal). For however intriguing the embryonic notions of alternative technology might be – such as energy-storing flywheels and solar-powered vehicles – one thing is certain. Those who have invested in the vast apparatus that attends the internal combustion engine are going to need a lot of convincing before they are won over to a new source of motive power, like the horse-riders of a hundred years ago.

A FUTURE FOR THE CAR

Paying toll, then and now. This scene at an English toll-gate early in the century *(left)* typifies the 'honeymoon' phase of the modern world's 'romance with the automobile'. The car – because it was a rarity – brought freedom and contact with nature. For a time. Today cars are still paying their dues, for the privilege of driving along superhighways which consume ever increasing tracts of the earth's surface. The problem is that new roads seem to generate more cars, which need yet more roads.

Looking back one can see that it was finally during the seventies, when the motor industry found itself faced by a more challenging situation than it had ever experienced before, that the man-in-the-street's car reached a rational, authoritative form. The fuzziness of design that characterised many products a few years previously – bodies that rusted away before your eyes, fittings that broke off, shapes that were pleasing but neither slippery nor sharp, mushy steering and plodding engines – was overcome at last, and the volume-produced cars of 1980 represented a stunning improvement on the predecessors of ten or fifteen years back.

It has taken, if you like, just about a hundred years of motoring to reach a point where the average car is efficiently packaged to give exciting, dependable transportation. Today a nimble small saloon like the Series 3 Alfasud is a quality product that even an enthusiast can enjoy without sacrificing his standards. And supercats like the new breed of Mercedes, the Porsche 928, the Audi 4 and the Ferrari Mondial are classics that collectors of the future will treasure as avidly as those from the golden periods gone by. Pioneer firms that stayed the course, like Daimler and Benz, Peugeot, Renault, Ford and, indeed, Cadillac and Oldsmobile, have become giants that will continue to shape the automobile of tomorrow. To be sure, as the car enters its second century of existence, there are exciting perspectives ahead. The rational machine of today will be old-hat soon. Within a few years the shape of cars will again be transformed – and that is not to say that the two box profile will have become three, or two and a half, or simply one (even as the Americans are introducing their new sharp-angled styling that harks back to those razor-edged silhouettes we knew in the thirties, Pininfarina and Giugiaro are experimenting with slippery, aero-spatial lines). Rather, the automobile, like so many other things, is on the threshold of a new technology made possible by electronics and microchips.

All the indications go to show that the next generation of cars will be designed by computers and constructed by robots. They will have electronic fuel injection, dispensing with the carburettor as we know it at present. And, despite all the alarms about world oil reserves, petrol and diesel engines are likely to be with us for a long time yet. It is difficult to say how much more development the internal combustion engine can take – Issigo-

nis, for one, maintains that it has hardly begun – but there are already refinements in the pipeline that will revolutionise output in relation to input, and thereby give higher levels of efficiency that cut both pollution and fuel consumption. Engines will become sealed units, such as refrigerators have, and micro-processors will monitor every component in the vehicle. One day there may be electric cars for shopping trips and nuclear-powered machines for long-distance use, but wheels are likely to be retained in the discernible future, despite research into vehicles that ride on a cushion of air, and ducted-fan flying cars. The steering wheel may disappear in favour of finger-touch sensitisors and automatic pilots that direct the machine by radar. In the short term, dashboards will become digital and gearshafts will disappear – even in Italy, where Fiat has announced a new automatic drive developed in conjunction with Van Doorne of Holland from the old Daf principle.

In the process of all this we stand to lose that sense of participation – of contact with the surroundings, of being part of the living stretch of ribbon in front – that has given such a zest to motoring during these first hundred years. Driving a car has been an intensely personal experience, like riding a thoroughbred hunter, handling a racing dinghy or schussing through fresh powder snow; even so, to sit behind the wheel of a Ferrari is a mere pub-crawl compared with driving a 1903 Mercedes at 70 miles a hour. So much the better, anyone but an old car fanatic will say. Yet the fun has been there, and what will be gained in exchange is something we shall discover during the next ten decades.

The car of tomorrow? The BMW 745i is now equipped with a dashboard mini-computer *(below)* which balances and coordinates as many as sixteen functions and accessories, such as speed, temperature, lights, ventilation, signals, for greater safety and comfort.

EPILOGUE

Throughout its long career the automobile has demonstrated that, with suitable modification, it can go just about anywhere. Up mountains, across water, over pack ice and deserts. There remained only one challenge unconquered – space. Then, in 1971, Apollo 15 blasted off for the moon, and aboard it was a car (or more accurately, a Lunar Roving Vehicle, folded up into three segments to be reassembled on arrival). On the moon it performed admirably, crossing small crevasses, climbing 25 degree slopes, and travelling several miles at 10 mph. Astronauts Irwin and Scott left it behind, parked on the lunar landscape for future generations of humans (or other beings) to inspect. A symbol of the automobile's expanding potential into the twenty-first century, or a monument to its final achievements in the twentieth?

PICTURE CREDITS

Original artwork:
Franz Coray, Lucerne: 32, 33, 55, 106, 107, 110, 111, 164, 165, 168, 169, 206, 207

Aston Martin Lagonda, Newport Pagnell: 2/3
Autocar, Magazine, London: 24 top left, 99 bottom
Baschet, Eric, Editions, Paris: 81
BBC, Hulton Picture Library, London: 15 top, 16 center, 35, 43 above, 73 bottom, 79 below, 84 left, 90, 98, 99 top, 117, 129, 130, 140 above, 144, 162, 171
Bertieri, Claudio, *Graphicar, l'auto, nella grafica,* Fiat Torino 1976: 1, 27 bottom, 28, 29 right
Biblioteca Ambrosiana, Milan: 8 left above
BMW, Munich: 217 below
Bourke-White, Margaret/Life Magazine © 1937 Time Inc., New York: 137
British Library, London: 83 right
Brown Brothers, Sterling: 114
Castelli Gallery: Photo Courtesy of Leo Castelli Gallery, New York: 186 top
Clymer, Floyd, *Early American Automobiles,* New York 1950: 118 left and center, 119
Comet-Photo, Zurich: 191, 193
Culver Pictures, Inc., New York: 121 left, 123 bottom, 124 above left, 127 right bottom, 145
Daimler-Benz AG, Stuttgart: 4 top and bottom, 6/7, 12 above, 13 above, 146, 167
Danmarks Tekniske Museum, Helsingor: 9 right
Datsun, USA: 213 right
Detroit Public Library, Automotive History Collection, Detroit: 26 below, 27 top, 128 above, 136 left
Deutsches Museum, Munich: 2, 8 left
Deutsches Patentamt, Bibliothek, Munich: 64 bottom, 65 bottom
Edita SA, *L'année automobile,* Lausanne: 50 top, 156 bottom
Environmental Communications, Los Angeles: 187 top, 188 bottom, 189 bottom right
Evans, Mary, Picture Library, London: 17 right, 38, 40, 50 right, 64 top left, 65 above, 147 left

Eyerman, J.R./Life Magazine, © 1958, Time Inc., New York: 172/173: © 1953: 175
Ford Archives: 57, 97 top, 115, 132 above, 214
Gamage, A.W. Ltd., *Everything for the Motorist,* London 1912: 50 left center, left below, 51 right center, right below, 66, 67, 70 left
General Motors Continental, Antwerp: 184
Graf von Seherr-Thoss, H.C., *Die Deutsche Automobil Industrie,* Stuttgart 1974: 158 right
Gritscher, H./Aspect Picture Library, London: 189 center right
Gullachsen/Daily Telegraph Color Library, London: 194 left
Herschtritt, Leon/Camera Press, London: 215 left
Hoffmann, Herbert, Berlin: 157 right
Honegger, Guido, Zurich: 176 below, 188 left top, 189 bottom left
How to Drive a Motorcar, London: 154
Imperial War Museum, London: 96, 96/97, 160 above left
IVB-Report, Dusseldorf: 217 above
Jakovsky, Anatole, Collection, Paris: 120 top
Jones, Michael Wynn, Stowmarket: 63, 64 top right, 77 top left, 86/87, 87 top and bottom, 118 right
Keystone Press Agency Ltd., London: 155, 186 bottom, 198, 199, 200, 200/201, 204, 215 right
Keystone Press, Zurich: 122 center left, 174, 177 below, 179 below, 190, 196/197
Kobal Collection, London: 123 above, 124 bottom, 125, 126/127
Kodak Museum, Harrow: 75 top
Lartigue, Jacques-Henri, Paris: 53 bottom, 74
Lee, Keith, London: 194 bottom
Library of Congress, Washington: 138
Lords Gallery Ltd., London: 29 left
MacDonnell, Kevin, Hampstead: 148 left
Malindine, Edward G./National Portrait Gallery, London: 147 right

Mansell Collection, London: 12 below, 13 below, 39, 59 bottom, 72 right
Motoring Illustrated, 1906: 91
Museum of Modern Art, Collection (Gift of A.A. Rockefeller), New York: 10

National Motor Museum, Beaulieu: 5 center, 14, 17 bottom, 18 right, 22, 23, 24, 24/25, 42 left, 44, 48, 49, 51 top, 56, 58, 62 bottom, 70 right, 75 right, 77 center right and bottom, 83 left, 84 right, 88, 94, 100 below, 102, 108 left and center, 109 center and right, 113, 116, 128 bottom, 131 top, 133 left, 139, 141, 142, 150, 151, 152, 153, 180 below, 192 left, 195, 208, 216
Noser, Peter, Zurich: 176 above left and right, 177 above, 187 bottom, 188 left center
Pininfarina, Carrozzeria, Torino: 185
Popperfoto, London: 95 below, 122 center right, 136 right, 170, 201 center, 205 top, 209, 210 top, 218/219
Portway, N., Stowmarket: 68, 69
Posthumus, Cyril, Epsom: 148/149
Prince, Tony/Camera Press, London: 189 top
Publisher's Archives: 41, 43 bottom
Punch, London: 77 right
Rainbird, George, Ltd., London: 101, 201 right
Ringier Bilderdienst, Zurich: 182, 182/183, 183, 212 below, 213 left
Roberts, Peter, Picture Collection, London: 4 center, 15 right, 18 left, 19, 20, 21, 26 above, 30, 31, 37, 42 right, 45, 47, 52, 53 top, 54, 59 above, 60, 61, 62 left top and center, 71 right, 73 right, 76, 78, 79 above, 80, 82, 85 right, 86 left, 87 center right, 89, 93, 97 center right, 100 above, 103, 104, 105, 108/109, 112, 120 left, 121 right, 122 bottom, 124 above right, 131 bottom, 140 bottom, 143, 178, 179 above, 180 above, 181
Roger-Viollet, Paris: 95 above
Sauer/Paris Match: 210/211

Saunier, L. Baudry de, *Das Automobil' in Theorie und Praxis,* Vol. II, Vienna 1901: 11, 16 left and right
Scagnet, Ernst, Lucerne: 202, 202/203, 203
Schall, Roger, Paris: 135
Schneider, Walter, Berlin: 71
Sigg, Hans, Vernate: 212 above
Süddeutscher Verlag, Munich: 126 left above, left center, left bottom, 127 right above, right center, 159
Sunday Dispatch, 1955: 192 right
Sunday Times, London: 205 bottom
Technisches Museum, Vienna: 9 left
Topham, John, Picture Library, Edenbridge: 5 bottom, 133 right, 163
Ullstein Bilderdienst, Berlin: 158 left, 160 bottom left and right, 161
Van Doren Stern, Philip, *A. Pictorial History of the Automobile,* New York 1953: 132 bottom, 156 above, 157 left
Von Frankenberg, Richard/Matteucci, Marco, *Geschichte des Automobils,* Künzelsau 1973: 5 top, 51 left
Wiesendanger, Gilbert, *Ein halbes Jahrhundert Automobil,* 1950: 8 left below
Williams, Kit/Collection Michael White, London: 186 center left
Worthington-Williams Collection, Hassocks: 36, 46, 72 left, 85 bottom

INDEX